Channels of Desire

Channels of Desire

Mass Images and the Shaping of American Consciousness

Stuart Ewen and Elizabeth Ewen

University of Minnesota Press
Minneapolis • London

Excerpt from "Lost in the Supermarket" words and music by Michael Jeoffrey Jones and Joe Strummer. Copyright 1979 Nineden Ltd/Virgin Music Publishers Ltd. International copyright secured. All rights reserved. Lyrics reproduced by kind permission of the publishers.

Excerpt from "America" from *Collected Poems 1947–1980* by Allen Ginsberg. Copyright 1956, 1959, 1984 by Allen Ginsberg. Reprinted by permission of HarperCollins/Penguin Books Ltd.

Excerpt from "The Pretender" by Jackson Browne. Copyright 1976 Swallow Turn Music. All rights reserved. Used by permission.

Excerpt from "We Shall Never Turn Back" by Bertha Gober Sawyer, 1955.

Published by the University of Minnesota Press
2037 University Avenue Southeast, Minneapolis, MN 55414
Printed in the United States of America on acid-free paper

Library of Congress Cataloging-in-Publication Data

Ewen, Stuart.
    Channels of desire : mass images and the shaping of American consciousness / Stuart Ewen and Elizabeth Ewen. — [New ed]
        p.   cm.
    Includes bibliographical references and index.
    ISBN 0-8166-1890-9 (acid-free paper)
    1. Advertising—Social aspects—United States—History. 2. Consumers—United States—History. 3. United States—Popular culture. 4. National characteristics, American—History. 5. Fashion—History. I. Ewen, Elizabeth. II. Title.
HF5813.U6E95   1992
302.23'0973—dc20   91-46917
                                                                              CIP

The University of Minnesota is an
equal-opportunity educator and employer.

Contents

Preface to the New Edition   ix

Acknowledgments   xiii

Prologue: In the Shadow of the Image   xv

1. *The Bribe of Frankenstein*   1

2. *Consumption as a Way of Life*   23

3. *City Lights: Immigrant Women and the Rise of the Movies*   53

4. *Fashion and Democracy*   75

5. *Shadows on the Wall*   189

   Notes   221

   Index   237

To Fran, Roger, Scotty, and Sol

Preface to the New Edition

THIS BOOK was originally published in 1982. In a series of five essays, we attempted to analyze the development of a culture in which the power of mass-produced, mass-distributed images and words had become all-pervasive. When *Channels of Desire* first appeared, the study of the mass media as powerful features of American life had already begun. Few studies, however, had examined the historical roots of this modern phenomenon. It was our purpose to take the familiar terrain of an image-laden culture and explore the social, cultural, and historical conditions out of which it had arisen.

A prime difficulty in assuming such a task is the seamless and all-encompassing nature of the contemporary cultural landscape. Where to start? What to focus on? How to make sense of an essentially ephemeral culture? How to evaluate the impact of this temporal culture on the modern imagination?

Rather than trying to present an unwieldy totalistic overview, we chose to concentrate on distinctive aspects of the cultural milieu, which, we thought, provided insights into the nature of the whole. The first essay, "The Bribe of Frankenstein," offered a look at the early beginnings of the mass media: the emergence of printing and of popular literacy. Beyond being an important historical benchmark by anyone's standards, these developments illuminate the ambiguous role of the media as instruments of perception. In the rise of print we can see the ways that the media served to open up new possibilities of human emancipation, while, at the same time, erecting new structures of authority that served the priorities and demands of an emerging industrial system.

In the second essay, "Consumption as a Way of Life," we traced the connection between the rise of a consumer society and the simultaneous breakdown of customary modes of survival. At the heart of this essay is the conception that *consumption*, rather than merely being an activity by which people survive, contains a special constellation of social relationships within it. As these relationships emerged, they demanded new definitions of work, culture, economics, and ecology. In this essay, we looked at some of the ways that the media served to transmit and inculcate these new modes of life in the United States over the past two centuries.

The next essay, "City Lights," examined one of the most persistent dynamics of the modern condition: generational conflict. In particular we looked at the dislocations experienced by turn-of-the-century immigrant women—mothers and daughters—in relation to the new culture they found in the United States. One of the most revealing examples of the interaction between these women and new forms of urban culture can be found in their responses as members of a nascent movie audience. First in the nickelodeons, and later in movie palaces, these new arrivals discovered America. Of specific interest here was the difference between the ways mothers and daughters responded to the silver screen. For mothers, still caught in the webs of tradition, the new culture was, in many ways, terrifying. For the daughters, anxious to become Americans, the movies became a place from which powerful lessons were drawn. Insofar as parents and children continue to battle over the value of *mass culture*, this essay sketches some of the contours of conflicts that continue to percolate.

In writing *Channels of Desire*, one of the basic premises we brought to our work was that the scope of *the media* extends beyond the limited way they are usually defined: print, film, radio, television, etc. Like Marshall McLuhan—who included *clocks, money, numbers, motor cars, weapons,* and *electric lights* within his purview—we viewed media as those aspects of culture by which people's perceptions about their world are shaped. Following this broad guideline, the fourth essay, "Fashion and Democracy," explores the ways that clothing harbors and communicates a complex social history. Pursuing fashion from the late Middle

Ages to our own time, we explored the rich connections linking clothing to changing issues of social class, gender, rebellion, self-improvement, urbanization, and mass production.

In the first edition of *Channels of Desire*, we concluded with an essay entitled "Mass Culture and the Moral Economy of War." Written toward the end of 1981, the essay confronted the coming of a new conservatism in the United States, and explored, in some detail, the ways in which the media were reforming a bellicose American consensus. That essay may still be of some historical interest, but much of it is, today, dated, locked into its time. We decided, in preparing this new edition, to write a new conclusion, one that benefits from a perspective gained over the ensuing decade. Entitled "Shadows on the Wall," this essay attempts to illuminate the perilous terrain of American culture as we approach the new millennium. It is, to borrow from the writer Brian Fawcett, both "an attempt to see things as they really are" and an invitation to envisage "the kind of world we might have."

Stuart Ewen and Elizabeth Ewen
New York City, Summer 1991

Acknowledgments

WITHOUT DOUBT, the issues, developments, and concerns raised in this book would not have come to our attention were it not for the groundwork laid by J. P. Morgan and Karl Marx. Beyond these two, a number of people have been particularly helpful to us in the writing and conceptualization of this book.

Karen Kearns conducted the interview with Anna Kuthan, under the auspices of the Oral History Project of the City University of New York. Laura Anker also provided us with rich interview materials.

Maria Spicciatie has been a patient and helpful friend, putting in long hours preparing the manuscript, making valuable editorial suggestions along the way. For her efforts we offer our deep-felt thanks. Others who worked on typing the manuscript include Maria Resurreccion and Marie Estime. Nancy Lane and Wayne Friedman offered valuable research assistance.

Over the years spent writing this book, we have been enlightened by the ideas and warmed by the support of Rosaalyn Baxandall, Herb and Anita Schiller, Eric Perkins, Steve Fraser, Stanley Aronowitz, Harry and Elaine Scott, Fred Ewen, Gail Pellett, Fina Bathrick, Andy Ewen, Paul and Wini Breines, Linda Gordon, Phyllis Ewen, Evan Stark, Margaret Schrage, Catherine Low, Onita Hicks, Sam Rosenberg, Larry Shore, Carmen Monteblanca, Bob Stanley, Allen Hunter, John Ehrenreich, and Kathryn Yatrakis. The friendships of M. J., Stolie, Pasta, and the Turk have sustained us through our wars with this book.

Much of our involvement with the cultural issues raised in the following pages was encouraged by the insights of teachers. For this we thank William Taylor, Loren Baritz, Harvey Goldberg, and George Mosse. We also remember the teachings and brilliant rage of Herbert Gutman, Hans Gerth and Micheal Cherniavsky.

To our students at Hunter College and the State University of New York College at Old Westbury, we offer our gratitude for their enthusiasm and their criticism while many of the ideas in this book were being worked out.

Our children, Sam and Paul Ewen, have provided us with a critical and illuminating perspective on our work. Without them, this book would not have been possible.

To our parents, Roger and Fran Wunderlich, Scotty and Sol Ewen, we dedicate this book. Their lives and those of *their* parents (Anna and Harry Scott; Mike and Rosa Campanile; Mollie and Sam Ewen; Hortense and Reginald Wunderlich) span the great transformation to which this book addresses itself.

Prologue: In the Shadow of the Image

MARIA AGUILAR was born twenty-seven years ago near Mayagüez, on the island of Puerto Rico. Her family had lived off the land for generations. Today she sits in a rattling IRT subway car, speeding through the iron-and-rock guts of Manhattan. She sits on the train, her ears dazed by the loud outcry of wheels against tracks. Surrounded by a galaxy of unknown fellow strangers, she looks up at a long strip of colorful signboards placed high above the bobbing heads of the others. All the posters call for her attention.

Looking down at her, a blonde-haired lady cabdriver leans out of her driver's side window. Here is the famed philosopher of this strange urban world, and a woman she can talk to. The tough-wise eyes of the cabbie combine with a youthful beauty, speaking to Maria Aguilar directly:

Estoy sentada 12 horas al día.
Lo último que necesito son hemorroides.

(I sit for twelve hours a day. The last thing
I need are hemorrhoids.)

Under this candid testimonial lies a package of Preparation H ointment, and the promise "Alivia dolores y picasonas. Y ayuda a reducir la hinchazón." (Relieves pain and itching. And helps reduce swelling.) As her mind's eye takes it all in, the train sweeps into Maria's stop. She gets out; climbs the stairs to the street; walks to work where she will spend her day sitting on a stool in a small garment factory, sewing hems on pretty dresses.

* * *

Every day, while Benny Doyle drives his Mustang to work along State Road Number 20, he passes a giant billboard along the shoulder. The billboard is selling whiskey and features a woman in a black velvet dress stretching across its brilliant canvas.

As Benny Doyle downshifts by, the lounging beauty looks out to him. Day after day he sees her here. The first time he wasn't sure, but now he's convinced that her eyes are following him.

* * *

The morning sun shines on the red-tan forehead of Bill O'Conner as he drinks espresso on his sun deck, alongside the ocean cliffs of La Jolla, California. Turning through the daily paper, he reads a story about Zimbabwe.

"Rhodesia," he thinks to himself.

The story argues that a large number of Africans in Zimbabwe are fearful about black majority rule, and are concerned over a white exodus. Two black hotel workers are quoted by the article. Bill puts this, as a fact, into his mind.

Later that day, over a business lunch, he repeats the story to five white business associates, sitting at the restaurant table. They share a superior laugh over the ineptitude of black African political rule. Three more tellings, children of the first, take place over the next four days. These are spoken by two of Bill O'Conner's luncheon companions, passing on to still more people the supposed voice of political wisdom.[1]

* * *

Barbara and John Marsh get into their seven-year-old Dodge pickup and drive twenty-three miles to the nearest Sears in Cedar Rapids. After years of breakdowns and months of hesitation they've decided to buy a new washing machine. They come to Sears because it is there, and because they believe that their new Sears machine will be steady and reliable. The Marshes will pay for their purchase for the next year or so.

Barbara's great-grandfather, Elijah Simmons, had purchased a cream-separator from Sears, Roebuck in 1897 and he swore by it.

* * *

When the clock radio sprang the morning affront upon him, Archie Bishop rolled resentfully out of his crumpled bed and trudged slowly to the john. A few moments later he was unconsciously squeezing toothpaste out of a mess of red and white Colgate packaging. A dozen scrubs of the mouth and he expectorated a white, minty glob into the basin.

Still groggy, he turned on the hot water, slapping occasional palmfuls onto his gray face.

A can of Noxzema shave cream sat on the edge of the sink, a film of crud and whiskers across its once neat label. Archie reached for the bomb and filled his left hand with a white creamy mound, then spread it over his beard. He shaved, then looked with resignation at the regular collection of cuts on his neck.

Stepping into a shower, he soaped up with a soap that promised to wake him up. Groggily, he then grabbed a bottle of Clairol Herbal Essence Shampoo. He turned the tablet-shaped bottle to its back label, carefully reading the "Directions."

"Wet hair."

He wet his hair.

"Lather."

He lathered.

"Rinse."

He rinsed.

"Repeat if necessary."

Not sure whether it was altogether necessary, he repeated the process according to directions.

* * *

Late in the evening, Maria Aguilar stepped back in the subway train, heading home to the Bronx after a long and tiring day. This time, a poster told her "The Pain Stops Here!"

She barely noticed, but later she would swallow two New Extra Strength Bufferin tablets with a glass of water from a rusty tap.

* * *

Two cockroaches in cartoon form leer out onto the street from a wall advertisement. The man cockroach is drawn like a hipster, wearing shades and a cockroach zoot suit. He strolls hand in hand with a lady cockroach, who is dressed like a floozy and blushing beet-red. Caught in the midst of their cockroach rendezvous, they step sinfully into a Black Flag Roach Motel. Beneath them, in Spanish, the words:

Las Cucarachas entran . . . pero no pueden salir.

(In the English version: Cockroaches check in . . . but they don't check out.)

The roaches are trapped; sin is punished. Salvation is gauged by one's ability to live roach-free. The sinners of the earth shall be inundated by roaches. Moral tales and insects encourage passersby to rid their houses of sin. In their homes, sometimes, people wonder whether God has forsaken them.

* * *

Beverly Jackson sits at a metal and tan Formica table and looks through the *New York Post*. She is bombarded by a catalog of horror. Children are mutilated . . . subway riders attacked . . . fanatics are marauding and noble despots lie in bloody heaps. Occasionally someone steps off the crime-infested streets to claim a million dollars in lottery winnings.

Beverly Jackson's skin crawls; she feels a knot encircling her lungs. She is beset by immobility, hopelessness, depression.

Slowly she walks over to her sixth-floor window, gazing out into the sooty afternoon. From the empty street below, Beverly Jackson imagines a crowd yelling "Jump! . . . Jump!"

* * *

Between 1957 and 1966 Frank Miller saw a dozen John Wayne movies, countless other westerns, and war dramas. In 1969 he led a charge up a hill without a name in Southeast Asia. No one followed; he took a bullet in the chest.

Today he sits in a chair and doesn't get up. He feels that the images betrayed him, and now he camps out across from the White House while another movie star cuts benefits for veterans. In the morning newspaper he reads of a massive weapons build-up taking place.

* * *

Gina Concepcion now comes to school wearing the Jordache look. All this has been made possible by weeks and weeks of after-school employment at a supermarket checkout counter. Now, each morning, she tugs the decorative denim over her young legs, sucking in her lean belly to close the snaps.

These pants are expensive compared to the "no-name" brands, but they're worth it, she reasons. They fit better, and she fits better.

* * *

The theater marquee, stretching out over a crumbling, garbage-strewn sidewalk, announced "The Decline of Western Civilization." At the ticket window a smaller sign read "All Seats $5.00."

* * *

It was ten in the morning and Joyce Hopkins stood before a mirror next to her bed. Her interview at General Public Utilities, Nuclear Division, was only four hours away and all she could think was, "What to wear?"

A half hour later Joyce stood again before the mirror, wearing a slip and stockings. On the bed, next to her, lay a two-foot-high mountain of discarded options. Mocking the title of a recent best-seller, which she hadn't read, she said aloud to herself, "Dress for Success. . . . What *do* they like?"

At one o'clock she walked out the door wearing a brownish tweed jacket; a cream-colored Qiana blouse, full-cut with a tied collar; a dark beige skirt, fairly straight and hemmed (by Maria Aguilar) two inches below the knee; sheer fawn stockings; and simple but elegant reddish brown pumps on her feet. Her hair was to the shoulder, her look tawny.

When she got the job she thanked her friend Millie, a middle manager, for the tip not to wear pants.

* * *

Joe Davis stood at the endless conveyor, placing caps on a round-the-clock parade of automobile radiators. His nose and eyes burned. His ears buzzed in the din. In a furtive moment he looked up and to the right. On the plant wall was a large yellow sign with THINK! printed on it in bold type. Joe turned back quickly to the radiator caps.

Fifty years earlier, in another factory, in another state, Joe's grandfather, Nat Davis, had looked up and seen another sign:

A *Clean* Machine Runs Better.
Your Body is a Machine.
KEEP IT CLEAN.

Though he tried and tried, Joe Davis's grandfather was never able to get the dirt out from under his nails. Neither could his great-grandfather, who couldn't read.

* * *

In 1952 Mary Bird left her family in Charleston to earn money as a maid in a Philadelphia suburb. She earned thirty-five dollars a week, plus room and board, in a dingy retreat of a ranch-style tract house.

Twenty-eight years later she sits on a bus, heading toward her small room in North Philly. Across from her, on an advertising poster, a sumptuous meal is displayed. Golden fried chicken, green beans glistening with butter and flecked by pimento, and a fluffy cloud of rice fill the greater part of a calico-patterned dinner plate. Next to the plate sit a steaming boat of gravy and an icy drink in an amber tumbler. The plate is on a quilted blue place mat, flanked by a thick linen napkin and colonial silverware.

As Mary Bird's hungers are aroused, the wording on the placard instructs her: "*Come Home to Carolina.*"

* * *

SHOPPING LIST

paper towels
milk
eggs
rice crispies
chicken
snacks for kids (twinkies, chips, etc.)
potatoes
diet coke, ginger ale, seltzer

cheer

brillo

peanut butter

bread

ragu (2 jars)

spagetti

saran wrap

salad

get cleaning, bank, *must pay electric*!!!

* * *

On his way to Nina's house, Sidney passed an ad for Smirnoff vodka. A sultry beauty with wet hair and beads of moisture on her smooth, tanned face looked out at him. *"Try a Main Squeeze."* For a teenage boy the invitation transcended the arena of drink; he felt a quick throb-pulse at the base of his belly and his step quickened.

* * *

In October of 1957, at the age of two and a half, Aaron Stone was watching television. Suddenly, from the screen, there leaped a circus clown, selling children's vitamins and yelling "Hi! Boys and girls!" Aaron ran terrified from the room, screaming.

For years after, he watched television in perpetual fear that the vitamin clown would reappear. Slowly his family assured him that the television was just a mechanical box and couldn't really hurt him, that the vitamin clown was harmless.

Today, as an adult, Aaron Stone takes vitamins, is ambivalent about clowns, and watches television, although there are occasional moments of anxiety.

These are some of the facts of our lives: disparate moments, disconnected, dissociated. Meaningless moments. Random incidents. Memory traces. Each is an unplanned encounter, part of day-to-day existence. Viewed alone, each by itself, such spaces of our lives seem insignificant, trivial. They are the decisions and reveries of survival; the stuff of small talk; the chance preoccupations of our eyes and minds in a world of images—soon forgotten.

Viewed together, however, as an ensemble, an integrated panorama of social life, human activity, hope and despair, images and information, another tale unfolds. They reveal a pattern of life, the structures of perception.

As familiar moments in American life, all of these events bear the footprints of a history that weighs upon us, but is largely untold. We live and breathe an atmosphere where mass images are everywhere in evidence; mass produced, mass distributed. In the streets, in our homes, among a crowd, or alone, they speak to us, overwhelm our vision. Their presence, their messages are givens, unavoidable. Though their history is still relatively short, their prehistory is, for the most part, forgotten, unimaginable.

This history that unites the seemingly random routines of daily life is one that embraces the rise of an industrial consumer society. It involves explosive interactions between modernity and old ways of life. It includes the proliferation, over years and decades, of a wide, repeatable vernacular of commercial images and ideas. This history spells new patterns of social, productive, and political life.

This book, in its various essays, attempts to plumb the social history that stands behind the apparent immortality of a consumer society; its universe of commodities; its priorities; its social forms. The pages that follow offer historical suggestions aimed at telling some of the story of how these disparate events, these "insignificant" details, took hold as the facts of life.

1

The Bribe of Frankenstein

Gears of Progress

To human consciousness, the epoch of the machine is one of hope and horror, ambiguous and confusing. While at one moment technology is equated with progress and the promise of a world of plenty, free from toil, in the next it evokes the vision of a world gone mad, out of control, the vision of Frankenstein.

In Mary Wollstonecraft Shelley's tale, on the verge of creating his terrible offspring, Victor Frankenstein sees only its utopian potential. Pondering his ability to replace kinship with science in the creation of life, the doctor proclaims:

> So much has been done . . . more, far more, will I achieve: treading in steps already marked, I will pioneer a new way, explore unknown powers, and unfold to the world the deepest mysteries of creation.[1]

This is the voice of eighteenth-century Enlightenment. The universe makes sense and it can be known, mastered, by its laws. Such knowledge of nature's secrets, once grounds for expulsion from Paradise, pointed Christendom toward the ultimate perfectability of human existence, as the "Great Mechanic" of the heavens gave way to the greater mechanic (and entrepreneur) on the ground.

Yet it is not long before Dr. Frankenstein's pride turns to a terror born of his own creation. The highly articulate monster of Shelley's story, betrayed by his father's fears, turns on his ambivalent creator with foreboding. He issues the following expression of a familiar technological predicament: "You are my creator," he says, "but I am your master." Then, for those of us not fully apprised of the extent of his mastery, he warns: "*I will be with you on your wedding night.*"[2]

The tale is recurrent within the industrial era. In one updated version, the film *Demon Seed* tells the story of a computer-monster that appropriates for itself all of the prerogatives of its creator. Securing its creator's home, the computer moves to help itself to the scientist's wife, raping her and impregnating her with the embryo of a new and ominous species—one that places humankind itself in jeopardy.[3]

Although the main theme in the Frankenstein legend lends itself to an Oedipal interpretation, the terror the story evokes should not be understood as purely or primarily sexual: neither is it purely or primarily about existence. Despite the unclear social relations expressed by the legends of Frankenstein, there is a particular social relation implicit within the legend. Historically, the story of human initiative as it is displaced by the demands of the "machine" is reflected most generally in the experience and consciousness of class. It is in the formation of the industrial working class that the visionary lullaby of technology is broken by the din of an ensuing nightmare. If the "machine" brings terror and pain to the human soul, it is because, for most people, the "machine" is not theirs. Like the monster, as "free laborers" they are but a part of it, pieces within a controllable universe that is out of their control.

Yet if for some the "machine" has provided a metaphor for domination, for others it has represented a guiding principle by which they might dominate. For an emerging bourgeoisie, the "machine" was no mere piece of equipment. First and foremost it was a way of perceiving the world. Historian Carlo Cipolla has argued that by the mid-seventeenth century, "the mechanization of the world view" was well under way. The machine provided a "reference-idea" by which the world could be understood, possessed, and mastered. In universities, speculative and contemplative philosophy and "traditional scholarship" were undercut by an "experimental and mechanical" philosophy, the aim of which was, very simply, "the whole 'management of this great machine of the world.' "[4]

Long before the rise of factory capitalism and the extensive use of power-driven machinery, the "machine" represented—

within evolving bourgeois thought—a vision of a world in which all human and material resources, even the power of creation, constituted a "complex apparatus of interrelated and moving parts."[5] In the nineteenth century, with the mammoth growth of industrialism, the stark contrast between the machine as a "reference-idea" and the machine as a social instrument of production became painfully apparent. Manchester, England, and other industrial hellholes revealed to a growing factory population the specter of "dark Satanic mills"—the impoverishment, disease, and squalor of working-class lives alongside the "wonders" of the machine age. Yet even amid the manifest contradictions created by industrial capitalism, machines themselves would often be publicly exhibited, not only as examples of scientific development, but as totems to the vision of a manageable universe. The "Corliss Engine," a gargantuan device exhibited at the Philadelphia Centennial Exposition (1876), was only one example. The engine, displayed in a tabernacle to industry, gave middle-class onlookers a modern religious experience. Viewers of the engine were often reduced to tears in its awesome presence, swept away by the apparition that they were witness to the power of the universe, tamed and harnessed by reasonable, enlightened science.[6] Separated from its industrial context, and enshrined within a house of secular worship, the engine stood as testimony to a world that could be controlled.

Behind this notion of a totally manageable world, there was an implicit cultural premise. For the world to be apprehended as a well-oiled machine, one must assume that the intricate fabric of daily life itself can be controlled by those who understand its workings. Within this entrepreneurial conceit lies the imperative to develop a means by which the law, knowledge, information, transactions, and priorities of an expanding world market economy can be regulated: a *technology of discourse*. The ability to accumulate, package, and disseminate knowledge represented the formation of new networks of understanding, prefiguring the slow abolition of autonomous and indigenous popular forms of "culture."

For more than five hundred years, the growth of capitalism has depended on the ability to manage and distribute standardized know-how and information. "Mass communication" is not an isolated phenomenon of twentieth-century capitalism, sustaining and reorganizing a society *previously* defined by the rise of factory production and discipline and by the development of heavy machinery. For capitalism, mechanical production and image making have long shared the same quilt. Though the rise of machinery, utilizing interchangeable parts and proliferating standardized goods, preceded the development of modern communications technology, it was the technology of communications that, within Europe by the mid-fifteenth century, offered the prototype for the machine age, for the era of factory industrialism. The first printing presses were ensembles of skills and tools from an artisan tradition. Scribal skills and papers, combined with artisan punches and a modified winepress, produced a mechanism that permanently altered social definitions of work and production. This mechanism — *the printing press* — was the first mass-production machine, and by the late fifteenth century it represented the most dramatic contrast available between the localized, erratic tempo of customary life and the worldly promise of capitalist enterprise. Not only were early printshops capitalist operations; some were *factories*. By 1480, less than forty years after Gutenberg's initial enterprise, the Koberger Press in Nuremberg employed a hundred men, operating twenty-four presses.[7]

To a large extent, the history of printing coincides with the history of an emergent world commerce; they were often intertwined. It is no coincidence that the first printer in the English language, William Caxton, was also the leading English wool merchant (*mercer*) at Bruges, Belgium. Printing enabled commerce to develop a more universal and consistent language, appropriate to mobile, contractual transactions. Printing could standardize texts and disseminate information and imagery in ways impossible within the constraints and imprecisions of the traditional scribal culture. Printing was a tool of revolution by which world commercial networks could be established and maintained; by which a mobile economy could be underwritten and secured.[8] Herbert Schiller has noted that in today's world, the integration of capitalism is ensured by the maintenance of a world information order.[9] Already by the sixteenth century, the printed word was, to a large extent, the connective tissue of what Immanuel Wallerstein has termed "the modern world system."[10]

Yet the machinery of print was not, from its inception, the whole or implicit monopoly of an unfolding world commerce. The power to reproduce and spread ideas and information served a variety of social forces and possibilities. Print was also a revolutionary, democratic tool, central in the unraveling of old, feudal seats of authority and power. The spread of knowledge and literacy that came in the wake of printing reached far and wide. Beyond its service in the development of commercial enterprise, print raised the possibility of a transportable popular discourse, explosive in the context of feudalism.

Throughout most of feudal Europe, the written word had been a monopoly of the church. Books were rare and costly, handwritten slowly and individually by scribes. Within such a world, literacy was unusual, limited to those clerics who had access to scribal texts. In addition, texts were for the most part written in Latin. While the clergy could read and understand them, they were indecipherable to those limited to vernacular tongues. This monopoly over the word gave the clergy enormous power, for they reserved the right to interpret what others could not read or understand. This power was particularly significant in the reading of the Bible.

The Bible was the word of God, the universal law, but its interpretation was left to those privileged few who could read it. Within the context of feudal Catholicism, biblical interpretation tended to underwrite the immense social, political, landholding power of the church. Exegesis underwrote structures of hierarchy and authority. Vast chasms between the material abundance of church and nobility and the scarcity experienced by peasants were represented as the immutable order of things. Salvation came from obedience to that order. According to the predominant clerical reading of the Bible, social inequity was the way of God. The sufferings of the poor were humankind's payment for *original sin*. Those who sat comfortably at the heights of social power did so, it was asserted, as a divine right; they were agents of God.

While feudal power was often held and defended by the sword, it was justified by the word. The monopoly over *the word*, over literacy, and over the ability to interpret what was read, was the fundamental aspect of rule.

Even before printing developed in the mid-fifteenth century, there were some radical challenges to this structure. If exclusive access to the word of God was used to justify the position and privilege of an often-profligate clergy, attempts to break that monopoly stood at the heart of social revolt. In England, John Wycliffe and the Lollards (literally, "Babblers") moved against the monopoly over the word in the early fourteenth century. Preparing a vernacular translation of the Bible, and consequently breaking the Latin cipher of the church, Wycliffe went throughout the countryside, reading the Bible aloud *in the vernacular.* Whereas the church limited access and interpretation to a clerical elite, Wycliffe and the Lollards sought to spread access to the Bible among people customarily banned from the power of interpretation. The results were explosive. With the word of God in the hands of the people, church hegemony and practices came under simultaneous attack. Implicitly democratic, the Lollard movement undermined church possession of the word and its interpretation. The spread of literature, the opening up of arenas of interpretation, cut deep into the traditional fabric of power. Denounced by Pope Gregory XI and later condemned by a synod in England, Wycliffe was branded a heretic, his writings and translation banned.

Printing made this democratic impulse behind Wycliffe's heresy all the more realizable. Within less than a hundred years of Gutenberg's first printed Bible, vernacular translations were widespread throughout Europe. In addition, a wide variety of literature began to appear in the vernacular, not only accessible to more and more people, but able to be interpreted in terms of those people's experience and perspective.

For increasingly mobile sectors of the European population —not just merchants, but also artisans, low-level civil servants, and rural and an emerging urban poor—the demand for printed, vernacular literature plowed into the static, entrenched soil of the feudal order. The spread of vernacular literature, and of literacy, enabled individuals to spread knowledge and ideas, to interpret the world in their own terms. Alongside commercial networks of printed materials, a radical vernacular tradition began to emerge. The reproducible and transportable capacities of print offered vast possibilities of popular knowledge and expression. Written knowledge, once the exclusive domain of elites, now might reach and permeate populations held down by ignorance. The power to speak through the printing press provided the link between literacy and struggle. Beyond serving as a tool of mercantilism, print was a tool of emancipation; much of the early history of printed materials is that of a vernacular literature of protest and revolt, of popular sentiment and activity. In addition to a commercial intelligence, printing expanded access to democratic ideas, notions of individual and natural rights.

Literacy and access to the printed word were cardinal elements in the overturning of social systems predicated on popular ignorance. For centuries following the development of the printing press, access to the word was an essential demand among people attempting to break the chains of autocracy.

One of the most eloquent and penetrating discussions of the liberating powers of literacy was voiced by the great black abolitionist Frederick Douglass. For Douglass, raised in slavery in Maryland, access to the word was a critical device of freedom. In his autobiography, *My Bondage and My Freedom*, he tells the story of his own acquisition of literacy, and some of the revealing lessons he learned along the way. As a boy, Douglass would frequently overhear his mistress reading the Bible aloud. Innocently, and without knowledge of the consequences, young Douglass asked her to teach him, so that he too might read from the Bible.

> . . . the dear woman began the task, and very soon, by her assistance, I was master of the alphabet, and could spell words of three or four letters. My mistress seemed almost as proud of my progress, as if I had been her own child; and, supposing that her husband would be as well pleased, she made no secret of what she was doing for me. . . .

Douglass continues, describing her husband's response:

> Master Hugh was amazed at the simplicity of his spouse, and probably for the first time, he unfolded to her the true philosophy of slavery, and the peculiar rules necessary to be observed by masters and mistresses, in the management of their human chattels. (He) . . . forbade the continuance of her instruction; telling her . . . that the thing itself was unlawful; that it was also unsafe. . . . To use his own words . . . he said,

"if you give a nigger an inch, he will take an ell"; "he should know nothing but the will of his master, and learn to obey it." "Learning will spoil the best nigger in the world"; "if you teach that nigger—speaking of myself—how to read the bible, there will be no keeping him"; "it would forever unfit him for the duties of a slave"; . . . "if you learn him now to read, he'll want to know how to write; and this accomplished, he'll be running away with himself." Such was the tenor of Master Hugh's oracular exposition of the true philosophy of training human chattel; and it must be confessed that he very clearly comprehended the nature and the requirements of master and slave.

For Douglass, the consequences of Master Hugh's oration were explosive and liberating:

The effect of his words, *on me*, was neither slight nor transitory. His iron sentences—cold and harsh—sunk deep into my heart, and stirred up not only my feelings into a sort of rebellion, but awakened within me a slumbering train of vital thought. It was a new and special revelation, dispelling a painful mystery, against which my youthful understanding had struggled, and struggled in vain, to wit: the *white* man's power to perpetuate the enslavement of the *black* man.[11] (Emphasis added.)

Douglass's words cut to the heart of the matter. As literacy had been a province of power among feudal clergy, slavery in the United States also depended on the exclusive literacy of whites, in order to maintain dominion over blacks. Access to the word—the ability to read, write, interpret, and spread ideas through print—was essential to the emancipation of blacks from the generations of bondage. Not only does Douglass speak to the emancipatory power of literary, he also illuminates the reluctance, on the part of ruling elites, to allow literacy and knowledge to spread beyond themselves.

Increased popular access to the word also inspired new interpretations. Often these interpretations were at odds not only with the feudal past, but with the outlook of new, commercial forces as well. If the predominant idea of a "world-machine" was consistent with the concentration of property and power in the hands of a few, radical appropriations of the printing press offered a different, more egalitarian worldview. Writing in 1649, Gerard Winstanley, a revolutionary English pamphleteer and a leader of the "True Levellers" (also known as "Diggers"), for example, offered a differed view of creation, one challenging the traditional notion that poverty was the legacy of original sin:

> In the beginning of time, the great creator, Reason, made the earth to be
> a common treasury, to preserve beasts, birds, fishes and man, the lord
> that was to govern this creation. . . . Not one word was spoken in the
> beginning that one branch of mankind should rule over another. . . .
> But . . . selfish imaginations did set up one man to teach and rule over
> another. And thereby . . . man was brought into bondage, and became
> a greater slave to such of his own kind than the beasts of the field were
> to him.[12]

Winstanley's words give us a good sense of the explosive capacity of vernacular printing. If in the traditional, clerical interpretation, poverty was the mark of sin, Winstanley sees property as sin, the result of bloody thievery. His reading of "creation" makes no allowance for autocratic control over land; Winstanley's God created the world as a "common treasury," motivated by Reason, not by vengeance against sinful humanity. Against a society marked by vast disparities of poverty and wealth, Winstanley appropriated the Bible on behalf of a world in which "the poorest man hath as true a title and just right to the land as the richest man." Diverting from definitions of *freedom* that accentuated the mobile needs of a commercial bourgeoisie, Winstanley posited a worldview in which "true freedom lies in the free enjoyment of the earth" for all.

Pamphlets, like those penned by Winstanley, were printed in the fields of battle, amid the Puritan revolution. Articulated in an accessible vernacular, they reached a population formerly proscribed from textual interpretation. By the latter years of the eighteenth century, this vernacular tradition of pamphleteering was an essential component in the flourishing of popular movements. In the words of Thomas Paine, for example, vernacular literature and increasing literacy merged with sensuous glory. *Common Sense*, published by Paine in January 1776, represented the triumph of the vernacular as a potent and compelling revolutionary form, one that spoke to and touched the experiences of its readers. Like Winstanley's, Paine's vernacular is a voice of Reason, an assault against tyranny. Its imagery, compelling and inspirational, was also accessible, written in terms that could be understood by nearly anyone:

> O! Ye that love mankind! Ye that dare oppose not only the tyranny but
> the tyrant, stand forth! Every spot of the Old World is over-run with

oppression. Freedom hath been hunted round the globe. Asia and Africa
have long expelled her. Europe regards her like a stranger, and England
hath given her warning to depart. O receive the fugitive, and prepare in
time an asylum for mankind.[13]

Paine's words offered an explosive, vernacular, political language, words waging war against the tyranny of British rule.
The ability to spread the word, rooted in the rise of a vernacular
literature and literacy, was essential to the popular mobilization
for the American Revolution.

Douglass, Winstanley, and Paine were powerful representa-
tives of a vernacular literary tradition, rooted in the development
of print and given impetus by developments that made printing
presses relatively cheap and extremely portable. Simultaneous to
the spread of printing throughout much of Europe was the circulation of an "underground" literature, using the new technology of discourse as a weapon against dominant structures of power and authority. The early history of the print media was not
one of a monolithic commercial development, but of a battle-
ground upon which struggles for social power and popular initiative were hotly contested.

Yet alongside the flowering of this vernacular tradition, the
most widespread implementation of print was in the accumulation, reproduction, and transmittal of information essential to an
unfolding world market. Well into the nineteenth century, one
of the most pervasive uses of printing was the dissemination of
commercial intelligence. Long before the "newspaper" became
known as a popular form of diversion, it was a vehicle of commerce, passing privileged mercantile dispatches from branch
office to branch office; from port to port; from seller to buyer
and back again. As the mechanic on the ground inherited the
creative powers of the mechanic in the sky, so too did the mysterious word and law of God give way to a worldly word and
law, informed largely by the priorities of commerce and industry.

By the 1830s, in the United States, this commercial tradition
in print took a new turn. Appealing to an increasingly literate
working class, and contending with a potentially dangerous vernacular tradition, farsighted entrepreneurs began to develop a

mass medium that was commercial in outlook and orientation, but that absorbed a vernacular idiom. The development of the "penny press"—a mass-circulation, commercial press—was the embryo of the twentieth-century mass media. As commercial ventures, these newspapers appropriated a common form of speaking, appealing to a wide, literate audience. Employing newswriting formulas that couched stories in fantastic, moralistic, and authoritative terms, these newspapers moved from being the limited, commercially oriented information sheets of the past, into commercial forms of popular entertainment and disclosure. Commerce was developing a popular "audience." While these papers built their readership by connecting their parlance to the terms of popular, urban experience, they were also vehicles that celebrated the mechanical worldview of the entrepreneurs. In the pages of this press, commercial enterprise was enshrouded in the magical liturgy of "progress." Science and invention were heavily promoted, presented in ways to capture the imaginations of a readership whose day-to-day confrontations with technological development might be considerably less entertaining. Newspapers offered readers a way of interpreting their world; moral lessons about urban life; fantastic visions of worlds unknown; and authoritative renderings of things to come.

Yet commercial information was still an exclusive currency within an expanding market economy. Commercially supported newspapers represented a hybrid between entrepreneurial interests and popular, vernacular forms of expression. Meanwhile, other forms of communication were promoted to provide exclusive channels for commerce. The early development of the telegraph, and later the wireless, reflected this priority.

While the first officially sent telegraph message—"WHAT HATH GOD WROUGHT"—suggested an invention that stood above pecuniary interests, it is noteworthy that the lines along which this message was sent were laid beside the roadbed of the Baltimore and Ohio Railroad between Baltimore and Washington, D.C. As new telegraph lines were established within the United States, they relentlessly followed the routes of commerce (or *war*, when required), providing a means for high-speed passing of information, analogous to the speed of carriage provided by the rails. Reflecting the centrality of communications to the rise of industrial America, the first major industrial monopoly (Western Union) was established over the field of telegraphy; the integration and control of commercial and requisite military information were at stake. By 1867, a specialized adaptation of the magnetic telegraph had been developed in the form of the stock ticker; once again, communications technology had elaborated upon the infrastructure of the "great machine of the world." It had done so using wires and code, circumventing the explosive lines of battle encompassed by the vernacular.

Following the pattern by which American telegraph and rail lines coincided, the British control of a global, oceanic empire was similarly integrated by the introduction of submarine telegraph cables. In 1851 a cable was laid across the English Channel from Dover to Calais. By 1864, another stretched to the Persian Gulf, providing near-instantaneous commercial and military contact between England and India; and 1866 witnessed the successful laying of a transatlantic cable. By 1871 (less than thirty years after the first overland lines had been established), the telegraphic cohesion of Empire was achieved with an underwater line to Australia.

The early development of the "wireless" had a similar pattern. Years before radio was commercially promoted as a vernacular medium of mass entertainment and impression, it was advanced by its developers as a refinement of the commercial orientation of telegraphy, allowing, for the first time, ship-to-shore communication. Wireless, like telegraph, was seen as a way of unifying and protecting commercial interests, for the carrying of market and military intelligence. Beyond Marconi, the prime developers of radio patents in the United States included the navy and the United Fruit Company; both saw radio as essential to coordinating their operations.[14]

By the end of the nineteenth century, the consolidation of information into a basic form of currency had become a keystone in the structuring of a capitalist world economy and in the establishment and maintenance of corporate industrialism. If Frankenstein provides us with a telling metaphor for a technological world out of reach and out of control, it is the development of communications systems, to a large extent, that has placed this world beyond the networks of popular discourse. Throughout its historical genesis, the apprehension of industrialism as a monster, as a machinery possessed of a pernicious intelligence, against which popular motives appear virtually helpless, owes much to the presence and elaboration of communication technologies. If print had once been a field of conflict between a vernacular and a commercial tradition, by the mid-nineteenth century the commercial tradition prevailed, in the process appropriating the vernacular, with the rise of mass-circulation newspapers.

By the dawn of the twentieth century, capitalism had come to mean an integrated, increasingly monopolistic interpenetration of market, scientific know-how, industrial and finance capital, and communications networks. Channels of popular sensibility and desire were themselves subject to the encroachments of a marketable vernacular. For triumphant industrial and finance capitalists, this was a moment when the management of the world-machine seemed almost within reach, when (to quote Victor Frankenstein once more) "unknown powers . . . (and) the deepest mysteries of creation" seemed there for the taking. Yet as the mechanical worldview became tangible in its formal structures, it was far from established within the social relations that guided them. If anything, the social experience of industrialism put the lie to the utopian idiom in which the world-machine had been articulated. The years leading up to 1900 were not only times of extreme exploitation and industrial hardship; they were also a time of concerted growing anticapitalist resistance and organization. The fantasy of a smoothly running mechanical world was eroded by the dislocation and unrest that it provoked. Beneath the reference-idea of capitalist development as a machine was a history of what Marx once termed "reckless terrorism." Capitalism, he reiterated, "comes into the world dripping from head to foot, from every pore, with blood and dirt."[15] For the industrial working class, and for those caught in the ever-widening sweep of capitalist dominion, it was a development that spelled continual and multiplying social crisis. Culture and social life were torn apart. As the machine represented a guiding principle for a maturing bourgeoisie, for those in its path it was the embodiment of the "white terror," threatening life itself.

For the industrial working class at the turn of the twentieth century, the social crisis was manifest and immediate. The sanguine and utopian rhapsodies of a new machine age were drowned out by the mechanical din of the shop. The bourgeois celebration of the machine was answered by a multitude of voices, drawing once again from the tradition of a radical vernacular. The contradictions and irony of the mechanical worldview can be heard in the words of Yiddish poet Morris Rosenfeld, writing of the sweatshops of New York City's garment industry:

> The machines in the shop roar so wildly that often I forget in the roar that I am; I am lost in the terrible tumult, my ego disappears, I am a machine, I work and work and work without end. I am busy and busy at all time. For what and for when? I know not and ask not! How should a machine ever come to think?[16]

Rosenfeld chants the subjective anguish of proletarianization. While the roar of the machines and the discipline of the time clock signal the root of despair, and stir the motive to retaliate, exploitation is understood not in the numerical terms of dollars and hours, not in the terms of the machine. The ironic phrasing "I am a machine" is a recognition that mechanical routine is an attack on the essential integrity of the subject. The revolutions of the machine, so glorious within the liturgy of bourgeois thought, are revealed as an abomination for those who must follow their drumming.

The Capture of the Eye

By the end of the nineteenth century, in the United States, the dissonance between the visionary celebration of the "machine" and the actual experiences of those employed in the mechanical processes of industry had reached crisis proportions. Labor militancy was on the rise and its socialist or syndicalist outlook posed a radical challenge to that of the "world-machine." Consistent with the traditions of the past, much of this militancy found expression in a critical and incendiary vernacular: song, poetry, journalism, political manifesto. While the ideology of mechanical progress permeated entrepreneurial thought, popular perceptions of the machine, and of capitalism itself, grew bitter and seditious. A torrent of antagonism was, more and more, carried by the channels of working-class opinion.

The 1905 *Manifesto* of the nascent Industrial Workers of the World (IWW) offered a depiction of the machine that clashed sharply with the dominating ideology, challenging the very social relations that upheld it:

> The *great facts* of present industry are the displacement of human skill by machines and the increase of capitalist power through concentration in the possession of the tools with which wealth is produced and distributed. (Emphasis added.)

Within such an arrangement, it was argued, the mechanical world becomes an arena of human degradation and destruction:

> As human beings and human skill are displaced by mechanical progress, the capitalists need use the workers only during that brief period when muscles and nerves respond most intensely. The moment the laborer no longer yields the maximum of profits, he is thrown upon the scrap pile, to starve alongside the discarded machine.[17]

Linked as they were to a flowering of revolutionary working-class activity, such ideas jammed the works of the "world-machine" outlook. They challenged the notion that the world could be mastered through the social application of mechanical principles, arguing that it was necessary to serve social needs, not vice versa.

Within the context of such combat, the commercial appropriation of the vernacular took on an increasingly important role in the forging of a modern, industrial ideology. Responsive to an environment shaken by proletarian rage and organization, commercial organs of public communication began to offer ideological concessions to the sway of popular desire. The idiom of a controllable "world-machine" became increasingly encoded with a vision of social promise. While the priorities of the marketplace continued to be asserted, they were phrased in the terms of the general good. "Industrial democracy" and social reform, previously the slogans of those opposing capitalist rapacity, began to enter the commercial dialect.

To an extent, the stage had been set for this development in the 1830s, with the emergence of the "penny" newspapers. As a mass-circulation press, its accomplishment had been based on the ability to translate the vernacular into a viable commercial form. The appeal to common experiences and perceptions provided an essential conduit between commercial institutions and the consciousness of an urban working class. During the latter decades of the nineteenth century, this fusion of perspectives provided the groundwork for a new, socially responsive iconography of capitalism, ostensibly more liable and accountable to its population.

From the mid-1870s to the 1890s, caught in a period of economic stagnation, American industry and federal policy pursued an increasingly aggressive search to expand markets and prosperity. As the domestic frontier was closing, the United States embarked upon assembling a world empire. Surely such a direction required, in a renewed sense, a deep commitment to the idea of a manageable "world-machine." Yet domestically — confronting a surge of class upheaval — the "machine" adjusted its verbiage in the direction of social amelioration, of defusing the roots of social discord. It was a "machine" that, in the name of effecting a more pacific home front, developed a public face that disowned the cold calculation of the mechanical worldview — at the same time pursuing it, internationally, with a vengeance. The "machine," and particularly the decisive machinery of mass communications, would hereafter serve as the public champion of universal possibility and well-being.

Communications assumed a new "progressive" phraseology, espousing the goals of social improvement and change, a palliative to demands being voiced by an increasingly militant working-people's movement. Continuing to develop a sophisticated apparatus as a passageway for privileged intelligence, communications technologies also increasingly entered into the spheres of public discourse. Underwriting a "socially minded" vision of capitalism, media technologies began to emerge, more and more, as the public vehicles of such a vision. The "yellow" journalism of William Randolph Hearst and Joseph Pulitzer, coming to prominence in and around the 1890s, foreshadowed the essential role of *the image* within the new, social strategy of capitalism. These papers made innovative and extensive use of il-

lustration, bold typeface, and sensationalistic style to command
the eyes and minds of their readership. The *photograph* provided
a model for the desired journalistic impact: objective, true to life,
mesmerizing. The photographic model for objectivity gave
Hearst and Pulitzer a vital command over the popular sensibility.[18] The mobilization of a visual world expanded the commercial terrain of the printed vernacular, and made it even more accessible. Yellow journalism gave corporate imagery an inspired
voice, couched in the idiom of social conscience. The papers put
together a broad audience, posing as champions of the industrial
poor and downtrodden, helping to forge the image of the United
States as a refuge for those scorned by the rest of the world.
Pulitzer's New York *World* mobilized a fund-raising campaign to
erect Bertholdi's Statue of Liberty on its pedestal in New York's
harbor, a mischievous promise to incoming immigrant labor.
*"Give me your tired, your poor, your huddled masses yearning to breathe
free. . . . "*

Carefully orchestrating and defending an image of capitalist
America as a land of social promise, Pulitzer and Hearst were
also propaganda architects for the imperial conquests that would
underwrite that promise. It has often been simplistically stated
that Hearst and his New York *Journal* brought about the
Spanish-American War to aid in a circulation war with Pulitzer's
World. Yet the war propaganda fomented in both of their papers
represented a wide-ranging political and commercial strategy,
within which the circulation of newspapers was but a small component. Building up a war fervor by printing a rash of articles
decrying "Spanish atrocities" against "freedom-loving" Cubans,
Hearst erected a massive, socially conscious smoke screen behind which American capitalism took hold of a Caribbean and
Pacific empire. The journalism of the yellow variety provided
the requisite imagery for a new corporate perspective, linking
the humanistic principle of a "full dinner pail" at home with aggressive and militaristic cultivation of markets abroad.

The yellow press, along with other emerging agencies of mass
impression, was a pioneer in the widespread dissemination of
photographic and other pictorial imagery. In the early years of
this century, the camera, particularly motion pictures, best revealed the charismatic social possibilities of communications

technology. The camera was a powerful mechanism for convey-
ing fantasy and suggesting transcendence; its imagery employed
a powerful, visual vernacular, understandable even to immigrants unable to speak English. Yet at the same time, in its
ability to codify and capture an objectivist "truth" it was also a
powerful mechanism of order and control.

Reflecting progressive corporate thought of the time, *Scientific
American* discussed the invention of the movie camera in its ency-
clopedic publication *The Book of Progress*, a three-volume work
that appeared in 1915.[19] Here the movie camera is situated first
in a long catalog of industrial accomplishments, discussed in two
entries on movie technology.

The first entry ponders the rise of the movies as a popular entertainment, one particularly appealing to the urban, immigrant
work force: the initial movie audience. The article is lyrical about
cinema's ability to portray an altered vision of reality, and its
ability to enlist the senses in such a vision:

> Here, at last, is the magic of childhood—appearances, apparitions, ob-
> jects possessed of power of movement and of intelligence. . . .
>   For the motion picture does for us what no other thing can do save a
> drug, or, in slight degree, long, long training. . . . It eliminates the
> time between happenings and brings two events separated actually by
> hours of time and makes them seem to us as following each other with
> no interval between them. Unconscious of this sixth sense of time, *be-
> cause it is so much a factor of our daily lives*, ignorant of the fact that it is
> this and not our eyes alone which have been tricked, we leave the dar-
> kened theater with wonder in our hearts and admiration on our lips.[20]
> (Emphasis added.)

Consistent with the way we see *advertised* goods today, the
machine is ripped from its association with the monotone of the
workplace; it is not the vehicle of direct commercial transac-
tion.[21] Revealing a significant break from the customary capitalist use of communications technology, this machine enacts a
symbolic assault on the conventions of *time* that rule in a society
where people make money, live, by selling their time. *The Book
of Progress* consecrates cinema as the carrier of utopian possibility.
While integral to the marketplace, this is a machine that apparently wages war on the "machine." It offered, in its imagery, the
language of dream in theatrical darkness; the possibility of escape

from the constraints of industrial ritual and routine. If the "machine" was, as in Morris Rosenfeld's poem, an attack on the integrity of the subject, the motion picture was a product framed in the imagery of a newly integrated subject, one that evoked transcendent desire within the whirring of its gears. Consumable leisure was ennobled as a subjective answer to the discipline of the "machine." Appropriating, to some extent, the language of the unconscious, of dream and of myth in its imagery, the movie camera could dissociate itself from the tedium of the mechanical process, and realign itself with those realms of existence repressed by the harsh rationalism of "world-machine" ideology. Like the medium in a seance, film crossed the boundary of material existence, evoking a spiritual world. Among the first to use cinema — and earlier, the "magic lantern" — as a public form of entertainment were magicians. It was a part of the spirit world they concocted, the "illusions" by which they captivated their audiences. Later on, these magicians contributed to the development of movie "special effects," further elaborating the link between cinema and apparent miracle.[22] To audiences embroiled in the banality of the mechanical routine, the movie camera was a machine that intimated transcendence and escape. For *The Book of Progress*, this capacity was basic to its achievement.

The second entry on the movie camera in *The Book of Progress* was in stark and sobering contrast to the first, discussing the development of a particular adaptation, the "Gilbreth Chronometer." This device was essentially a moving-picture machine linked to a clock. Invented by management expert Frank Gilbreth, this movie camera was used in performing time-motion studies on industrial workers. In the wake of a rhapsody on the ability of the moving picture to lift people from the time constraints of industrial life, the following description of Gilbreth's movie camera appears:

> Every film [frame] reveals the successive positions of a workman in performing each minute operation of the task entrusted to him. The position of the chronometer pointed in successive films indicates the length of time between successive operations. These films are studied under a microscope, and a careful analysis of each operation is made to develop the standard time for each. . . .
>
> Any workman may, for a time, deceive an inexperienced efficiency

engineer . . . but *the camera cannot be deceived.* . . . . The film records faithfully every movement made, and subsequent analysis and study reveal exactly how many of these movements were necessary and how many were purposely slow or useless.[23] (Emphasis added.)

Implemented within the realm of production, film becomes a mechanism of bald social control. As the movies constituted a consumable form of leisure, predicated on escape, this movie camera reinforced the entrepreneurial idea of an objective "world-machine" from which no variation or escape is possible. Broken from and doing battle with the relentless rhythms of the industrial machine, it is at the same time a faithful servant to capitalist order — on one hand as a transcendental vehicle of mass illusion, on the other, an instrument of "truth" ("*the camera* cannot be deceived"). Its hold on truth consumes our own.

In this and other examples of communications technology, the dialectic of mass culture is manifest. For popular consumption, leisure, the technology is the carrier of visionary escape. Elsewhere, the technology performs, organizes, stores surveillance. We become data, facts, in the "world-machine." Here the traditional use of communications technology continues unabated. Mechanical control is maintained as the reference-idea of capitalism.[24]

The unity of illusion and control, presented by *Scientific American* in 1915, has established the terms that have characterized industrial culture in the twentieth century. This is a theme, a concern, that runs through the essays that follow. This pattern has informed the development of the "consciousness industries." Machinery is both the monster of Frankenstein and the bribe by which that monster is endured. The mass media and the industries of fashion and design, through the production and distribution of imagery, have reconciled widespread vernacular demands for a better life with the general priorities of corporate capitalism. The growth of the advertising industry, beginning in the 1920s, is *the* fundamental expression of this development. Built on expanded production and the economic potential of consumer markets, advertising created the imagery, the aesthetic, of a social-democratic capitalism, one that understood and would claim to solve the most basic contradictions of modern life.

Within this altered landscape, technologies of communication stand prominently. If previously they had served as a blood-stream nourishing the "world-machine," in the decades leading up to the twentieth century they emerged, more and more, as vehicles by which capitalist culture offered a way out. Altering the meaning of industrial social control, communications technologies were employed to convey an intelligence that was seemingly at odds with the mechanical discipline of industrial productivity.

2

Consumption as a Way of Life

"The System Is the Solution"

The scene opens: A pair of hands interlocking the pieces of a three-dimensional wooden "Chinese" puzzle. As the puzzle is solved, a softly modulated man's voice explains that most "industrial problems" or "business problems" are actually "communications problems."

Businessmen and industrialists, take note! An effective, well-designed, integrated system of *communicating* is the key to a smoothly running enterprise.

At last the disembodied hands complete their task. The puzzle is complete. Behold! It has formed the logo of the American Telephone and Telegraph Company, the largest corporation on earth.

Now the screen goes black, and a white-lettered message crosses it, proclaiming:

The system is the solution.

Like stars in the firmament.

This television ad ran during evening national news broadcasts. As people within a highly technological, consumer society, the message addresses us as a philosophical statement about the world in which we live. A quintessential example of the communications industry's self-projected image, it offers total control as a positive ideal, an absolute good. Elsewhere, the same corporation claims that its channels provide us with the where-   *23* withal to "reach out and touch someone." Families are kept to-gether, friendships maintained as we purchase the services of AT&T.

The image, the commercial, reaches out to sell more than a service or product; it sells a way of understanding the world. The basic premise is that in a corporate, industrial world, it is the agencies of communication that provide the mechanisms for so-cial order. The notion appeals to the businessman's desire for effective management. For the rest of us, as mobile, often-isolated individuals in an industrial consumer society, it promises that which is increasingly elusive: kinship and com-munity.

Mass imagery, such as that provided by AT&T, creates for us a memorable language, a system of belief, an ongoing channel to inculcate and effect common perceptions, explaining to us what it means to be a part of a "modern world." It is a world defined by the retail (individualized) consumption of goods and services; a world in which social relations are often disciplined by the ex-change of money; a world where it increasingly *makes sense* that if there are solutions to be had, they can be bought. Such reminders as those seen in the above ad are commonplace. Con-sumption is our way of life.

Commercial imagery — ads, packaging, public relations, film, television, and so on — plays an ongoing part in the reinforce-ment of this way of life. Yet for us, images merely reaffirm that which is structured within the terms of existence. A question — rarely addressed within commercial depictions of the world — remains. How did this way of life come about? Also, since mass imagery plays such an important role in our kind of society, what role has it played historically in the directing of people into consumption as a way of life, a way of understanding?

An American Metamorphosis

As a seven-year-old girl, Anna Kuthan worked in a small textile factory in Czechoslovakia. She was born into a world of home production and self-sufficiency, but with her leaving home, her

daily labors already represented a compromise with a new unfolding world of mass production. Each day she went to the factory and applied her small young body to the task of unloading
bales of cotton, sent there from a faraway place called Texas, in
the United States.[1]

These bales of cotton provided Anna with more than her
childhood labors; they also gave her a first glimpse of America.
On the wrapping of each bale, a colorful lithographed label
provided her with a utopian vision of the world from which they
had come. In the "big beautiful pictures" she saw a vision that
contrasted sharply with the tedium of her own daily chores.
They showed "the plantation and the colored people, you know,
pictures of how everybody worked and was happy." The children in the factory in Czechoslovakia looked at these pictures
each day, weighing them against the hardships of their own experience. For the time being, the pictures served to bring a piece
of beauty into their lives. "We got them off nicely," she recalls,
"and we decorated everything" with them. But the labels also
provoked the wellsprings of desire, pointing her, and others of
her generation, toward America as a place to go, to live: "Oh my
God! I save every picture and I was always saying I wish I could
get to this country. I was dreaming already about this country.

But from the perspective of years of life in America, she
found—in this instance—a fissure between image and reality.

> I came to this country and worked with the colored people and hear
> about and read about the history of the slaves and everything. . . .
> Then I realize that—Oh my God—how they have to work on the big
> plantation in the cotton fields, all those black people and children for
> nothing . . . you know, like slaves.

Nevertheless, the images had stood by themselves: promising
and alluring. A way of life was heralded by a colorful label, pasted on the side of a cotton bale, and planted in the imagination of
a seven-year-old Czech girl in the first few years of this century.

It was during the First World War that, as a young woman,
Anna Kuthan came to Vienna, where she took work as a domestic servant to a wealthy Viennese woman. One of Anna's jobs
was to pick up Red Cross packages filled with goods from
America, and bring them to the home of her employer. Even

though, as a domestic servant, she was denied access to these provisions, she saw the packaging in which they arrived. Like the labels on the cotton bales, those she saw on the Hecker's flour, the Nestlé's cocoa, and the Carnation milk helped to form in her mind a vision of America as a land of plenty:

> I saved all the labels, even from the Hecker's flour. I says, "Oh my God, they must have everything so good if they pack everything so good. If I could only come to this country."

While she was permitted to save the labels from empty containers, their contents were forbidden. "The lady locked everything up," she tells us. She could only imagine that wondrous goods must reside within such brightly decorated packaging. One day, she remembers, her questions were answered. Her employer was away from the house and had forgotten to lock up the provisions. This was Anna's moment of discovery:

> You know what I did? I just put the can in my mouth and it was dripping like honey right in my mouth. And one, two, three she opened the door. I says, "It's inside already, you can't get it out of me!" I got a taste for it. I never forgot it.

After the war was over, Anna made her pilgrimage to the United States. Her experiences of denial and getting caught in the act of stealing were constantly on her mind. To a large extent, she recalls, what she saw in America was a dream come true:

> When I came to this country, the first thing I see is those big stores. I said, "There is the Hecker's flour . . . there is the condensed milk!"
> I was married. . . . One day I was shopping and I came home. [My husband] says, "What happened to you?"

She responds:

> "All the things I bought in the stores . . . what I got in Vienna and I could only dream about, not even taste it. And here I see it on the shelf. I bought everything and I'm gonna go there every day and I'm going to buy it!"

As a domestic servant in Vienna, Anna Kuthan saw the consumer products of America as magical objects. Here were the fruits of the land sealed mysteriously in beautified vessels, with painted scenes gracing their outsides. Never before had she seen such things. When, on the occasion described above, she was able to taste from one of these enticing containers on the sly, her experience only served to verify the magic. Like honey the milk flowed past her lips! Yet what was magic for her had for others become a means of day-to-day survival. Already, among the elite of European society, American exports were beginning to make their mark on everyday existence. The terms of luxury were being redefined, and they were coming in cans.

For Anna these cans took on great significance. Beyond their mystical properties, they were concrete embodiments of her own deprivation, of what she desired. From the home of her employer she could take the gaily colored cans, emptied of their content. She was allowed to keep the packaging—the image of a good life—but was denied its contents. The brand names of this new, consumer economy became symbols of her own denial, her class-bound status; they also became channels for her desires, emblems of a world denied, embodiments of wishes unfulfilled. Mere objects, mass-produced in factories, held a highly personal significance; they were benchmarks of servitude, carriers of fantasy. The stolen taste of these products was, in part, an impetuous attempt to break through that world of denial; to assert her own needs and tastes. Before Anna ever set foot in America, her subjectivity had become intertwined with the brand names and products of a young and burgeoning consumer society. Through these she came to understand and define "America."

Arriving in the United States, Anna found these objects of denial flamboyantly displayed in store windows and in advertising. They beckoned to her as symbols of a heretofore unfulfilled expectation. Hecker's flour sacks and Carnation milk cans stared out at her with a promise: What had been denied to her as a servant in Vienna, or as a child laborer in Czechoslovakia, was now available for her own consumption. It was only up to her and her ability to buy. The availability of these products, even on the shelves of stores in which she shopped, was symbolic of a new social position. She was becoming a "free consumer" in an increasingly universal, consumer marketplace. The new constellations of the consumer economy defied the class-bound world of Europe; what was possible only for the upper class in Europe

was for her a part of the storehouse of goods that might be purchased for money wherever one turned.

Tears streaming down her face, Anna Kuthan rushed into the
grocery store to buy with her small earnings the goods that had
become so important, so pregnant, in her previous history. The
ability to buy these goods in America was not just an objective
act of consumption; it was an act of transcendence, and the realization of a new social status. The brand names and trademarks
of America's flowering consumer society formed a historical
unity in Anna's passage from a European domestic servant to a
new consumer in an industrial society. The image, along with
more conventional means of transport, was a vehicle for historical travel.

Anna Kuthan's experience was widely shared. For many people, abroad and even in rural America, the proliferation of mass
images provided an introduction to a new way of life promised
by industrial America. One such introduction was a flyer circu-
lated and posted in Italy's *mezzogiorno* (southern tier) at the turn
of the century, addressed to a decimated peasantry plagued by
taxes and rents, historical victims of the ascendancy of the industrial north. One of countless circulars inviting viewers to come
to America, this flyer was distributed by woolen manufacturers'
agents from Lawrence, Massachusetts, and showed a "picture of
a mill on one side of the street and a bank on the other—and
workers trooping from one to the other with bags of money under their arms." Linking "ancient utopian motives" to an as-yet-
unknown future in industrial America, this ad functioned as an
initiation into the terms of *modernity*.[2]

Likewise, within the United States, many rural people who
moved into the industrial cities of the north had held similar
hopes. Herbert Gutman tells us of an advertisement distributed
among black Alabamans during a Kansas coal strike of 1896–97:

> WANTED! COLORED coal-miners for Weir City, Kan., district, the
> paradise for colored people. . . . Special train will leave Birmingham
> the 13th. Transportation advanced. Get ready and go to the land of
> promise.[3]

Industrial wages held a utopian promise for many freedmen
historically denied any claim to the land. Wages could provide

the wherewithal for former slaves to return south and establish, for the first time, a sovereignty on the land—a hope instilled by the broken promise of Reconstruction: "Forty acres and a mule."

Unlike the later ad from AT&T, which assumes a viewership well-schooled in the logic of the consumer metropolis, these flyers—wooing people from one world into another—offered an unknown, which—through an image—promised to alleviate the hardships of immediate experience. It is only fitting that the first contact with an emerging consumer society should have come in the form of an advertisement, an artifact so characteristic of such a world.

The flyer, and the broad ensemble of alluring imagery to which it belonged, offered a first glimmer of a distant society where industrial development and a triumphal ideology of *progress* were forging new and unfamiliar precepts of survival. America was not a land where existence proceeded according to the venerable laws of nature. Industrial growth was premised on the taming of the natural world, molding it to the expansive imaginations of technological dreamers. Man would create a *nature* of his own, beyond that to which people had historically been bound. Unbeknownst to these peasants, whose axioms of survival had been instructed by a reciprocal engagement with the land, they were beckoned to a place where the transcendence and domination of nature was a project of loud-spoken and evangelical proportions. The world that called was one without a peasantry; its landed wealth had been amassed by means of large-scale capitalist agriculture.[4] The claim of the New World was that here basic goods came from no apparent source. The ecology of the land, and the finger-knowledge of home and workshop production, were memories in the process of being annihilated.

While the America depicted in the circulars offered itself as a land of money and of promise, we cannot assume that the circulars were understood in their own terms. Millions came to the "land of dollars," but they did not necessarily want to abandon the "old culture." Because they needed and sought money does not mean that they consciously embraced a worldview in which the abstraction of money (*false estate*) provided the basis of "value" or of "worth." Born of the land, many of these people held on to a notion of value bound to the tangible utility of the land (*real estate*) and the knowledge that it was the land—ultimately —that supports life.

Indeed, many saw money as a device, something to be saved and consolidated to replenish and revitalize their connection to a customary means of survival, while those who paid these immigrants their wages were merely concerned with sustaining them as laborers in the here and now. The immigrants themselves often hoped to bankroll a return to their roots. Many saw migration as but a temporary foray, one that would allow for a prosperous reunification with an old and more familiar way of life.[5]

Such hopes persist today among people who, over a lifetime, are caught in the dynamics of an unequally developed world; "guest workers," migrant, industrial laborers in Europe flock to industrial centers with the hope of returning home to enjoy a new prosperity. But now that the return home is systematically enforced at the completion of one's contracted work, it is a return more likely to be accompanied by impoverishment and extreme alienation. Such alienation is rooted in the unclouded recognition of oneself as a movable and malleable object in the design of others.[6]

In the United States, even at the turn of the century, this sense of alienation was widely expressed among the millions who made the journey. In Mike Gold's autobiographical immigrant novel, *Jews without Money*, the author's father put this sense of cultural disruption succinctly when he called America "the thief." Initially interpreted as a vehicle for replenishing a familiar way of life, wage labor and the practice of selling time were soon revealed as a new structure of domination.[7] Wages did not behave like capital. Capital behaved a little like land; it was a form of wealth that sustained those who owned it; it replenished itself. Wages, on the other hand, were different. The little money that working people gathered in America was something to be spent, to be used up. It involved no posterity, held out little hope. Among people whose agrarian and handicraft backgrounds taught them that consumption was anathema, consumption was being proffered as a necessary definition of citizenship in the New World. Each day they *used up* the means to survival.

This new physics of survival, and the cultural transformation it entailed, can be seen in language itself. In Raymond Williams's historical etymology of the word "consumer," the alteration of meanings reflects alterations in the way of life.[8] In its original usage (rooted in French) to *consume* was an act of pillage. It meant to "take up completely, devour, waste, spend." "In almost all its early English uses," Williams contends, "*consume* had an unfavorable sense; it meant to destroy, to use up, to waste, to exhaust." It is the meaning expressed in the old term for tuberculosis: "consumption." The implication was clearly that using up such a basic resource as land was contrary to the interests of survival. The negative connotation remained dominant in English through the sixteenth century. In the seventeenth century, as a world market economy grew, based on the new media of exchange, "using up" and the demand it created became increasingly linked to prosperity; as exchange left the ancient sense of natural propriety behind, the term "consumer" took on a neutral, then a self-congratulatory meaning. Today, in the United States, people unselfconsciously refer to themselves as *consumers*.[9]

In a context where value and survival were evidently and directly derived from the land, or from the direct appropriation of nature, consumption on a mass scale would have meant suicide. For the agrarian and handicraft people who came to populate industrial America, the wage system represented an intrinsic violation of a basic assumption, derived from a sensuous proximity to nature, now increasingly hidden in the mire of industrial production, marketing, and urban life. Even here there was a common compulsion to try to *save*; an often-futile attempt among immigrants to appropriate their money *as if it were land*. In a world increasingly marked by mass industrialism and a nascent consumer market, the separation of people from nature was becoming axiomatic, entailing what Raymond Williams has called "a triumphalist version of 'man's conquest of nature.' "[10]

In the society to which immigrants came, waste and exhaustion were already the keys to the creation of new, industrial markets. In the cases of those people who made steerage to Gotham, the consumption of their traditional understanding of nature, the destruction of skills coming from that way of life, and the exhaustion of the familiar social patterns of customary life (family, community) were primary elements of American mass industrialism as it took shape in the early years of this century. Repeated calls for the "Americanization" of these immigrants came from many decisive and decision-making sectors of American society. In 1925, Edgar Furniss, a social scientist at Yale, expressed an American conviction that was held by many in business and politics, in service bureaucracies, and by academic intellectuals.

"Americanization," Furniss implored, "is the paramount need, not only for the immigrant, but for the very existence of the Republic. Unless the millions of immigrants present and future are made an integral part of the population, understanding our institutions, sharing the standards and ideals of the democracy, the Nation itself is imperiled."[11] While the call for "Americanization" was couched in the terms of eighteenth-century nationalism, immigrants were hardly being invited to join the ruling Yankee-Calvinist brotherhood. Rather, the "American nation" that was raised before them as a social standard was a nation in the process of taking form, becoming standardized and mass-marketed. It was a nation that not only called out to the newly arrived from southern and eastern Europe, but also to an increasingly large, increasingly mobile domestic population. "Americanization" was as process by which a cultural transformation was enacted, a process by which memory came under assault as people were encouraged and/or coerced into equating consumption with survival.

A more biting and satiric definition of "Americanization"—one that spoke eloquently to the pains of this transformation—came from two American social workers, Simon Lubin and Christina Krysto, at the height of a massive "Americanization" campaign in 1919. Offended by the barrage of propaganda that assaulted recently arrived immigrants, Lubin and Krysto insisted that "Americanization" was aimed at the obliteration of traditional culture and its substitution by new, marketplace values:

> Come on all you foreigners, and jump into this magic kettle. You are colored and discolored with things that do not fit in well with affairs here. . . . In fact to speak frankly, there is a certain taint about you, a stain brought by the old world . . .
>
> Your clothes are ill-fitting and ugly. Your language is barbaric. Of course, we do not hold you personally responsible; for you have come from backward and antiquated civilizations, relics of the dark ages. . . .

Jump into the cauldron and behold! You emerge new creatures, up to
date with new customs, habits, traditions, ideals. Immediately you will
become like us; the taint will disappear. Your sacks will be exchanged
for the latest Fifth Avenue styles. Your old-fogey notions will give way
to the most modern and new-fangled ideas. You will be reborn. In
short, you will become full-fledged Americans. The magic process is
certain. Your money back if we fail.[12]

The promise of the "melting pot" was inextricably tied to the
consumption of American goods. It equated the utilization of
consumer products not only with citizenship, but with a demon-
strable and necessary transformation of the self. To be "reborn"
meant a profound metamorphosis in the culture of daily life: a
change in habits and understandings demanded by the new, unfolding agencies of consumption. The message leveled at immigrants found its corollary aimed at vast sectors of the domestic
population as well. "Americanization" was a process through
which all Americans had to pass, whether they were greenhorns
from the old country or rural "hicks" from the new; it was a metaphor for the transition from the age-old logic of agriculture and
handicraft to the logic of consumption.

The first stage was the integration of migrants into the wage
system of labor, which created enormous fissures in people's
comprehension of the material world. Money was an abstract
system of value that was necessary to life, yet it seemed to operate according to an autonomous and lifeless code. It rendered
useless much of the way in which agricultural and handicraft
peoples understood themselves and daily life. The money system
itself functioned as a *mass medium* that restructured people's
needs, transplanting these into a soil nourished by the "rationality" of corporate industry and the retail marketplace. Robert
Park, Chicago School sociologist, was one of the most ardent
chroniclers of this transplanting and a vocal champion of "Americanization." In an enthusiastic, typically progressive discussion
of the transformative powers of money in 1925, Park described
what must have been for immigrant people a wrenching experience:

Money is the cardinal device by which values have become rationalized
and sentiments have been replaced by interests. It is just because we feel
no personal and no sentimental attitude toward our money, such as we

do toward, for example, our home, that money becomes a valuable means of exchange. We will be interested in acquiring a certain amount of money in order to achieve a certain purpose, but provided that purpose may be achieved in any other way we are likely to be just as well satisfied. It is only the miser who becomes sentimental about money.[13]

Like many developments that are forged in the heat of historical transformation, the purge of the "sentiments" by modern "rationality" was a double-edged sword. As mass production and the wage system uprooted people from traditional worldviews, they undermined traditional seats of local authority. For women and children this subversion involved something new — the possibility of freedom from the formerly unassailable power of patriarchy. Similarly, the idea of rationality at the heart of the new society undermined the sometimes unjust power of religion. Equally important, the money economy and industrial production raised the historically elusive possibility of material abundance, a development that has had a resounding appeal worldwide.

But what Robert Park celebrated as the eradication of sentiment meant — for most people entering the metropolis — the experience of a social fabric torn asunder. Bonds of family and community, traditions of mutual dependency, customary patterns of work, all of these were jeopardized by a world whose self-proclaimed destiny was the transcendence of nature itself. The results of this process were often devastating and continue to be so, decades after the "Americanization" of the great waves of European immigrants was completed.

In the Canadian Northwest Territories live twenty-three thousand Eskimos — "Inuit," they call themselves — who only recently have experienced the process of cultural transformation. Conventionally hunters and handicraft producers, the area in which they live — Frobisher Bay in Canada — has, since the late 1970s, become an area of massive industrial development, centering around oil exploration and production. Their traditional nomadic existence disrupted, the Inuits have been forced into permanent settlements with the trappings of modern life: "medical care, schools, telecommunications and a range of Government services." All of these, argued an article in the *New York*

Times, were "designed to give them a decent living and the ability to cope in a modern waste economy."[14]

For the people, however, the results have been disastrous. John Amagoalik, an Inuit rights leader, reports that he has seen his father transformed from "a proud and independent hunter, the master of his own destiny" into a man ravaged by alcoholism. "Proud people" have been reduced to "beggars outside a bar." Violence consumes a society of people whose traditions were rooted in the "primary responsibility" of survival. Another *Times* article, two months later, reported that "the Inupiat Eskimos of Alaska's North Slope, whose culture has been overwhelmed by energy development activities, are 'practically committing suicide' by mass alcoholism . . . violence is becoming the most frequent cause of death as a result of the 'explosive and self-destructive abuse of alcohol.'" Dr. Samuel Z. Klausner, a researcher from the University of Pennsylvania who has studied the development, commented—with little apparent sense of irony—that "their culture cannot contain the sudden enrichment."[15] While the severity of this instance is extreme, the cultural crisis of these Eskimo people throws light on the experience of Americanization among immigrants at the turn of the century. The magnetism of a consumer culture so eloquently recalled by Anna Kuthan meant a disruption of momentous proportions.

"The Magic of the Marketplace"

If entry into the modern metropolis posed a social crisis to newly industrialized people, key aspects of this new world generated a powerful appeal. Modern consumerism presented new arrivals with new kinds of institutions and a compelling ideological panorama. The failure of traditional cultural modes and the unraveling of customary human bonds made people particularly receptive to the lure of the new.[16] It is no accident that a *mass culture*—a social landscape marked by consumer industries, mass media, and merchandising—developed just when a formerly rural or otherwise nonindustrial people were being transformed into a permanent, mass industrial population. The panorama of a mass culture was a bridge between the aspirations of an old culture and the priorities of a new one.

On a narrowly economic level, the origin of mass culture can be seen as an extension of the necessity to generate and maintain an industrial labor force and expand markets. Yet both of these imperatives were inextricably linked to cultural and perceptual processes of change. The creation of an industrial force and of markets necessitated an abolition of social memories that militated against consumption. A consumptionist ideology required a worldview in which people and nature were not merely separate, but at odds with one another. Consumerism posed *nature* as an inhospitable force, a hopeless anachronism. Industrial production and enterprising imaginations claimed for themselves the rights and powers of creation. Though the question of how such a momentous upheaval in perception could have taken hold cannot be fully answered here, it is clear that, by the early twentieth century, the double prong of "Americanization"—mass production and mass consumption—had dramatically altered the social landscape of American life. The Jeffersonian ideal of a country of self-producing farmers was receding in the dim twilight of American consciousness, even if poets, sociologists, and ordinary folk each in their own idiom bemoaned the ways by which industry and its products had stepped between farm and home, country and city, people and their habits of survival. Edward Devine, a social worker and editor of the *Survey* magazine, distilled these feelings in 1907 when he exclaimed that the "home has ceased to be the glowing center of production from which radiates all desirable goods and has become a pool towards which products made in other places flow—a place of consumption, not of production."[17]

What Devine and others saw was the result of a historical redefinition of the nature of daily life. By 1900, in many critical arenas of life, the home had ceased production; the factory had taken its place. People now purchased what they had once produced for themselves. Production and consumption had become distinct activities, a fundamental rearrangement in the way people apprehended their material world. More and more, it was the *wage* that determined how well people could satisfy needs and desires. In large cities this relationship between people and survival was accentuated, but even small towns and farms were drawn into the network of influence. The elaboration of this network was a process that had unfolded in the preceding century; its story was the evolution of the modern, American consumer market.

In the late eighteenth and early nineteenth centuries, such a market was inconceivable to most people. As the continent was being settled, the maintenance of home and/or farm was a formidable and diversified project. Most goods were produced in the home. The demands of farm work and home production encouraged large families with many children. Women were the fountain from which many basic necessities flowed. As a source of survival, an inclusive arena of existence, the home was, in a sense, rooted. Even if families moved, over a lifetime, the arrangement of the home itself reflected its productive and sustaining nature. Alongside such a pattern of sufficiency, the consumer market — insofar as one existed — was an itinerant and picaresque phenomenon. It provided those few items home production could not; it existed on the fringes of necessity. Individual peddlers plodded the country roads of rural America, making house calls. Poorer peddlers trudged the byways with tin boxes on their backs; a prosperous peddler had his horse and wagon. Loaded down with "city" goods — nails, wood plates, tinware, a shovel or two, buttons, and so on — these nomads traveled the length and breadth of settlement, establishing a mobile marketplace of goods and notions. Here was the consumer society in its primitive essence, still operating often by barter, dealing in whatever goods were on hand — straight pins, combs, eyeglasses, musical instruments, clocks, shoelaces, window glass, and farm tools. Some combined their traffic in goods with artisan craftwork: carpentry, shoemaking, portrait painting. Others provided what today might be called "professional" services, as legal advisers, doctors, preachers.[18]

These traveling salesmen also, in embryonic form, dealt in images and desire for the unknown. They were forerunners of modern advertising and public relations. As people in motion, commercial adventurers, peddlers brought the world of the city to country people, employing the language of allure, glamor, and spectacle. Women whose hands had spun drab, homemade

cloth were treated to the attractive promise of gaily colored cali-
co and gingham, which showed no trace of the working conditions in the early textile mills from which they came. For those
exhausted by the deadly routines of rural life, peddlers brought
tonics and pills designed to alleviate or distract from the cares of
everyday life. Other items — clocks, for example — offered *status*
to those who made the purchase. Though relatively insignificant
as sources of basic survival, the peddler offered the allure of that
which might be had in another way of life.

By the mid-nineteenth century, the once-itinerant market had
gained a more stable place within rural and small-town life, in
the form of local general stores, which eclipsed the peddler as the
herald of the marketplace. The appeal of the general store to rural
Americans was twofold: it centralized goods under one roof; and
it was run by "trusted" people, who lived in the area and sought
to maintain the goodwill of their neighbors. Familiarity and con-
venience were the hallmarks of the general store, and with them
community life was increasingly touched by the channels of an
emerging industrial commerce. Anxious to establish a monopoly
over local trade, local store owners branded the peddler as an unscrupulous stranger, shrewd, morally questionable, greedy.
Playing upon common distrust of the commercial world, general
stores brought it closer. Store owners drew upon vernacular notions of the virtues of rural simplicity, and altered the face of rural life, making consumption more a part of it.[19]

Meanwhile, peddlers developed techniques in response to this
ethos of rural distrust. One notable example was Benjamin Babbitt, a peddler whose innovations in marketing and packaging
contributed to the commercialization of what had, previously,
been home-produced. Before Babbitt, soap was a common
product of the home, made from the fat of animals. He began his
commercialized soap business when he bought a large number
of hog carcasses. Producing a batch of soap, Babbitt now traded
soap for hog fat. Eventually, he made enough deals with farmers
to form a specialty business in soap, setting up a factory in New
York. With an eye to aesthetics, Babbitt produced soap and sold
it not in long loaves, but in individual bars, which encouraged
its greater use. He also wrapped his cakes, labeling them with an
attractive trademark, a personal claim of quality. Such innova-

tions made his soap far more costly than home-produced, but with the cost came the allure of the packaged product, the mundane surrounded by finery. To encourage customers to spend, Babbitt established a premium system: in return for a few wrappers, one might receive some inexpensive but useful item.

Besides becoming millionaires, Babbitt—and other innovators like him—wrought massive changes in the daily life of Americans. Taking a staple of home production and turning it into an attractive marketable commodity, he established a basic principle of American marketing—masking the ordinary in the dazzle of magic.[20]

Jim Fisk, known primarily as a railroad baron, was another trailblazer of the consumer culture. Born into a successful peddler family, Fisk was expected by his father to go into the family business. Before settling down, however, Jim ran away and joined a circus, serving a few apprenticeship years. When he returned to take on his father's wagon, his head was filled with the ideas of P. T. Barnum, the first great adman. Fisk had learned, for example, that towns would be receptive to the circus if they were properly seeded with publicity beforehand. Aware of the distrust of rural folk for strangers, Fisk employed the technique of "advance billing." First he decorated his wagon according to circus conventions—brightly colored, hung with flags. He wore a black silk suit, boots to the knees, and a large-brimmed white hat. Before entering a town, he hired people to plaster it with handbills and posters, depicting him and his gaudy wagon. When he finally arrived, hired musicians greeted him ceremoniously. If not familiar in the sense of the general store, Fisk had assembled a familiarity out of spectacle. His approach has become a fundamental component of a consumer society; the proliferation of images makes things known in advance. The dull familiarities of daily life were now confronted by the dazzling familiarity of promise; the challenge was formidable. To people schooled in the ways of home production, the inventions of the marketplace appealed to magic and wish fulfillment, altering the terms by which objects were to be understood. The techniques of Babbitt and Fisk anticipated Elmer Wheeler's First Commandment of Salesmanship: "Sell the sizzle, not the steak!"[21]

Although peddlers and local merchants broke the ground for

consumerism, by the late nineteenth century the scope of their commerce was becoming "quaint" and outmoded. Only in immigrant ghettos, filled with new generations of people unused to modern consumption, did peddlers thrive. Even there, their success was to be short-lived, for in more general terms, capitalist industry had begun to complement mass production with systems of mass distribution. Railroads were national avenues of commercial goods; mass production was turning home production into a relic. Ready-made clothing, canned goods, store-bought bread, and factory-produced furniture each made headway into a wide variety of homes. Price lines were established according to the structures of social class.

As rural and artisan people made the trek into cities, they left much of the rootedness of the home behind them. In the city, life was more mobile, less predictable, and peopled with strangers. If the commercial world of the peddler had been itinerant and marginal, the new industrial city presented commerce as stable and entrenched. Campbell's soup, Heinz ketchup, Hecker's flour, Carnation milk . . . trademarks and brand names became the familiar: these were what began to make people feel at home. This familiarity became a bond between people who were otherwise culturally heterogeneous.

The cement of such familiarity was further strengthened by important innovations in retailing, increasing the presence and impact of the marketplace in day-to-day existence. In rural and small-town areas, and to some extent in cities, *mail-order merchandising* was a "natural" outcome of mass production, with a particular appeal to people who held on tenaciously to a preindustrial way of life; a way of life dominated by land, nature, and home production. Among these people, mail-order companies helped to mold a large-scale consumer market where none had previously existed.

The success of mail order was built on some of the weaknesses of the general-store system. Widespread by the 1870s, these stores had become known for high prices and usurious credit practices. Goods, it was reported, were often misrepresented and/or shoddy.[22] As an expansive decade for mass production, the 1870s offered another retailing possibility, one that circumvented the general store. Eager to find outlets for their products, manufacturers were generally willing to offer low prices on large orders of goods. Such entrepreneurs as Montgomery Ward and Richard Sears (founder of Sears, Roebuck) built their empires on this premise. Buying large lots of merchandise, Ward and Sears distributed provocative and alluring picture books—catalogs— from which potential customers could order goods. Both Ward and Sears understood that the penetration of local, rural markets depended on the ability to present new, often-unfamiliar goods in a vernacular of "trust" and "friendship." Ward initiated the idea of a catalog, filled with beguiling images and text, designed to appeal to current folk wisdom. He offered customers that which the general store would not: "Satisfaction guaranteed or your money back." Appointed the official supply house of the Grange, and using its membership to develop a market, Ward sent out a one-page catalog by 1873. Within ten years his annual sales exceeded a million dollars.

Writing the catalog copy himself, in an amateurish, folksy vernacular, Ward became a source of information, an adviser, a self-proclaimed "personal friend" to millions of anonymous customers. As a benign progenitor of consumerism, his money-back guarantee signaled the generosity of a benevolent, if unseen, patriarch. The catalog—which came to be known as "The Great Wish Book"—pushed the need and desire for mass-produced goods beyond the established limits of contemporary imagination. It inspired promising fantasies of consumption among its customers. To people with little to read, and a desire to transcend the limits of their immediate environment, the combination of image and text was compelling; whole families reached for finery previously beyond their grasp or imagination.

The success of this "Wish Book" was phenomenal, growing from a one-page sheet in 1873 to a 24-page booklet in 1874 to a 544-page catalog in 1893. By 1890, Ward's enterprise had authoritative legitimacy. His catalog was used in rural schools as a modern reference on the new, emerging material culture. People eagerly awaited the coming of the catalog; through this window on a world of apparently unlimited possibility they caught a glimpse of things to come and received advice on how to get these things in the here and now. Home producers of clothing were instructed on how to order the latest fashions, ready-to-wear, easily through the mails. "In ordering clothing please be particular to send your size. Measure for coat around the chest, just under the arms; for pants take size around waist and length of leg. . . . Give your age and general build, and we will nine times out of ten give you a fit!"

Ward's expanded its market among immigrants as well, providing instructions for ordering products in ten languages. Here was an American institution that seemed to reach out, to embrace new arrivals with a sympathy that was rare. Customers were urged to use their native tongues in ordering. The catalog was a perfect vehicle for "Americanization": the pictorial images spoke an easily understood, universal language, demonstrating what an American appearance was all about and actual transactions could be performed in one's language of origin.[23]

With his Sears, Roebuck catalog, Richard Sears, known as the "Barnum of merchandising," a man who could "sell a breath of fresh air," built the largest retail institution in the United States. Sears, Roebuck & Company was an ingenious blend of evocative propaganda and superbly orchestrated distribution system. Sears's warehouse was so efficient that it was one of the models cited by Henry Ford for the development of his assembly line.

Sears called his catalog "The Farmer's Friend." Early catalogs were introduced by a personal letter, designed to allay fears people might have about writing letters to the big city. "Don't be afraid that you will make a mistake," he assured potential customers. "We receive hundreds of orders every day from young and old who never sent away for goods. . . . Tell us what you want, in your own way, written in any language, no matter whether good or poor writing, and your goods will be promptly sent to you."

The symbiosis between new commercial channels and traditional community networks that fed them is manifest in Sears's "Iowaization" scheme of 1905. Sears improvised a plan, first implemented in Iowa, to distribute catalogs and recruit customers. The company wrote to all of its current customers in Iowa and asked each to pass on catalogs to friends and neighbors. The customers, in turn, sent to the company the names of people given the catalog. The company kept track of who was ordering, and gave each "distributor" premiums on the basis of the number of incoming orders from among the friends and relatives of each. Accepting the role of "distributor," participants implicitly presented themselves as satisfied customers among their peers. Sears was trading on mutual bonds established autonomously, but which now entered the market. "Iowaization" was the most successful word-of-mouth campaign in the company's history, because word of mouth had been commercially structured. Sales from Iowa soon outstripped all other states; Sears went on to "Iowaize" America.[24]

Customary rural networks became pathways along which modern channels of commerce were established. In the process, social relations themselves were metamorphosed. Originally built on patterns of mutual reliance and barter, now these relationships provided an arena within which people became individualized agents and consumers of goods. Utilizing the patterns of friendship, Sears altered community networks into new avenues for the distribution of goods, providing benefits to individuals at the expense (literally) of their friends. Perhaps most important, people who had lived, to a large extent, apart from a money economy were now embroiled in it.

Another factor in the success of mail-order merchandising was the creation of rural free delivery and the parcel-post system. Prior to rural free delivery (RFD), rural people had to travel to town to pick up mail and packages; once in town they frequented local merchants and general stores, and bantered with friends. Proposed in 1891 and endorsed by Postmaster General and Philadelphia department-store magnate John Wanamaker, RFD was a system of direct-to-the-home mail delivery. Local merchants lobbied against it for years, to no avail. Eventually it was installed, converting the farmer into a modern consumer; it made the promise of mail-order merchandising all the more possible, as it eroded the turf of local, small-scale enterprise. Made from a catalog in the comfort of the home, each selection was a negotiation between customary life and the attractive network of an emerging national consumer market.

Such far-reaching innovations were not made without protest. Given smaller volume, higher costs, and limited stock, local merchants could not easily compete with the new, national marketplace. Often desperate in their responses, midwestern and southern store owners appealed to parochialism and xenophobia among their customers: fears of the big city; of foreigners; of blacks and Jews. Exploiting the distant anonymity of mail-order companies, local merchants peddled rumors that Sears and Ward were black men, or that Sears was a Jewish company. They argued that these companies used the mails because "these fellows could not afford to show their faces as retailers."

By the turn of the century, some local merchants were encouraging people to turn in catalogs for Saturday night bonfires. Prizes of up to fifty dollars were offered to those folks who collected the largest number of "Wish Books" for public immolation. For the most part, Sears and Ward responded with little concern; theirs was the conceit of an unfolding commercial power. Ward proclaimed assuredly, "We are honorable and we know we are. So do three million of our customers. Thus are curses turned to blessings." In response to racial innuendo, Sears published "photos of its founders to prove they weren't 'colored.'" Ward offered a hundred-dollar reward for the name of the person who had initiated the rumor that he was a mulatto.[25]

If mail-order merchandising was a spectacular refinement of a mobile market, reaching out to a rooted clientele, other institutions evolved in areas where the population itself had become itinerant. Filled with immigrants and migrants from another way of life, the cities became sites for massive, imposing structures of consumption, beginning in the mid-nineteenth century. The department store was the city equivalent of the mail-order catalog, employing compelling visual dramas within which mass-produced goods played the starring role. As forms of home production slipped from the hands of city women, the department store provided an evocative, image-laden context for industrial modes of survival. Not all city dwellers flocked to department stores. Immigrant women still purchased goods from itinerant street peddlers, thinking that the display of the department store only added to the price of goods. Yet while the initial clientele of the department store was largely middle class, its conspicuous presence as a new, urban institution gave consumable products the aura of modernity and gentility, while newspaper and display advertising spread the connotation even among people who could not afford the emporiums.

The department store was more than a site for consumption, it was a *sight* of consumption; goods were graced in monumental splendor. Shopping was a perceptual adventure. In the department store, industrial retailing created a place where the ideologies of progress and magic encountered the manifold needs of everyday life. From their beginnings, department stores were publicized as "cathedrals" and "palaces." This mixing of sumptuous metaphors was revealing; the department store surrounded practical concerns with a religious intonation, a touch of royalty, the promise that the mundane could become glamorous.

Innovators in the retail trade, men such as R. H. Macy, Marshall Field, and John Wanamaker, built mammoth structures replete with rotundas, Grecian columns, and grandiose courts where elaborate balconies and gaslit chandeliers surrounded and dazzled their customers. As a theater of goods, the department store combined sheer immensity with regal forms of display. Wanamaker's, in Philadelphia, contained 129 counters totalling two-thirds of a mile in length, with fourteen hundred stools in front of them. Lighting was supplied by lead-glass skylights by day, gas chandeliers by night. In 1896, Wanamaker built a nearly life-sized replica of the Rue de la Paix in his store — "a consolation for Americans who could not go to Paris." In 1911, Wanamaker opened a new twelve-story structure featuring a Grand Court and the second largest organ in the world, the latter punctuating the shopping day with sacredness.

In addition to lavish retailing, the department store offered itself as a palace away from home. For middle-class city women, the traditional needs of the household had been ministered to by servants and merchant callers; the home was a blend of productive and social activity. Daily life had revolved around the dinner meal, a family occurrence. With the separation of work life from home life, dinner meals began the long march toward the TV dinner; home preparations began to recede in importance. As the mass production of goods and external activities cut into duties of the customary home, department stores offered themselves as arenas for spending newfound "leisure" time. Myriad services were designed to lure women into the nest of the Big Store. Macy's, for example, housed elegant lounges and rest rooms, special writing rooms supplied with paper and pens, an art gallery filled with oil paintings (historically the property of the wealthy), rooms for reading newspapers, restaurants for luncheon get-togethers. Other department stores had nurseries, beauty parlors, live music, and post offices. Lecture halls and meeting rooms were also included in some stores' facilities. Shopping at Macy's, claimed one advertisement, would "yield you more than you dreamed possible."[26]

Along with mail-order merchandising, department stores helped shape consumption as a palpable system of belief by providing an institutional structure for mass marketing. Goods became actors in the pages of catalogs and in store displays. As customers, with free time from the activities of production, increasingly were invited to be admiring spectators, the social process of consumption drew upon the imagery of royalty, of religion, and of magic to elaborate its atmosphere of promise. Things customarily defined in terms of the long labor of home production reappeared as primarily aesthetic objects. Beauty and ease were claims that spoke loudly to people schooled by historic denial, and these were the blandishments proffered by consumer marketing as it evolved.

By the turn of the twentieth century the marketplace had evolved from a local and itinerant structure, servicing a rooted economy of self-sufficiency, into a formidable and "permanent" institution. Against the disruptive changes experienced by people undergoing industrialization, apparent stability and aesthetic allure began to reorganize the structure and meaning of *need*. If consumption was alien to a customary way of life, the genesis of the national marketplace was the historic passageway for the transition. A new way of life did not arrive merely as a cold, economic structure—wage labor, factory production, corporate goods. Its evolution was wrapped in the history of mass imagery and need, a complex amalgam that made the experience of transformation so conflicted—a conflict giving rise to such tensions as those of Anna Kuthan, so bitter over the false promise of happy plantations, waxing eloquent over Hecker's flour. Within such ambivalence, the human and ecological contradictions of the rise of consumer culture are blurred.

Changing the Subject

Out of the social pains of industrialization, its spiritual and material deprivations, a consumer culture was born. In its imagery and ideology were powerful appeals from hitherto denied realms of leisure, beauty, and pleasure. Mail-order catalogs and department stores were prime examples in an array of institutions that provided vehicles for this new way of seeing. In exchange for adopting a consumerized understanding of survival, people could hope to enjoy aesthetic pleasures traditionally the province of the very rich or even unimaginable in times past. This enrichment was not proffered as a quantitative change, however. In order for people to enjoy the pleasures of the new order they had to abandon many old expectations. Simon Patten, one of the most important and outspoken apostles of industrial consumerism, argued in 1892 that the leap from "scarcity" to "abundance" demanded a break with the past. The universe of nature would be transcended by one of artifice; the old, familiar world would recede; a new one would take its place: "It is the reduction of old pleasures that forces the consumer to resort to new pleasures to make up for the loss of old ones."[27]

Patten clearly perceived that the pleasures of a consumer society took root in a turbulent soil, a soil soaked in the blood of decimated traditional cultures. It was worth it, he argued: the benefits of this new culture justified its costs. Anticipating Walter Benjamin's insights into the mechanical reproduction of images, Patten understood the decisive appeal of these images in the new order. Mass imagery would bring what he termed *"the beautiful within reach of all"* (emphasis added). Advocating the metamorphic and democratic powers of such images, Patten — by the 1890s — already knew the eventual magnetism that mass advertising would hold within American society.

> So cheap are many kinds of pictures that they are largely distributed as means of advertisement. Everywhere the homes of the poorest people are full of beautiful objects, many of which have no cost; and when their taste is improved by contact with these objects, others more suited to the new condition can be obtained at a slight increase in cost.[28]

According to Patten, imagery would infuse the mass production of products, and the logic of consumption — much in the terms outlined in Raymond Williams's etymology—would take over. Continual waste and spending would be elevated as a social good, driven by a cycle of continual dissatisfaction. Patten celebrated this eventuality, setting out its logic this way:

> The standard of life is determined, not so much by what a man has to enjoy, as by the rapidity with which he tires of the pleasure. To have a high standard means to enjoy a pleasure intensely and to tire of it quickly.[29]

Patten's vision provides a description of the ways in which the demands of the market were shaping a new national identity, a philosophy of life. Although still undeveloped in many ways in Patten's day, the following patterns of modern life were established:

a powerful break with the past had taken place;

the basic groundwork of a consumer culture had been laid;

the tunnels of vision had been dug.

It is upon these that ultimately shopping centers and urban malls have been built. Under this order, we have come to live in a visual space consumed by the imagery of commerce, a society organized around the purchase.

From the vantage point of late-twentieth-century America, this existence is familiar to us; its alternatives are not. While Patten's enthusiasm for consumption seems blind to the spiritual and ecological drawbacks we have come equally to know, his explanation of the *American standard of living* and the logic of consumption hits the nail on the head. Recognizing that industrial capitalism had severed people from their roots, from customary relationships with one another and with the natural world, he sketched out the shape of new drives that propelled the activities of life. Implicitly, and unwittingly, Simon Patten provided a sketch of the antisocial and destructive premises of the consumption process: life would be a competitive struggle, continually using up the *old*, seeking and anticipating the *new*. Replenishment and the preservation of resources, systems of mutual interdependence were part of the old patterns of survival; they were of no concern within his vision of progress.

Patten also understood the importance that the mass production and distribution of commercial imagery would have in American material culture. They would tap the wells of need and desire. Commodities would be wrapped in an aesthetic of seduction. If, as Freud argued, precivilized humanity was propelled by insatiable drives for immediate, inconsequential gratification, the consumer culture appealed to these repressed drives with abandon. Today, the promise of ecstatic delight permeates everything from floor wax to toothpaste to mechanical vibrators. It is the undifferentiated, universal promise of the marketplace. Utopia is spectacle! Pain is only a reminder to those who have not yet bought the right product.

The acceptable arena of human initiative is circumscribed by the act of purchasing, given the status of *consumer* or *audience*. Within the logic of consumer imagery, the source of creative power is the object world, invested with the subjective power of "personality." History itself takes the shape of a succession of technological and commodity forms, forms propelled by the exigencies of the market economy. "The new basis of civilization" that Patten saw at the turn of the century really amounts to one in which the human subject has been expelled from history. Progress was to be measured by the extent to which social life, relations between people, had become what has been termed a "mirror of production." A consumerist cosmos was taking shape.

Insofar as this consumption cosmos liberated people from certain forms of oppression of the past, it assumed a certain cachet. Were not new realms of possibility being explored? Yet at the same time, it was an exploration within the limited confines of new, industrial institutions with their unprecedented ability to diminish the activity and imagination of individual human beings. Consumerism engendered passivity and conformity within this supposedly ever-expanding realm of the *new*, which put leisure, beauty, and pleasure in the reach of all. Customary bonds of affection and interdependence, born of other circumstances, disintegrated. Most important, the old bond of humanity and nature collapsed. The new survivor was the "wise shopper."

Alongside the considerable achievements of industrial development, the logic of consumption has become increasingly universal in our way of life. It is embroiled in our intimacies; tattooed upon our hopes; demanding of our energies. The "constant rapidity" with which we are encouraged to tire of consumable objects, of our elusive pleasures, is generalized as an axiom for existence. To buy is to succeed. Soon, this success becomes failure. A recent song by the English rock group The Clash angrily laments the dissatisfaction that is simultaneously played upon and exacerbated by consumption:

> *I'm all lost in the supermarket*
> *I can no longer shop happily*
> *I came in here for the special offer*
> *A guaranteed personality*[30]

In the areas of love and sexuality, consumptionism is rampant, signaling its grip on the reproduction of life itself. Divorce rates climb amid the clichéd "search for meaningful relationships." The insatiable urge for new things, a hallmark of Patten's definition of industrial progress, finds its painful corollary in the insatiable need for new and different love objects. The separation from nature is exacted at the expense of reliable social bonds. Within such a framework, sexuality among strangers becomes the logical ideal. No matter how shattering the experience, we are continually enticed toward more of the same. In a society with its social fabric shredded, the models of love and friendship are most conspicuous among the illusory propaganda of the consumer industries. Only goods and images seem really to be *there*. Political and religious leaders aggressively bemoan the moral crisis that has beset us, yet their criticisms steer clear of the commercial environment from which they themselves have often achieved their goals of power.

As we have seen in the United States, the adversarial interpretation of the relationship between people and the natural world is prominent in commercial ideology and production. Waste and *throwaway* are signatures of what is often termed "the American way of life." It is still a basic component of marketing and of our expectations. An extreme expression of this philosophy can be found in the words of Reagan's Secretary of the Interior, James Watt. A man with the job of administering and protecting the natural environment, Watt was asked whether he "favored preserving the land for future generations." Expressing his unabashed commitment to consumerism as a way of life, and re-vealing the hopelessness of it, Watt replied: "I do not know how many future generations we can count on before the Lord returns."[31] In the name of God, pillage is performed on behalf of Mammon.

The politics of consumption must be understood as some-thing more than what to buy, or even what to boycott. Con-sumption is a social relationship, the dominant relationship in our society — one that makes it harder and harder for people to hold together, to create community. At a time when for many of us the possibility of meaningful change seems to elude our grasp, the question of consumption has immense social and po-litical implications. To establish popular initiative, consumerism must be transcended — a difficult but central task facing all people who still seek a better way of life.

3

City Lights: Immigrant
Women and the Rise
of the Movies

FROM 1890 to 1920, over twenty-three million
people from eastern Europe and southern Italy
came to the United States and settled in primarily urban centers.
Though they were to labor in and populate a maturing industrial society, they emerged from semi-industrial peasant and artisan backgrounds where the social institutions of family and
community organized and maintained a customary culture. For
these people, the migration represented an unraveling of the
fabric of their lives, felt most deeply in the home and the family,
the customary realm of women. The new urban world undercut
the basis of traditional womanhood, forcing women to look in
two directions simultaneously: to the past for strength to sustain life in the present and to the future to find new means of
survival. This split impinged directly on family life and created
strains on the customary expectations of the mother-daughter
relationship. One generation, the mothers, had grown to matu-
rity in European society. Urban life challenged the sense of survival and perception they had brought with them when they
migrated to the United States. The daughters, the next generation, although touched by the experience of the Old World,
were much more the children of the metropolis. Their lives
were caught up in social dynamics beyond the frame of Old
World understandings.[1]

In the cities new cultural images—billboards, signs, advertising, the electric lights of Broadway—pressed themselves on people's attention and created a new visual landscape of possibility.
An urban and distinctly American culture proclaimed itself in
image form, demanding response and notice, as strange to small-

53

town Americans as it was to incoming immigrants. Viola Paradise of the Immigrant Protective League analyzed the social complexity of this new cultural formation:

> The very things which strike the native born [Americans] as foreign seem to her [the new immigrant] as distinctly American: the pretentiousness of signs and advertisements, the gaudy crowded shop windows, the frequency of fruit stands and meat markets, her own countrymen in American clothes . . . she sums it all up as "America."[2]

One of the most powerful components of this new urban culture was the development of moving pictures. For immigrants in a world of constant language barriers, the silent film was compelling and accessible. Silent pictures spoke primarily to urban immigrant audiences of women and children, themselves caught up in the social drama of transformation.

Like radio and television after them, the movies were an exemplary piece of a cultural environment that interacted, over time, with the social history of its audience, playing a crucial role as an "agency of mass impressions" in the large-scale displacement of people.[3] Changing demographic and industrial patterns created the context for an audiovisual culture designed to fill the gaps and fissures of experience. As an agency of mass impression, movies became a new electronic presence in the social landscape of everyday life, explaining away the past, preparing people for participation in a new present.

The world these movies addressed was in crisis. Adaptation to city life required a constant struggle. Old World societies, whether in eastern Europe or southern Italy, were still rooted in resources drawn from nature: gardens, home production, and systems of family and community support.[4] In the New World, wages and money were the key to survival. In the old cultures, the social labor of women had converted raw materials into household goods; New World immigrant mothers had to confront the industrial marketplace to secure the goods necessary for their families' survival and well-being.

In order to make ends meet, immigrant families adopted a new division of labor. The facts of urban economic life made family cooperation essential. A study of wage earners' budgets in New York in 1907 revealed that the number of families entirely dependent on the earnings of one person is small when compared with the numbers whose incomes include the earnings of husband, wife, several children, some boarders, gifts from relatives. . . . Several or all of these resources may enter into the total resources of that family in a year. Perhaps this income should more accurately be called the household income, for it represents the amount which comes into the family purse, of which the mother usually has the disbursement.[5]

While the father and older children worked for wages outside the home, the mother was central to the family's well-being, and in a certain respect, the customary pattern adapted itself to the new situation. As one social worker noted at the time:

It is the mother around whom the whole machinery of family life revolves. The family economy depends on her interests, skills and sense of order. Her economic importance is far greater than that of her wealthier sisters for as income increases . . . the amount of it controlled by the wife diminishes. . . . But in her humble status, her position is thoroughly dignified.[6]

Robert Chapin concluded in his 1909 study of New York working-class life:

While the personal factor does operate in the case of every family . . . the limits with which it may affect the actual sum total of material comforts that make up the living of the family are set by *social forces*. These social forces find expression on the one side in the income which the family receives—that is, in the rate of wages received by the father and others who are at work; on the other side, they are expressed in the prices that have to be paid to get housing, food and other means of subsistence.[7] (Emphasis in the original.)

The common experience for immigrant women on arrival was to "figure the dollar in their home money. They thought they were rich until they had to pay rent, buy groceries, clothing and shoes. Then, they knew they were poor."[8] To maintain home and family in the urban economy demanded a range of skills from the daily negotiations in the marketplace for basic needs, to the careful accumulation of money for rent, to taking in boarders to help make ends meet, to occasional finishing work brought back from the garment shops. In addition, the social demands were equally pressing: from the care of young children, to the daily grind of housework, to the care of the sick, to providing help to neighbors and relatives.

In all of these activities, immigrant mothers faced impossibly high rents, the fear of eviction, high prices for food and clothing, sickness, noise, inferior housing, and times of unemployment and poverty. Barred from access by reasons of sex, class, nationality, language, and custom to most of the institutions of American society, most mothers relied on those most familiar and immediate: family and community. Many sought out relatives, neighbors, and other women of the same ethnicity to establish networks of support and common concern. Within the congested tenement districts of New York, new forms of community developed in which women learned from each other and shared the problems of urban life. Elsie Clew Parsons, the well-known contemporary anthropologist, observed:

> One of the most noticeable traits in the life of the average tenement dweller . . . to the eyes . . . of the private visitor . . . is the more or less intimate and friendly intercourse of the families of the house. Washtubs and cooking dishes are borrowed from one another at any hour of the day; a mother leaves her child with a friend across the hall when she goes shopping . . . ; a kindly soul sits up all night with a sick child; yet, in spite of all the little individual acts of service, the whole round of economic activity is entirely independent of every other family.[9]

The borrowing of tools, the lending of service, the exchange of activity became a buffer against the isolation imposed on women as housewives and a mediation between an older, more familiar culture left behind and the chaotic individualizing forces of urban life.

While immigrant mothers were coping with the new realities, fathers and elder children were engaged in the outside world of wage labor and urban life. On the surface, there seemed to be a split between first-generation immigrant mothers and their daughters. The urban environment created a historic division in the customary expectations of the mother–daughter relationship. The industrial city separated the home-centered experience of mothers from the more social experience of daughters in ways that were painful and difficult to understand. New urban institutions such as the public school, the settlement house, the dance hall, and the diversions of the street made claims on the lives of some immigrant daughters, redirecting their activity. Unlike that of their mothers, the immigrant daughter's sense of self, although halting and incomplete, was directed outward. American society was based on a conception of family life that demanded that female adolescents identify with a social world outside the domain of family. Access to that world meant having time and money for it. The price of admission to the new culture was the negation of Old World notions of womanhood; "needs" arose for clothing, hairstyles, and cosmetics to create the external appearance of an "American" and for other forms of economic and sexual independence from maternal authority.

This, of course, put pressure on the immigrant mothers, who on the one hand needed their daughters' outside earnings to help maintain the fragile household economy, but on the other, felt threatened by the separate social life demanded by some daughters. Patriarchal culture had deemed the outside world the proper place for men and boys, while young women were expected to stay close to home by the side of their mothers. The struggle against family bonds was harder for daughters to win than for sons.[10] In general terms, the outside world of American culture was viewed with hostility by most immigrant mothers, who saw it as a direct threat to their ability to carry on cultural traditions and achieve economic viability.

One American institution, however, was a realm of shared cultural experience for mothers and daughters: the movies. While immigrant parents resisted their daughters' participation in most of the recreational opportunities of the city, *everyone* went to the movies, which were the one American institution that had the possibility of uniting generations and was cross-generational in its appeal. Most film historians agree that the first audiences for motion pictures came primarily from the immigrant working-class neighborhoods of America's largest cities. The movies were a welcome diversion from the hardships of daily life in the communities. By 1909, New York City alone had over 340 movie houses and nickelodeons with a quarter of a million people in daily attendance and a half million on Sundays. *Survey* magazine, the journal of social work, observed that "in the tenement districts the motion picture has well nigh driven other forms of entertainment from the field" and that "it was the first cheap amusement to occupy the economic plane that the saloon [had] so exclusively controlled."[11] Like the saloon, it was cheap: a nickel per person, twenty-five cents for the whole family. Unlike the saloon, it was not sex-defined; anyone who had a nickel could enter. There, for a low price, families could be enveloped in a new world of perception, a magical universe of madness and motion.

The movies became for immigrants a powerful experience of the American culture otherwise denied to them, surrounding them with images, fantasies, and revelations about the New World: "More vividly than any other social agency, they revealed the social typography of America to the immigrant, to the poor. . . . From the outset, the movies were, besides a commodity and a developing craft, a social agency."[12] In *Sons of Italy*, Antonio Mangano described the effects of motion pictures on the typical recently arrived Italian: "Moving pictures were a great attraction, and he went every day to see what new pictures there were on the billboards. . . . Cold chills crept up and down his back as he witnessed thrilling scenes of what he thought was *really* American life."[13] The movies became a translator of the social codes of American society, which could now be unraveled, looked at, interpreted, made fun of, understood. They formed a bridge between an older form of culture inadequate to explain the present and a social world of new kinds of behavior, values, and possibilities; their images and fantasies were a text of explanation, a way of seeing. Like their audience, early movies had not yet found a voice. Silent movies spoke in a more comprehensible language of silence, image, sign, and gesture.

The movies also presented themselves as a release from daily troubles, a world where the realities of daily life were rendered emphathetically in comedic or melodramatic form. Movie advertisements pitched themselves to working-class audiences in a tone of compassion:

If you're tired of life, go to the movies
If you're sick of trouble rife, go to the picture show
You'll forget your unpaid bills, rheumatism and other ills
If you'll stop your pills and go to the picture show.[14]

In a sense, movies were a form of community. Families went together; local merchants advertised on the screen; people sang along and read or translated captions out loud; the organ played. Moreover, as one observer commented: "Visit a motion picture show on a Saturday night below 14th Street when the house is full and you will soon be convinced of the real hold this new amusement has on its audience. Certain houses have become genuine social centers where neighborhood groups may be found . . . where regulars stroll up and down the aisles between acts and visit friends."[15] The *Jewish Daily Forward* in 1908 commented on the growing popularity of this medium for women and children during the day. "Hundreds of people wait on line. . . . A movie show lasts a half hour. If it's not too busy you can see it several times. They open at one in the afternoon and customers, mainly women and children, gossip, eat fruit and nuts and have a good time."[16]

The content of some early films bore a direct relationship to the historical experience of its audience. Some films depicted a landscape outside of immigration; these brought American history and culture, in the form of westerns, news clips, and costume dramas, to ethnic eyes. Some movies were nativist, racist, and sexist. But many early movies showed the difficult and ambiguous realities of urban tenement life in an idiom that spoke directly to immigrant women. The new medium attracted many immigrant and working-class entrepreneurs into its ranks. Before Hollywood took center stage, the movies were created in primarily urban settings. As Lewis Jacobs, the film historian, observed, "The central figure of adventure comedies was always a common man or woman—the farmer, fireman, policeman, housewife, stenographer, clerk, servant, cook. . . . Such characters were selected because the audience and filmmakers alike were of this class and because of the growing popular interest in the everyday person."[17] From 1903 to 1915, he argues, poverty and the struggle for existence were "favorite dramatic themes." In films with such titles as *The Eviction*, *The Need for Gold*, *She Won't Pay Her Rent*, *Neighbors Who Borrow*, *The Miser's Hoard*, *Bertha, the Sewing Girl*, and *The Kleptomaniac*, everyday situations were depicted, the causes of poverty were held to be environmental, and economic injustice was deplored.[18]

More important, these films spoke directly to tensions and contradictions in the world of immigrant mothers. For example, Edwin S. Porter's 1905 film *The Kleptomaniac* treated justice in a class-defined society. The first sequence shows the arrest of a wealthy woman for shoplifting trinkets in a department store, the second that of a poor woman, on the brink of starvation, for stealing a loaf of bread. The third sequence brings both women to court, where the poor woman is jailed and the judge discharges the rich woman. An epilogue sums up the three sequences; we see a figure of Justice blindfolded, holding up a scale. On one side of the scale is a bag of gold; on the other, the loaf of bread. The scale moves in favor of the gold. The blindfold is removed, and the figure of Justice has only one eye, which is fixed on the gold.[19] In *Eleventh Hour* (1911), the slum dwellers are Italian. The father, a street peddler, goes to jail for fighting with a bully who constantly harasses him. When the bully dies, the husband gets a life sentence. The wife pleads with the governor to no avail, as do the children. At the "eleventh hour," the father is released, the family reunited.[20] This film spoke clearly of the defense of the family against legal injustice and harassment.

Sometimes the immigrant experience itself was the subject, as in Chaplin's *The Immigrant*. In Thomas Ince and Gardner Sullivan's *The Italian* (1911), a series of dramatic contrasts is used to depict the social transformation and economic dislocation of immigrant families on New York's Lower East Side. It begins with a romanticized image of Italian life in Venice, where the audience is introduced to Beppo, a gondolier, and Gallia, a young peasant woman. The film develops images of a bounteous and festive Italy. The scene then shifts to the Lower East Side; the new landscape is framed by stark, bleak, realistic images. Beppo has become a poor bootblack, Gallia a housewife in a stifling tenement apartment. Aided by neighbor women, Gallia gives birth to a son, who rapidly becomes sickly. The doctor explains that the baby is sick from the heat and the impure milk he has been fed. In 1911, pasteurized milk was sold in bottles at high prices, but lower grades of unpasteurized milk were sold "loose" in tenement neighborhoods and carried home in glasses or pails. John Spargo, a well-known social reformer, argued in 1908 that in immigrant neighborhoods "one third of all babies die before five years old of diseases chiefly connected to the digestive tract and a considerable percent of these diseases are definitely known to be caused by milk."[21] In contrast to the bountiful imagery utilized to frame peasant life, the image of poisoned milk spoke to the inversion of nature and mothering in industrial America.

At this point in *The Italian*, a new level of contrast is presented. While Beppo and Gallia try to raise money for a supply of bottled, pasteurized milk, the baby languishes and dies. Beppo tries to raise money from "The Boss, The Wealthiest Man of the Slums." The Boss refuses him, throws him off his car, and has him arrested. Beppo is imprisoned. The Boss also has a sick child, so he uses his money and influence to rope off his elegent house from the public noise that would be fatal to his child. Beppo, out of prison and consumed with hate, sneaks into the Boss's house to harm the child, but he cannot bring himself to do it. While the Boss's child lives, Beppo and Gallia grieve. The contrasts between peasant and urban life, rich and poor, class and family, spoke directly to immigrant mothers: the maintenance of family and the care of children was a class question, since only through access to money could these conditions be transformed. This film provided a prism through which the audience could look at and recognize itself.

In *The Eviction* (1907, director unknown), a poor man, drunk with his friends, dreams that his wife has sold her wedding ring to save their home and furniture. On awakening, he hurries home to see the landlord removing the furniture from their tenement apartment. Passersby chip in to pay the rent, the husband repents, the wife forgives, and a new life begins for the family.[22] This movie would have made perfect sense to urban immigrant women. Maria Ganz, in her autobiography of New York tenement life, recounts a similar incident:

> The evicted woman kept staring at the litter of cheap things in which she must have taken no end of pride and pleasure while she had been gathering them one by one in the making of her home, now left in pieces on the street, a symbol of eviction and destitution. She brought out a china plate from the folds of her dress and placed it on one of the chairs. . . . People would drop pennies, perhaps even nickels and dimes into that plate — enough to save her from being wholly destitute.[23]

Mike Gold, in *Jews without Money*, explained this system of community support: "This is an old custom on the East Side; whenever a family is to be evicted, the neighborhood women put on their shawls and beg from door to door."[24]

Early movies existed outside of the moral universe of correct and respectable middle-class society. Comedies also mocked respectable ruling elites and looked at authority, social conventions, and wealth with a jaundiced eye. In the Sennett and Chaplin comedies, the artifacts of the new consumer culture became objects of ridicule. Mack Sennett explained the attraction of his films:

> Their approach to life was earthy and understandable. They whaled the daylights out of pretension. . . . They reduced convention, dogma, stuffed shirts and Authority to nonsense and then blossomed into pandemonium. . . . I especially like the reduction of authority to absurdity, the notion that Sex could be funny, and the bold insults hurled at Pretension.[25]

Yet, despite the affinities between audience and early film, the movies were primarily an institution of the larger society, subject to its shifts and pulls. If some of the silent movies registered, to some degree, the social and economic problems of urban life, others spoke increasingly to the social and sexual dynamics, the ideological superstructure of an evolving consumer culture. The outlines of this development are to be seen in the contradictory experiences of immigrant daughters and their interaction with the silent screen. The concerns and experiences of immigrant daughters, as opposed to those of their more homebound mothers, led in some cases to active participation in the trade-union movement, political life, and involvement in the suffrage movement.[26] For others, contact with American culture was mainly involved with educational aspirations and cultural transformations.

For many, contact with American culture at work or at school created compelling new definitions of femininity, which spoke to a sense of independence from the constriction of family bonds; ready-made clothes, makeup, dance halls, and amusement parks all symbolized a cultural environment that assumed greater individual freedom and less formal relations with the opposite sex. As one social worker noted at the time:

Inevitably, the influences of her new work life, in which she spends nine hours a day, begin to tell on her. Each morning and evening as she covers her head with a crocheted shawl and walks to and from the factory, she passes the daughters of her Irish and American neighbors in their cheap waists in the latest smart styles, their tinsel ornaments and gay hair bows; a part of their pay envelopes go into the personal expenses of these girls. Nor do they hurry through the streets to their homes after working hours, but linger with a boy companion "making dates" for a movie or affair.[27]

While most immigrant mothers became reconciled to the fact that their daughters would leave home to go to work or school, they still expected their daughters to obey and adopt their own standards of sexual deportment. For the second generation, the gap between home life and work life was acute: "It wasn't that we [the younger generation] wanted to be Americans as much as we wanted to be like other people. . . . We gradually accepted the notion that we were Italians at home and Americans elsewhere. Instinctively, we all sensed the necessity of adapting ourselves to two different worlds."[28] A social worker noted: "The old standards can scarcely be maintained in a modern community where girls work in factories side by side with men. . . . It was impossible for the parents to supervise young women in school or at work . . . the girl naturally thinks that if she can take care of herself at work, she is equally well able to do so at play."[29]

Some immigrant daughters developed strategies for claiming a part of their income for themselves. Ruth S. True, in her study of working-class life, recorded this example:

> Filomena Moresco, whose calm investment of $25 in a pretty party dress, a beaver hat, and a willowed plume was reported as little less than the act of a brigand. If she had withheld twenty cents out of her pay envelope, she probably would have been beaten by her mother. As it was, she appropriated $25 and her high-handedness was her protection.[30]

On the one hand, adolescent daughters were reared in the morality of family obligation; "good girls" returned their unopened pay envelopes to their mothers and were obedient to the needs of their families. "Bad girls" snuck or took money out of their envelopes to spend on themselves and defied the wishes of their mothers. Having money to spend on the self was intimately connected to breaking out of the family circle; yet personal ideas of independence were against the tradition of feminine sacrifice. For example, Agnes Mazza, an Italian garment worker, was a good girl: "I gave my pay envelope to my mother. I wouldn't dare open it up. I'd give it to my mother because I knew she worked for us and I thought this was her compensation. I always stayed close to my mother." Her sister, however, was different:

> She used to open the envelope and take a few dollars for herself if she needed it. They [sister and friends] would come home at twelve o'clock —this was terrible, especially for the Italian people. The neighbors would gossip, would say "Look at that girl coming home by herself." My mother would talk to her but it did no good. And then one day, my sister wanted to pay board. She was eighteen. My mother said, "What do you mean, board?" She said, "I give you so much and keep the rest." So my mother said, "Alright, do what you please."[31]

Independence from the family obligation implied not only the right to wages, a new physical appearance, and a social life, but, most important, the right to a mate of one's own choice. At issue were not ultimate goals, for both the bad and the good girls had severely limited options, but the means to the future, the means to marriage. In a sense, the initial stages of the sexual revolution of the twentieth century can be identified with this desire for independence on the part of those daughters who broke with family tradition and control to marry men of their own choosing.

Despite the enormous energies and activities of some immigrant daughters in the trade-union and women's suffrage movements, the options open to most women at this time were limited to the appropriation of urban adolescent culture as a wedge against patriarchal forms of sexual control. New, often-bewildering dating, courtship, and sexual patterns caused pain and anguish for mothers and daughters alike. While family-dominated culture was repressive, it did present a familiar form of courtship and sexual relations. The more anonymous nature of sexual relations in the city created traps for women, and immigrant women were often taken advantage of by strange and unscrupulous men.[32]

It was ironic that those immigrant daughters who worked in the ready-made clothing industry were not paid enough to purchase what they produced and, consequently, had to engage in a family battle for the right to the fruits of their labor. Their inability to purchase an American "appearance" led to anguish and frustration. This problem was not associated only with immigrant life; the conflict between family obligation and more individualized definitions of social life was also felt in the homes of the prosperous middle class.[33]

While the old family ways of understanding seemed inadequate as a guide to industrial culture, the movies seemed more shaped to the tempo of urban life. Increasingly, the social authority of the media of mass culture replaced older forms of family authority and behavior. The authority of this new culture organized itself around the premise of freedom from customary bonds as a way of turning people's attention to the consumer marketplace as a source of self-definition. This new cultural thrust took on the culture of Victorian America as much as that of first-generation immigrant parents.

The movies became less identified with family entertainment as young people increasingly turned to them for a place away from family life, a place to escape, to use a hard-won allowance, to sneak a date. As True observed:

> There is a signal of restlessness beneath the surface. . . . Into her nature
> are surging for the first time the insistent needs and desires of her
> womanhood. She is the daughter of the people, the child of the masses.
> Athletics, sports, discussions, higher education will not be hers to divert
> this deep craving. . . . The city bristles with the changes she longs
> for—"to have fun and see the fellows."

Because of these needs and the limited options for their expression, "the control of a little money is far more essential to these girls in their search for enjoyment than to girls in another class. There are many doors which a very small coin will open for her."[34]

One of these doors was the movies, where "flashing gaudy posters lined the entrances. . . . These supply the girls with a 'craze.' These same needs send them . . . to the matinees. There pictures spread out showing adventure and melodrama which are soul-satisfying."[35] Filomena Ognibene, an Italian garment worker brought up by strict parents, claimed that "the one place I was allowed to go by myself was the movies. I went to the movies for fun. My parents wouldn't let me go out anywhere else, even when I was twenty-four. I didn't care. I wasn't used to going out, going anywhere outside of going to the movies. I used to enjoy going to the movies two or three times a week. But I would always be home by nine o'clock."[36] Sometimes the movies were used to subvert the watchful eye of parental supervision. Grace Gello recounted that she met her future husband in 1918 through her father. "We kept company for a year and a half. We weren't allowed to go out alone, even with groups of people. My father or mother always accompanied us. But we did meet on the sly. Occasionally, we would take the afternoon off to go to the movies. We didn't do this too much because we were afraid of my father. He would say, 'If I catch you, I'll break you neck.'"[37]

By 1915, the year of D. W. Griffith's *Birth of a Nation*, the movie industry had expanded its initial audience to include middle-class patrons, had moved to the remote environs of Hollywood, and had established the studio and star systems. The thematic content showed the transition; the earlier images depicting the urban housewife embattled by the economic forces of the New World were increasingly displaced by images of women in flight from or redefining the meaning of home, family, sexual behavior, and social codes. The first female "stars" of the industry were cast in new roles: the vamp, the gamine, and, of lesser significance, the virgin.[38] Through the creation of these feminine archetypes, the silent screen began to raise sexual issues and develop imagistic fantasies that spoke directly to the confusing sexual experiences of immigrant daughters.

The vamp was the symbol of the war between passion and respectability. Theda Bara, born Theodosia Goodman, daughter of a Jewish garment worker from Cincinnati, was created by Fox Studios as one of America's first movie stars. In over forty films from 1915 to 1919, she played the vamp, the woman who flaunts men and social convention to get what she wants. In the American lexicon, the archetype of the sexual woman was European, a woman who used her beauty and passion "to lure some helpless and completely dumb man to his ruin."[39] Underneath this image was a new consciousness about sexual relations. In Theda Bara's own words, "Believe me, for every woman vamp there are ten men of the same . . . men who take everything from women, love, devotion, youth, beauty and give nothing in return. *V* stands for Vampire and it stands for Vengeance too. The vampire that I play is the vengeance of my sex on its exploiters. You see . . . I have the face of a vampire, perhaps, but the heart of a 'feministe.' "[40] For example, in *A Fool There Was* (1914), Bara portrayed a woman who reduced respectable middle–class men to bumbling idiots, leaving a trail of madness and suicide along the way. Its imagery depicts a woman who has broken with so-cial convention, who drinks and smokes with abandon, and who reverses the traditional assumptions of the male-female relation-ship. In doing so, her image points to a clear critique of the dou-ble standard.[41]

The gamine, epitomized by Mary Pickford, was an archetype of female adolescence whose pluck and determination allowed her to create a more independent future. Born Gladys Smith into a poor family and forced at an early age to become "father" to her family,[42] Mary Pickford often played a battling tomboy "pro-voked by a sense of injustice and motivated by the attempt to bring happiness to others."[43] In her many films, she took on repressive fathers, ministers, and moralistic community values and defined for herself her own space. While she was part sweet-ness, she was also part "hellion . . . morally and physically committed to all–out attacks against the forces of bigotry and malicious snobbery that sought to frustrate the proper denoue-ment of a triumphant lovely girl."[44] Playing a spirited adolescent girl in such movies as *Rags* and *Little Annie Rooney*, she was an ap-pealing example for women attempting their own fights against barriers. Although Mary Pickford occasionally played adult roles, her screen projection of independence was usually circum-scribed by childhood. She herself stated the irony of her position. For Mary Pickford, "the longing for motherhood was to some extent filled by the little children I played on the screen. Through my professional creations, I became, in a sense, my own baby."[45]

While the vamp and the gamine projected images of sexual freedom and social independence, the virgin—the Griffith hero-ine—was, in many ways, the last holdout of the patriarchal tradi-tion. The virgin, played by Lillian Gish, was the good woman firmly devoted to the protection of her virtue against the menace of male passion. While the virgin, as the male symbol of American womanhood, registered the existence of the new sexual wilderness, she recoiled against it, seeking protection from its claims through patriarchal solutions.[46]

The history of these transitional female archetypes parallels the social and sexual struggles of the immigrant daughters. If they were torn between fresh notions of sexuality and constricting family structures, the vamp and the gamine, who seemed to point the way to new definitions of femininity, were locked into a constricting star system, which severely limited their expression and development. Their images were used by the new studios as building blocks of an expanding industry. By 1919–20, the movie industry had become a major corporate enterprise, committed to a national rather than a class audience. To create this audience, some movies opted for images from the consumer marketplace. Some of the content and form of postwar movies revealed a new definition of "Americanization," the consumer society as an ideal way of life. Perhaps early movies had shown an ambivalence toward urban industrial society, but by 1920 American capitalism's consumer culture was in full force.[47]

By 1920, a new "formula" for movie-making had been developed, most notably in the films of Cecil B. De Mille. Realizing that "a new generation of movie goers, not in sympathy with its elders,"[48] was growing up, De Mille redefined the subject matter of film. While the De Mille films continued to explore the sexual dynamics of urban culture, they also began to demonstrate the maturation of a new sexual logic. Instead of the traditional settings of the prewar movies, De Mille "withdrew the curtains that had veiled the rich and fashionable and exhibited them in all the lavish and intimate details of their private lives."[49] The new De Mille movies created a fantasy world where sex, romance, marriage, and money were intertwined to create a new frame of reference. In such movies as *Old Wives for New* (1918), *Male and Female* (1919), *Why Change Your Wife?* (1920), and *Forbidden Fruit* (1920), De Mille gave voice to a crucial myth of modern culture: metamorphosis through consumption.

In the De Mille formula, the key to modern marriage lay in the ability of women to maintain a sexually attractive appearance. In *Old Wives for New*, the plot hinges around a slovenly, lazy wife in danger of losing her dapper husband. In *Why Change Your Wife?* a dowdy, modest woman interested in high culture is embarrassed by her husband's gift of a risqué negligee. The marriage breaks down. The wife then experiences a metamorphosis: she realizes that sexual appeal is crucial and thereafter transforms her appearance by purchasing new clothes. In brief, the vamp had become respectable.[50]

In *Male and Female* and *Forbidden Fruit*, De Mille explored class relations through the lens of sexuality and consumption. *Male and Female*, a satire of aristocratic manners, contrasts the exquisitely coiffured and well-mannered mistress (Gloria Swanson) with the sloppy and ill-mannered servant girl, Tweeney. For example, in the first part of the film, each of them eats breakfast. Edward Wagenknecht, a De Mille defender, argued that there was a social purpose to the scene: "From Tweeney's eating habits in *Male and Female*, it is just possible that some of the comfortable gum chewers in our 'movie palaces' may have learned that it is not good form to leave your spoon standing in your cup or to cover a whole slice of bread with jelly and then bite into it."[51]

In *Forbidden Fruit*, De Mille gave the Cinderella myth a modern twist. The heroine, Mary Maddock, is the wife of a lazy, working-class husband who lives off her earnings. In contrast to a film like *The Italian*, the depiction of working-class marriage here assumes that husbands live off the labor of their wives. Mary is asked by the oil magnate for whom she works to help him and his wife "vamp" another oil magnate in order to close a business deal. They offer her twenty dollars, and she agrees. Replete with Cinderella fantasies, the film details her transformation. The wealthy wife phones for "jewels from Tiffany, gowns from Poiret, and perfumes from Coty." The servants dress her, and a hairdresser does her hair; she has become an object subject to the manipulation of experts. Her new appearance is quite convincing: she has transcended her class. The only obstacle to her success now is her manners. In a key scene, Mary, through cues and imitation, triumphs by choosing the correct fork. The rest of the film revolves around her duty to her husband versus her newly found life and "love" in the upper classes. Ultimately, "Cinderella" wins her love choice and escapes her husband and her class.

In contrast to the earlier movies, the De Mille films demonstrate the new logic of consumption as a way of presenting the self in the urban world, as the essence of the promise of modern life for women. In doing so, these films openly attack the customary assumptions, behavior, and style of the audience and point the way to a new self-definition. In this sense, they became an agency of Americanization. After the success of *Why Change Your Wife?* and *Forbidden Fruit,* many producers "turned their studios into fashion shops and the screen was flooded with imitations. . . . Wise wives, foolish wives, clever and stupid wives were portrayed in every variety of domestic situation that gave an opportunity for displays of wealth, money getting, money making, smart clothes and romance."[52] In imitation, movies with such titles as *The Amateur Wife, The Misfit Wife, Poor Men's Wives,* and *Behold My Wife* "all lectured to the frump who learns that it is important to remain stylish and good looking after marriage."[53] They emphasized that the metamorphosis of the female self was the new condition for securing the means of survival in modern society — getting and keeping a husband.[54]

For second-generation immigrant women, one step away from arranged marriage and family obligation, these new movies were manuals of desire, wishes, and dreams. What was remarkable about them was the combination of new ideas of romance and sexuality with practical guidelines for change. Out of De Mille's movies came a visual textbook to American culture, a blend of romantic ideology and practical tips for the presentation of self in the new marriage market of urban life. Here was guidance their mothers could not offer. By presenting an illusory world where "a shop girl can marry a millionaire,"[55] these movies evoked a vision of the American dream for women and the means to its feminine realization.

The appropriation of Americanized styles of dress, manners, and relations to the opposite sex were experienced as a gap between immigrant mothers and their daughters. In this sense, the imagery in the films — supported by the rapid growth of the ready-made clothing industries, the cosmetics industry, and new forms of advertising and display — made possible the liquidation of traditional culture. Maria Zambiello, who migrated here in 1903 and was the mother of three children, explained:

I don't feel as good as the American women because I am old-fashioned, from the other side. . . . When I am with American women, I am afraid I don't talk good enough for them. Then sometimes they serve tea or coffee in nice cups and napkins—I feel ashamed . . . and they got different manners. We put the hands on the table, they don't. That's why I don't feel so good. But the young Italian girls, my daughters, they're up to date, just as good, just as polite like the Americans. They were born here, they go to school together, they see the same movies, *they know.*[56]

In other cases, an uneasy compromise between cultures developed. Maria Frazaetti articulated this possibility:

There are no old-country customs prevailing in our house. My children follow the American customs. I would like them to remember that the parents must be considered as an authority. I approve of allowing my children the freedom they desire; by doing so, they learn for themselves. My children misunderstand me when I advise them what style clothes they should wear. I blame styles and clothes on some of the stuff in magazines and the movies of this country. If I had my way, I would like my children to follow some of the old disciplinary laws of the old country.[57]

Filomena Ognibene measured her distance from American culture by contrasting her real life and style of dress with those she saw in the movies:

We dressed plainly. We wore long dresses that were different than the styles in the movies. I knew about flappers from the movies, but I never dressed that way. None of my friends dressed that way. There was a flapper in my building. I guess . . . it was her nature. She was Italian and went to speakeasies. Her mother was upset at her daughter's behavior, but she didn't bother anybody.[58]

With the change in content came a dramatic change in form. The nickelodeons gave way to movie houses designed to win over "the steady patronage of a new class"[59] and to hold their audiences in the dark somnambulism of celluloid fantasy. Starting with the construction of the Strand Theatre in New York in 1914, these palaces, in the words of one of their architects, were designed as "social safety valves in that the public can partake of the same luxuries as the rich."[60] Another critic commented that "the differences of cunning . . . and wealth that determine our outside lives are forgotten. . . . Our democratic nation reserves its new democracy for the temple of daydreams."[61] The form itself was a demonstration of new content. If the old noisy neighborhood nickelodeons were an experience of community, the new palaces were a reprieve from community, a vision of wealth, a touch of royalty. If there were sexuality and romance inside the frame, the dark interiors, away from the watchful eyes of parents and neighbors, encouraged sexuality outside the frame, creating a new definition of a participatory audience. One critic observed:

> In the dim auditorium which seems to float on the world of dreams
> . . . an American woman may spend her afternoon alone. . . . She can
> let her fantasies slip through the darkened atmosphere to the screen
> where they drift in rhapsodic amours with handsome stars. In the isola-
> tion of this twilight palace . . . the blue dusk of the deluxe house has
> dissolved the Puritan strictures she had absorbed as a child.[62]

Some early films spoke sympathetically to the confused cultural experience of uprooted women—to the tasks of maintaining home and community in a world threatening to tear them apart. They helped to unify generations caught up in the divisive experiences of urban life. To the daughters, also the children of cultural transformation, film spoke differently. As themes of traditional family and community began to fade, the cinema spoke increasingly in the idiom of an urban, individualized culture. At first, these films briefly revealed new archetypes of feminine possibility that bore a relationship to the dynamics of cultural change. Yet in affirming the daughters' break from the traditions of family life, these films also pointed, as teachers and guides, to a mode of existence predicated on a commitment to individual survival and satisfaction within the social relationships defined by the consumer marketplace.

The ability of film to speak, in various ways, to the experience of its audience provides us with a key to understanding its appeal and power. In the first instance, film as a component of mass culture became a mediation between a historic uprooting and an unknown and threatening urban society. In the second instance, it was a mediation between traditional culture and the emergent terms of modern life. Film as a part of mass culture has the power to act as a force of unity as well as becoming an aspect of "the liquidation of the traditional value of the cultural heritage."[63]

While some of the contents of early films reflected a trend toward the liberation of women from patriarchal constraints, the social order was able to utilize this new release for the construction of a new form of domination. As women moved from the constricted family-dominated culture to the more individualized values of modern urban society, the form and content of domination changed, but new authorities replaced the old. In the name of freedom from tradition, women were trapped anew in fresh forms of sexual objectification and bound to the consumerized and sexualized household.

Nonetheless, moving pictures were the most universal form of cheap and satisfying entertainment in urban immigrant communities. As escape, education, or pleasure, they constituted a major source of new ideas and social experience. For immigrant women, motion pictures were a community-sanctioned form of urban mass culture, beguiling in its presentation of dress, manners, freedom, and sexual imagery. They provided an escape, but they also extended the world as a visual universe of magic and illusion.

4

Fashion and Democracy

"The Ends Justify the Jeans"

*Have we worked out our democracy further in regard to clothes
than anything else?*

—Jane Addams (1902)

July 14, 1980. Bastille Day. On Broadway, at Seventy-second,
a bus rattles to its stop. Above, a blur of color—bright red, or-
ange, shocking saffron, lavender blue, marine, livid, purplescent,
raven—invades the corridor of vision. Looking up, we see a
poster ad that, running along the entire roof of the bus, offers an
outrageous display: an assembly line of female backsides, pressed
emphatically into their designer jeans. On the right hip pocket
of each, the signature of an heiress.

We see the figures from waist to midthigh, yet we *know* they
are women. We have seen it before. These buttocks greet us from
a rakish angle, a posture widely cultivated in women from time
to time, in place to place. What was termed in nineteenth-
century America the *Grecian bend*. The bustle. Foot-bound
women of China. Corsets. High heels. Hobble skirts. Here it is,
women hobbled in the finery of freedom.

The bus moves along. Pinned to its rear, we see its final
reminder: "The *Ends* Justify the Jeans . . . Gloria Vanderbilt
for Murjani." Today's freedom is molded and taut. An animal in
perpetual heat. Individuals are identical, but come in colors.
Over *this* rainbow lies the promise of perpetual pleasure.

Calvin Klein makes a similar promise. These jeans are blue;
their double-stitched seams mottled by the *image* of wear. But

75

there all evidence of toil evaporates. The shirt—white, casual, rolled at the sleeves—is satin. His model stands locked at the knees, flexed in a paroxysm of ecstasy. She too assumes the Grecian bend; a moment of submission, captured for you, by a pair of pants. She purrs; she growls—restrained by the cloth, caressed by the seams. Calvin Klein has done this for her. He will do it for you.

Bon Jour Jeans are "built to look like you're moving even when you're idle." The Protestant ethic creeps in. Ben Franklin would have loved it.

A simple pair of pants is infused with a multiplicity of meanings. in the 1850s, denims were the unemotional, durable garb of miners and others among a newly mobile work force that came to California in the aftermath of the gold strike. Seams were riveted to make them hold, a technology borrowed from the construction of horse blankets.[1] Cloth for beats of burden was translated to the needs of men of burden. These were the clothes of hard-laboring people. Loose and ill-fitting, these pants were mass-produced for men separated from their homes and from the clothing those homes had customarily produced. These pants held little promise for the men who wore them, save the promise that they would be ready for the next day's labors.

For others during the same decade, horse blankets were hardly enough. In the court of Empress Eugénie, "the dress worn by a fashionable lady in attendance contained 1,100 yards of material used in the construction of flounces and worked into tucks, folds and various trimmings."[2] American women of means were also wrapped in an abundance of cloth. While such makers of overalls as Levi Strauss and John H. Browning worried over how many men could be fitted into a given yardage of cloth, for women of wealth the concern was with how many yards of cloth could be pleasingly draped upon a given individual. This was the mark of prosperity: to wear enough material on one's back to clothe many of a more common caste.

"Three-flounce skirts were commonly seen" on women of property:

> Full sleeves were split in front revealing the white sleeves of the soft
> blouse underneath. . . . The skirt and bodice were often separate be-

cause of the immense weight of the full skirt with the stiffly boned point of the bodice coming over the fullness to flatten it. . . . Braid trims the skirt flounces; split sleeves, and bodice. It covers the curved bodice side-front and dropped-shoulder armhole seams too. Wide grosgrain ribbon sashes, caught up in poufs, decorate the skirt. Sometimes flowers were added to them.[3]

While merchant burghers in America were not as fancily dressed as were the women of their estate, neither did they wear horse blankets. Box coats, edges "trimmed with dark braid accenting the lapels and cuffs," provided a sporty prototype for today's "business suit." For those more tied to an elegant past, the "double-breasted coat has a fitted bodice and flared skirt with a split. . . . This man wears a black satin vest with a collar and a black cravat on his high shirt collar."[4] The display of cloth was the mark of substance and, most certainly, profit.

In the 1850s, the *fashionable* rich could not imagine themselves wearing the dungaree pants of proletarians and "peasants."[5] Neither could working-class people realistically imagine themselves in the finery of wealth and power. The only fashion link between them — subtle at best — was the austere, coal-black stovepipe hat of capitalist wealth, symbolizing the factory smokestacks that brought profit to one, toil to the other. Blue jeans wore the signature of deprivation and sweat.

Success in that world required a dramatic change of clothes. In Horatio Alger's *Ragged Dick* (1866), it is a neat gray suit of clothes, a gift from a fortuitous benefactor, that signals Dick's impending metamorphosis from a ragged bootblack to "Richard Hunter, Esq.," a gentleman of substance:

> When Dick was dressed in his new attire, with his face and hands clean, and his hair brushed, it was difficult to imagine that he was the same boy. . . . He now looked quite handsome, and might readily have been taken for a young gentlemen, except that his hands were red and grimy.[6]

Years later, the clothing of nineteenth-century laborers would assume new and different meanings. Functional beginnings became increasingly obscure within unfolding imagery. In the movies, the range hands of the early cattle industry were reborn as icons of a noble, rural simplicity; rugged individualism; primal morality and law. Blue jeans were conspicuous within the moral landscape of media Americana. On the screen these pants taunted the imaginations of city folk as emblems of a simpler and uncorrupted life. While laborers would continue to wear them at work, now the well-heeled might don a pair — a symbolic escape from the regimen of the marketplace, at home or in the garden. Democracy in action!

In the fifties, blue denim became part of a statement, a rejection of postwar suburban society and of the tyrannies of the fashion-conscious consumerism that gave that society its definition. In James Dean's *Rebel without a Cause*, or Marlon Brando's *Wild One*, dungarees provided a channel of contempt toward the empty and conformist quietude of cold-war suburbia, and for the "rural idiocy" of small-town life. The affirmative images of American consumer capitalism were under cultural siege. What had been a piece of Americana — blue jeans — became a rejection of Americana. These images found a responsive audience among those for whom gray flannel suits and crinoline shirtwaist dresses had been elevated as ideals of the age. In blue jeans, men and boys found relief from the priorities of the business world. Women and girls found relief from the Grecian bend. Even some suburban gardeners slipped into their Levis for their moments of casual comfort, for a nap on the porch.

By the mid-sixties, blue jeans were part of an essential ensemble within an emerging commitment to social struggle. In the Deep South, where tenant farmers and sharecroppers, grandchildren of slaves, continued to wear denim in its mid-nineteenth-century sense, they were joined by college student activists — black and white — in a battle to overturn the deeply embedded centuries of segregation and race hatred. Blue denim — pants, jackets, overalls — became a sacred bond between them. The garb of toil was sanctified by the dignity of struggle. The blue *image* moved north with the song:

> We've been 'buked, and we've been scorned.
> We've been talked about, sure as you're born.
> But we'll never turn back.
> No we'll never turn back.

Until we've all been freed,
And we've got e-qual-i-ty.

In the student rebellion and the antiwar movement that followed, blue jeans and work shirts provided a counterpoint to the uniforms of the dominant culture, whether fatigue green in Southeast Asia, or police blue in Chicago, or gray flannel on Madison Avenue. Denim provided an antifashion, an antiuniform.

With the rekindling of a long-dormant feminism in the late 1960s, the political configurations of dress became increasingly explicit. Rejecting the sex roles of convention, blue jeans were a feminist weapon against restrictive fashion, sexual objectification, passive femininity. This was the cloth of action, a challenge to the social fabric of sexuality. The cloth of labor became the emblem of liberation.

If blue jeans were renegade in the 1960s and early 1970s, by the 1980s they had become the mainstay of fashion—available in a variety of colors, textures, fabrics, and fit. These simple pants have made the long trek "from workers' garb to counter culture revolt to status symbol." According to a newspaper article:

> As American families back away from having their used-to-be requisite 2.3 children, they're snapping up jeans at a rate of 2.3 pair per person *per year*. That's 16 pairs of jeans bought per second, or 50,000 pairs per hour. Annually, that adds up a cool $5 billion industry figure.[7]

On television, in magazine advertising, on the sides of buildings and buses, jeans and backsides call out to us. Their humble past is obscured in the imagery. In ads, "horse blankets" are infused with "a surrealistic, new-wave flavor." Functional roots are rendered aesthetic; corporate sources are hidden. Dan Carroll, advertising director for Bon Jour Jeans, explains his task simply. "We try to stay away from commercial-looking ads. . . . We try to make advertising artistic."[8] The exploitative labor system that underwrites these fantasies of freedom in capitalist America is nowhere in evidence. The image is seductive; the name is French; the signature is personal; the cotton is American; the weavers and dyers and cutters and sewers and finishers toil in the sweatshops of Hong Kong.[9]

The contradiction between promise and production resides in

the image of itself. Jeans are the facsimile of freedom, brought to us by models who are tucked — painfully — into a skintight fit. They are the universal symbol of individualism and Western democracy; mass-produced clothing of workers, embellished by the imprimatur of Paris, the home of *haute couture* since the time of Louis XIV. They are the vestments of liberated women, cut to impose the postures of Victorianism: corsets with the *look* of freedom and motion.

Their allure is compelling. A student writes to the Soviet youth newspaper, *Komsomolskaya Pravda*. He explains that when he went to a dance wearing the clothing available in the Russian stores, "Nothing happened." He continues:

> The next night I dressed entirely in foreign clothes and brought some Western records with me as well. You should see what happened. Invitations and telephone numbers came raining down on me. Now I have jeans, good suits, records and all that sort of junk. I have plenty of friends who can get me anything I want. I have gone into businesses, but now I dictate my own conditions.[10]

The ideological attraction is international in scope; fashion is the "bounty" of capitalist culture. Growing up in the cold war of the fifties, fashion was the dividing line between friends and enemies. Russians and Chinese could be known by the uniformity of their dress; Americans were brightly packaged.

In blue jeans, the most functional and least ritualistic of clothes, fashion reveals itself as a complex world of history, promise, and change; as a capturing of continual "truths." Opposite worlds collide violently and then mesh in fashion. Social conflict and contradiction are displayed . . . and diffused. Resistance and conformity coexist within "the mirror of fashion."

What are we to make of all this? Do we dismiss it as a meaningless frivolity, irrelevant and immaterial? Paul Nystrom, a writer on fashion and economics in the 1920s and 1930s, and a father of modern mass-merchandising techniques, contended that it was "foolish and shallow-minded people" who refused to take fashion seriously. "The wiser ones," he said, "have tried to find explanations and to understand."[11] Yet looking at fashions, in and of themselves, provides explanations that often defy understanding. Our ability to interpret a specific fashion — the current one of jeans, for example — shows us that as we try to make sense of it, our confusion intensifies. It is a fashion whose very essence is contradiction and confusion.

To pursue the goal of understanding is to move beyond the artifact of cloth itself, toward the more general phenomenon of fashion and the world in which it has risen to prominence. It is a piece in the political discourse of consent, and of revolution. It is a keystone in the shifting architectures of class, sexuality, national identity. Fashion is situated within the framework of industrial development; it interacts with the rise of consumer capitalism and mass-media imagery. It is a way in which people identify themselves as individuals and collectively.

What events, what developments, what forces proceeded to make *fashion* a more considerable concern than *function* among increasing numbers of people? In what ways have fashion and sexuality coincided, particularly in the context of palpable transformations in the structure, ceremony, and economy of family life? How does fashion provide a social language that infuses the historic emergence of women's liberation?

Exploring the role of fashion within the social and political configuration of industrial America helps to reveal the parameters and possibilities, the fantasies of freedom, the industrial democracy of American capitalism. Blue jeans alone suggest that politics and fashion may be the warp and woof of American culture in an era of mass production and mass merchandising. The ultimate question is whether the incorporation of images of rebellion into mass-produced fashions has been a meaningful component of social change.

In the Beginning . . .

And when the woman saw that the tree was good for food, and that it was pleasant to the eyes, and a tree to be desired to make one wise, she took of the fruit thereof, and did eat, and gave also unto her husband with her; and he did eat. And the eyes of them both were opened, and they knew that they were naked;

*and they sewed fig leaves together, and made themselves
aprons. . . .*
*   And the Lord God said unto the woman, "What is this that
thou hast done?"*

—Genesis 3:6–13

Within the biblical account of creation, the first appearance of
clothing was the mark of sin. Adam and Eve, born naked into
Paradise, get dressed at the threshold of perdition. With the putting on of clothes, the future life of humanity is cursed. In the
leaves of the fig tree, standing before God, man and woman
received the dire sentence of "the Fall."

For these "sinners in the hands of an angry God," the penalty
was monumental. Once a garden of universal bounty and
reciprocity, the earth was now bounded by hierarchy, scarcity,
and denial. As the most cursed of all the animals, the serpent was
relegated to eat dust all the days of its life, crawling upon its belly; yet the curse on humanity was also severe.

For woman, who bears primary guilt in this venerable tale, the
judgment carried sorrow and pain in the bringing forth of children. It also established her subjugation as a class. From that time
forward, she was destined—so generations have been told—to
submit willingly to the desire and the rule of her husband. The
prototype of domination, one human over another, was inscribed upon history.

With sin, and with the assumption of clothing, Adam's sufferings were likewise multiplied. Sorrow would pursue him all the
days of his life. Labor and toil were his miserable inheritance. So,
too, was death: "For dust thou art, and unto dust shalt thou return." For each person, the miracle of creation would be
ceremonially and inevitably undone.

As the trappings of sin, clothing is infused with these wretched conditions of existence. Hierarchy and domination are elevated as the way of God on earth. The common lot of humanity is
to persevere under the constant reminder that we are essentially
scorned, sinful. The sexual divisions of labor and of power are
also established concurrently with the assumption of clothes.
Clothing bore witness to this world-historic, tragic moment,
and would continue to do so in the millennia to follow. It was

the word of God, emblazoned upon the very surface of humanity.

This injunction informed and permeated the structure of European feudalism. Within this static and landed society, hierarchy and caste had the underpinning of religion. The social world was cut deep with the imprint of power and inequality. The prerogatives of nobility and clergy were seen as God-given, as was the subordination of the peasantry. Obedience to God, to an eternal law, was defined by an unhesitating acceptance of one's station within the existent hierarchy. Salvation itself was predicated on compliance.

As in the realm of *the word*, in the decisive arena of clothing, the dominant biblical interpretation was one that perpetuated the rule of landed nobility and church. Among a degraded peasantry, historically bound to the land and wedged at the bottom of an immobile social order, the curse of Adam was the characteristic definition for life. Labor and sorrow were a continual plight, and the dominant interpretation of the Bible offered no possibility of escape. In the lives of those who worked the land, the wages of sin were exacted perpetually.

The structure of material life in general, and clothing in particular, was sustained by this presupposition. Scarcity and abundance coexisted as in a great chain of being. While evidence is slim regarding the clothing worn by poor people in that era, certain general parameters can be deduced. The social misery of peasant life was embodied in the inelegance of their clothes. Peasant clothing was simply made and rough of cut and cloth. The phenomenon of "fashion," whereby clothing design undergoes a general and discernible process of change, was unknown among the poor.

> For 1,500 years the essential lines of dress had hardly changed . . . a shepherd of the Fourteenth Century might have inherited his garments from his great, great, great grandfather many times removed. The usual attire was a coarse gray smock, trousers, leg wrappings and shoes.[12]

Needless to say, such garments were a part of the broad home production of the peasantry. This was a society of self-sufficiency, and needs were addressed within the immediacy of the locale. Weaving and sewing were performed at home, as was dyeing where it was employed.[13]

Against this rustic backdrop of peasant simplicity, the clothing of the feudal landowner was something to behold. If the shabby togs of plowmen betrayed a kinship to fallen man, a life defined by labors of the soil, the vestments of clergy and of nobility bore no such shame.

While those at the bottom of the feudal hierarchy bore the weight of sin most heavily, those at the top acknowledged a servitude only to God. Otherwise they bore the weight of life with little difficulty. Within the structure of feudalism, the nobility was — it would seem — largely immune from Adam's curse. While others' God-given station required a commitment to the invocation "*In the sweat of thy face shalt thou eat bread*," the stature of the nobility and priesthood was defined by a life of consummate leisure.

"The nobleman, like the lady, was a creature incapable of useful work," argues Quentin Bell in his evocative study of fashion, *On Human Finery*. Idleness, within the prevalent reading of the Bible, was a mark of favor in the eyes of God, insofar as it exempted the nobility from the judgment of labor. For the nobility, stewardship over cursed humanity defined them, along with clergy, as agencies of the Lord. This role was imprinted upon the practices and material conditions of their lives. Bell continues on the life of the nobleman:

> A high degree of conspicuous leisure was expected of him. Equally, it was important that he should be a consumer; if he had relied simply upon the vicarious consumption of his household, it would have appeared that he was working to support them. He had to establish the fact that he was a rentier (which until the eighteenth century almost implied the ownership of land).[14]

Idleness and waste were symbolic of a God-given freedom from the ecological terms of common life.

Clothing was an essential part of this conspicuous display of sloth and needless expenditure of resources. It was the material embodiment of what Thorstein Veblen called "conspicuous leisure" and "conspicuous consumption."[15] Clothing was a palpable and powerful expression of a social relationship. Among men

and women of nobility, cloth — in abundance — was an achievement of their prosperity. The immense amount of labor and intricate needlework required in assembling and embellishing their
clothing was testimony to the immense amount of labor that was
held under the sway of their domain. In a world of general scarcity, their birthright was a surplus. Cloth was worn in billows
and tucks. The God-given powers they claimed were underwritten by a visually tangible differentiation between themselves
and the common lot of humanity. Their clothing was cut and arranged to reveal the depth of its sumptuosness. These clothes had
no functional association with work. Indeed, their function was
largely to convey the message that their owners lived beyond
work. Freed from the biblical inscription to labor, they stood
within their world, somewhere between God and humanity.
Sartorial aesthetics, clothing imagery was their province and
their prerogative. To violate this prerogative was to violate not
only the dominant structure of power, but also the dominant
structure of religious belief.

As in the Bible, where the assumption of clothing immediately precedes the demarcation of gender, there was some distinction between the clothing of men and of women. If noblemen
were immune from the curse of Adam, Eve's sin was not so easily
expiated. By recent standards, however, these distinctions were
minimal.[16] Among peasant folk, the distinction was almost
nonexistent. In the clothing of the rich, a sexual division is evident, yet in both men's and women's clothing, leisure and consumption are dramatically proclaimed. Within the order of
feudalism, such a claim was an essential component of inequity.
In their clothes, and — as Anne Hollander has pointed out — in
their portraits, "cloudlike, flame-like rivers of cloth" were the
honoraria of religiously ordained status over society.[17]

With the development of a "democratic" challenge to this
structure, among peasants and among an incipient bourgeoisie,
the prerogatives of nobility took on an increasingly legalistic
character — an attempt to stem the tide of history. Elaborate systems of "sumptuary law," governing consumption along class
and caste lines, developed in Europe in the Middle Ages, and
continued to be established — in certain places — into the twentieth century. According to Frances Elizabeth Baldwin, a scholar

of sumptuary legislation in England, the enactment of such laws between 1327 and the early seventeenth century — when they begin to disappear from English canon — was motivated by three general concerns. First and foremost was to "preserve class distinctions, so that any stranger could tell by merely looking at a man's dress to what rank in society he belonged."

Second, sumptuary legislation was designed to "check practices which were regarded as deleterious in their effects, due to the feeling that luxury and extravagance were in themselves wicked and harmful to people." Initially, this concern was leveled by the upper echelons against the lower, and applied selectively throughout society. Only later, with the rise of new forms of mobile wealth and the ascendancy of Puritanism and other Protestant sects, were such invocations directed at the sumptuary practices of the church or the nobility, per se.

The third concern was economic. Laws were designed to promote home industries, as in the case of late eighteenth-century America where homespun was seen as a patriotic resistance to British domination over the American market. It could also mean that consumption was restricted to "encourage savings" for the purposes, often, of supporting the political, military, or sumptuary demands of a sovereign.[18]

It is clear that the first concern — that of maintaining hierarchy and convention — was the preeminent impetus behind the enactment of such statutes. "Sumptuary laws," argues clothing historian Pearl Binder, "constituted a means of enforcing class privilege in a regimented social structure. . . . In the Middle Ages, both Church and State rigorously enforced social distinctions. 'Men may be equal in the sight of God, but on earth they are commanded to stay in that status of life into which they are born.' "[19]

Under the broad canopy of sumptuary law, "men and women, in literal truth, were regulated from the part in their hair to the soles of their feet."[20] Behind these laws lay the word of God.

> Each man's place was appointed to him in a common scheme; he must, in general, be content to live in that state of life unto which it had pleased God to call him at his birth. . . . Since each man's place in life was thus fixed by social custom, it was heresy for him to attempt to rise above his class either in his manner of living or in his dress.[21]

Such laws were overwhelming in their detail, and categorized according to the lines of social power. An English law, enacted under the reign of Elizabeth I (1582), gave specific directions to apprentices regarding their acceptable mode of dress. "No apprentice whatsoever should presume," it began, "to wear (1) any clothing except what he received from his master; (2) a hat, or anything except a woollen cap . . . ; (3) ruffles, cuffs, loose collars . . . ; (4) anything except canvas, fustian [a stout fabric of cotton and flax], sack cloth, English leather, or woollen doublets, without any silver or silk trimming." Punishment for violation of the statute was at the discretion of the master for a first offense; a public whipping for a second offense; and six months added to the period of indenture for the third offense."[22] Likewise, a proclamation of July 6, 1597, lists a vast array of cloth and accessories that "none shall wear," save those of high rank. In an elaborately drawn document, indicating what is forbidden and who is exempted, we discover that "Cloth of gold, sylver tissued," and "Silke of purple color" are forbidden in garments, save those of "Earls and above that rank and Knights of the Garter in their purple mantles." Among ladies of nobility, only "Knights' wives and all above that rank" might wear velvet in their upper garments. In "Kirtles [a skirt or outer petticoat] and Petticoats, however," velvet was permissible for "Wives of knights' eldest sons, and all above that rank."[23] Within that same statute we see the arrival of another significant realm of status within the arena of hierarchical dress codes: *money*. While the highest levels of sumptuary practice are still reserved for those landed lords of inherited lineage, we see that "those with net income of 500 marks per year for life" share the same level of exception as "Barons' sons and all above that rank," as well as "Gentlemen attending upon the queen in house or chamber," and "those who have been employed in embassies" as emissaries of a monarch.[24] As the ranks of nobility are solidified within the structure of law, the law itself betrays a portentous vulnerability to a class of people whose wealth is defined not in the static tenure over land, but in the mobile negotiations of a money economy.

In Augsburg, somewhat earlier, in 1530:

Only princes, knights and their ladies were permitted to wear brocade, velvet garments were for patricians. The upper bourgeoisie were allowed three ellens of velvet to decorate their headdresses. Those dedicated to learning wore silk, damask or satin, whereas wool and homespun materials were for simple folk. Furs were regulated in the same manner: ermine and sables for princes and aristocrats; fox and polecat for simple townspeople; goat and lamb skins for the peasant.[25]

Sources indicate that while sumptuary law became increasingly prevalent at the dawn of the modern era, it was rarely imposed and almost impossible to enforce. In England, the reign of Elizabeth I saw the most vigorous development of sumptuary legislation in British history, yet only a short time after her death, early in the reign of James I, sumptuary legislation was altogether abolished.[26]

Like censorship, which arose rapidly in the aftermath of the European development of the printing press, sumptuary law may be seen — in part — as a desperate gesture to maintain entitlements of customary power in the face of mounting pressures. Clothing, like *the word*, was essential to the mediation of feudal powers. Control of both *the word* and the sartorial image was the province of elites. The possibility of diffusion of these media to those previously excluded threatened social revolution and gave rise to state-sanctioned regulation.

Particularly in the arena of clothing, the development of mercantile wealth posed a serious challenge. Regardless of law, it was unlikely that a peasant or an apprentice would have the resources available to violate the code surrounding "cloth of gold." Occasionally, the idiom of rebellion would assume a sartorial component, as in sixteenth-century Germany, where "rebellious peasants . . . demanded the right to wear red cloaks like their masters," but — for most — the garb of wealth was forbidden by economic rather than legalistic circumstances."[27]

In reality, it was from an emerging mobile class of monetary wealth that the greatest threat to social prerogative was perceived. Merchant trade, often feeding the luxurious practices of the nobility, elevated an embryonic bourgeoisie to circumstances of prosperity, if not political franchise.[28]

Over time, with the ascendancy of a mercantile and later an industrial bourgeoisie, exclusive possession of a sartorial eloquence eroded as an aristocratic privilege. Initially, incipient capitalists had access to the material comforts born of the purse. Eventually, their successors in mass industry, and then in merchandising, would transform that eloquence into the profitable terms of mass production, establishing a vernacular imagery of consumption. Insofar as clothing constitutes a generally understood language of society, however, the categories of adornment, dating to the aristocratic tradition, still hold sway. The great difference, as will be discussed later, is that this continuity of meaning has persisted more in the clothing of women than of men in the era of capitalism.

While significantly diminished from the standards of the past, even today the signs of aristocracy assert a considerable — if now mass-produced — presence. Much of this persistence is rooted in the particular history of France, as is, ironically, its renunciation. During the reign of Louis XIV, a pregnant admixture of absolute monarchy and mercantile capitalism produced an economy geared toward the fabrication of luxuries. The Sun King's principal financial advisor, Jean-Baptiste Colbert, happened to be the son of a cloth merchant in Reims. Colbert bound his mercantile roots to the splendor of the court and "gathered together all the plans and expedients of his predecessors for a prolonged attempt to establish an entirely self-sufficing national economy." At the heart of this enterprise lay Colbert's particular strategy: "With our taste," he proclaimed, "let us make war on Europe and through fashion conquer the world."[29] A central part of the program was the promotion of French luxury industries and their products.

Colbert "used many methods: encouragement through the giving of honours and monetary rewards; regulation through the *Code de Commerce* which set forth exactly what was to be produced and by which methods it was to be manufactured."[30] In addition, import tariffs, state subsidies, and relaxed guild regulations contributed to the realization of this economic program, and since that time, the predominance of French *haute couture* has been unchallenged. Expressing perhaps Colbert's own mercantile roots, the continuity of aristocratic influence has been dependent on the growth and success of the bourgeoisie and on the mobile market economy.

Alongside this tendency, the bourgeois revolutions altered the terms of politics and ushered in a whole new mode of life. A broad alliance of classes assembled around the explosive banner of "natural rights." One aspect of this revolutionary process played itself out in the area of fashion. Against the aristocratic clothing customs that accentuated social inequality, a new, egalitarian fashion developed. We can see this in the rise of Puritanism, where a "plain style" of dress was a mark of opposition to feudal waste and privilege, paralleling the rise of a "plain style" in language as Latin texts were replaced by vernacular ones and popular access to Scripture became key to the Protestant notion of salvation. A Puritan could be known by the simplicity of his garb and by the Bible carried under his arm.[31]

The renunciation of aristocratic modes crested dramatically, and prophetically, with the French Revolution. Before the revolution, the conventions of clothing were deeply entrenched along lines of class. In the *ancien régime*, men and women of nobility wore the conspicuous apparel of their caste. Ladies of the court were decked in elaborate gowns, deeply layered, and inscribed with labor and lace. Their waists were constricted by corsets, driving powdered breasts upward beyond the frontiers of a plunging neckline, and pushing faint sighs from their lips. While the hobbled habit accentuated a demeanor of erotic availability, it also asserted a leisurely existence.

Men, too, were marked by privilege: *culottes* (knee breeches); silk stockings; the *justaucorps*, an ornate body coat, close fitting and reaching to the knees. Men and women alike wore elaborate wigs upon their aristocratic heads. In a society sharply divided by broad restrictions on social and political rights, these garments were notorious as symbols of domination, just as motor cars would be viewed in urban working-class neighborhoods in the early years of the twentieth century, before the mass production and merchandising of auto-mobility.[32]

In contrast to this splendor, the laboring poor of Paris were known simply as *sans-culottes*; they wore ankle-length trousers or rough smocks. With the revolution and its egalitarian idiom, *culottes* fell into disrepute, as did silk stockings and *justaucorps*. Wigs disappeared in the spirit of democracy and emancipation. Breaking with the aristocratic past, and adapting the public im-

ages of popular sovereignty, fashion and democracy were symbolically fused. Asserting solidarity with the Parisian masses, the
dress of middle-class men adapted a vernacular cut, the cut of
modern-day trousers. For a time, women of means also took on
the garb of social equality, wearing simple and flimsy shifts.[33] If
France would be the fountain for the continuation of aristocratic
elegance in fashion, so too was it a source for the revolutionary
imagery of emancipation.

The Cloak of Morality

Cloth stands prominently at the heart of capitalism's development from the sixteenth century to the present. It is woven deeply into the massive social transformations wrought by capitalism. In England and northwestern France, the shift from crop
production to the raising of sheep for wool irrevocably altered
the course of world history. Cloth was conspicuous in the *sinews*
of trade by which a world-market economy was created and
mobilized. The isolation of local self-sufficiency gave way to a
"modern world system."

Dealings in cloth were essential to the development and
prosperity of an urban bourgeoisie. From the end of the eighteenth century, the city as a social and economic network, the
bourgeoisie, and the growth of technology coalesced to define
the contours of modern commerce.

If laborers in agriculture and industry were not at first motivated by the impetus of "fashion," they were decisively affected
by it. After initial inroads established by the cash crops of sugar
and tobacco, the plantation system of slavery — particularly in
the southern United States — was driven forward by seemingly
insatiable markets for cotton. The industrial factory system in
England and America was likewise propelled by textile production. Factory labor had its harsh birthplace at the side of a loom.

Cloth provoked a horrific uprooting of peoples, across frontiers and oceans. While a handful prospered in trade, the vast
majority of the rest labored out of necessity, often against their
will. Factory production of textiles moved women from the are-

na of home production and engaged them in the public spheres of modernity as mill workers. Customary definitions of womanhood and of family life were shattered in the process.

Over the course of the nineteenth century, the development of the ready-made clothing industry began to alter the very terms of popular survival, signaling a shift from home production of goods to the general consumption of factory-made products. With the input of emerging structures of mass merchandising around the turn of the twentieth century, and urged on by the burgeoning agencies of mass impression, clothing and fashion began to take their central place in the proper imagination.

For an urban bourgeoisie at the beginning of the nineteenth century, clothing was a matter of principle, a statement of purpose. If the Protestant Reformation had split sumptuousness from the realm of the sacred, mercantile capitalism had erected a bastion of power and wealth whose emblem was diligence, not idleness.[34] In his *Autobiography*, Benjamin Franklin — Max Weber's archetype of the "protestant ethic and the spirit of capitalism" — presented a clear picture of the importance of surface appearance:

> In order to secure my credit and character as a tradesman, I took care not only to be in *reality* industrious and frugal, but to avoid all appearances to the contrary. I drest plainly; I was seen at no places of idle diversion. . . . To show that I was not above my business, I sometimes brought home the paper I purchas'd at the stores thro' the streets on a wheelbarrow. Thus being esteem'd an industrious, thriving young man, and paying duly for what I bought . . . I went on swimmingly.[35]

In this late-eighteenth-century account, the man of business is engaged morally in the world. Simplicity of attire was a hallmark of that morality. In violent juxtaposition to the customs of the landed aristocracy, a secular saintliness was inscribed, proudly, with the mark of one's worldly activity. In Franklin's Philadelphia, where Quaker businessmen forged a powerful unity between commerce and Christianity, the "plain style" of dress was a visible sign of their commitment to hard work and simple justice. Under no circumstances did this mean that their garments were cheap or inelegant. The "plain style" was, indeed, a style. While simply cut coats signified a break from the visual language of sumptuousness, they were at the same time made of the finest cloth and employed a time-consuming artisan dexteri-ty in their creation.[36]

The "plain style" was also not totally plain. Like the business suit of today, which derives from this shift, it had vestigial rem-nants of the sumptuous mode. Coats and vests were cut to reveal the layers of linen beneath them—tangible evidence of prosperi-ty, although understated in comparison with the tradition they rejected. Surely a man of means could still be known by the clothes he wore, but the image conveyed had changed from one of idleness, waiting to be served, to one mobile and self-serving.

In certain areas, the "rich but grave" aura of the commercial garb did not take hold, even within the capitalist epoch. Ceremonial garments continued to betray a commitment to sumptuosness, as is still in evidence in formal academic attire. In a world of mundane commitments, the doctoral hood allows for the mystification of unearthliness. In military attire as well, epaulets, braids, and other ornamental flourishes functioned to ennoble the practice of war.[37] Perhaps, as Quentin Bell suggests, this is rooted in war itself: giving symbolic legitimacy to the conspicuous consumption of human life. The separation of busi-ness from evening or leisure dress also left certain areas of mas-culine bourgeois life more ornamental or languid than others.

Overall, however, the trend was toward the tangibility of in-dustry, thrift, and action. Even such figures as Beau Brummell or Beau Nash, whose names come to us with the reputations of archetypal dandies, stood in stark contrast to the dash of courtly splendor. They were exemplars of the elevation of the "plain style" to the height of fashion around the turn of the nineteenth century. Both avoided what Victorian writer and critic John Ruskin was to call "that flabby flutter, wrinkled swelling, and puffed pomp of infinite disorder."[38]

The elegance of their garb was a costly investment in "simplic-ity, good fit and cleanliness." This fixation with cleanliness was a characteristic development of the capitalist ethic, set against the unbathed—if perfumed—bodies of the nobility.

> Beau Brummell hated dirt and was meticulously tidy. . . . His clothing was distinguished by its perfect fit and extreme cleanliness. He changed his linen three times a day, and he had the soles of his boots polished

like the upper part. . . . He wore a cambric shirt with valuable buttons
and an immaculate white cravat, which he spent three hours tying every
day. Beau Brummell usually wore black or navy blue, the garments
fitting so well that not a single crease was ever formed.[39]

Brummell was an architect of a simple, unflamboyant form of
ostentation, where fit and workmanship began to replace the
weighty display of cloth in the perfection of "elegance."

As industrial capitalism developed in the nineteenth century,
bourgeois men's clothing continued to develop in a mode of
fastidious austerity. As the wealth of industrialists grew, "an industrious life no longer implied a poor or laborious existence.
. . . Masculine dress betokened a complete abstention from industrial labour, but that was all; it was not 'highly sumptuous.' "[40] Even immense power was understated. Dark colors
were both resistant to the dirt of the industrial landscape and
consistent with the democratic ideology of enlightenment.[41]
Black coats and cylindrical "smokestack" hats betrayed a sartorial commitment to a new, industrial aesthetic. In industrial areas
of the United States, this mutation was fairly complete by about
1830, while among the landed wealth of the plantation South, an
aristocratic motif persevered.[42]

While men of capitalist wealth employed highly skilled tailors
and demanded fine, if substantial, fabrics for their clothes, the
idiom of their garments was one of engagement and social ethics.
An emanation of precisionism was implicit in the fit. A suggestion of asceticism was projected by the dark gravity of the cloth.
In the midst of these vestments, men of extreme wealth claimed
a moral penance, a righteous place in the world. Capitalist fashion had freed men from the evidence of rapacity and waste, from
the guilt and conceit of gluttony that marked the aristocratic tradition.

Yet if capitalists, merchants, and somber professionals made
sartorial claims of self-denial and egalitarianism, the social world
they forged and administered offered a very different picture.
Those who stood outside the stewardship of capital did not have
access to the conspicuous symbols, these finely tailored emblems
of austerity and moral purpose. The cloak of morality was not
available to those who labored beneath its threads. The hypocri-

sy of capitalist wealth was revealed most glaringly in the lives of those who stood in the shadow of its righteous image.

The Three Faces of Eve

In 1868, an eight-year-old girl named Jane Addams prepared herself for a weekly trip to the Union Sunday School in Cedarville, Illinois. Dressed proudly in a beautiful new cloak — "gorgeous beyond anything I had ever worn before" — she stood before her father for his approval. The owner of a sawmill and a flour mill, Mr. Addams was the epitome of middle-class substance. Himself a teacher of a large Bible class at the Union Sunday School, Jane's father cut "a most imposing figure in his Sunday frock coat, a fine head rising high above all the others." He wore the cloak of morality with pious pride.

His Quaker eyes looking sternly down at his daughter, Mr. Addams suggested that Jane forgo her illustrious garment in favor of more humble garb.

> I was much chagrined by his remark that it was a very pretty cloak — in fact so much prettier than any cloak the other little girls in the Sunday School had, that he would advise me to wear my old cloak, which would keep me quite as warm, with the added advantage of not making the other little girls feel badly. I complied with the request but I fear without inner consent, and I certainly was quite without joy of self-sacrifice as I walked soberly through the village street by the side of my counselor.

Yet after moving beyond an initial response of confused reluctance, the event proved to be a moral lesson:

> My mind was busy . . . with the old question eternally suggested by the inequalities of the human lot. Only as we neared the church door did I venture to ask what could be done about it, receiving the reply that it might never be righted so far as clothes went, but that people might be equal in things that mattered much more than clothes . . . and that it was very stupid to wear the sort of clothes that made it harder to have equality even there.[43]

Whereas for Benjamin Franklin the appearance of diligent piety was essential in the carrying on of business, for Jane Addams appearances provided an external symbol, a visible testimony of social morality. In a world that said that clothes shouldn't matter very much, the one thing that was clear was that they mattered completely. "Above everything else," her father's message conveyed the admonition that "mental integrity" should be there to be seen. Sumptuous dress, in a world of inequality, was a manifest mark of greed.

In her life in social work, Addams kept to the lesson, and to the faith. She appropriated the "plain style" not for business, but in the name of community service. A worldly calling in the thoroughfares of commerce was the province of men. The general morality of the time instructed bourgeois women to dedicate themselves unswervingly to what Jane Addams referred to as "the family claim." Yet this was not for her. As one of an early but significant band of "educated" women, she perceived the family as a trap, one that would deny her outlets or activities in which she could adhere to the social morality inherited from her father.

Caught between the masculine principle of social engagement and the stark inequity of feminine reality, she translated the Protestant ethic into the terms of nurturance and service, rather than productivity and industry. In the early 1880s, while a junior at Rockford seminary, Addams proclaimed her calling, prophetically setting the terms for a life's work:

> As young women of the 19th century, we . . . proudly assert our independence, on the other hand we still retain the old ideal of womanhood—the saxon lady whose mission it was to give bread unto her household. So we have planned to be "Breadgivers" throughout our lives, believing that in labor alone is happiness, and that the only true and honorable life is one filled with good works and honest toil.[44]

Despite her hopeful claims for a generation, Jane Addams stood prominently as a heretic to the Victorian standards of femininity. Her "plain style" of dress and her blunt commitment to a social world placed her outside the conventions of womanhood. Her transgression—unwittingly encouraged by her father's stern morality—must be placed against the panorama of a more dominant social tradition. To a large extent, Addams's embracing of social works, and of a "plain" attire, was at the same time a rejection of *woman* as "a family possession, whose delicacy and polish are but outward symbols" of subservience to male prosperity.

For most wealthy women in nineteenth-century America, social engagement was relatively minimal. Their dress was not as "plain," nor did it evince the moral claims borne by the somber clothing of men. If men of money scorned sumptuous claims for themselves, the ideals propagated for women of their class were far less economical. Similarly, while the social language of men's clothing tended to denote activity and industriousness, the idiom of women's clothing was fragility, idleness, and the conspicuous consumption of cloth.

In the United States, as in much of western Europe, most nineteenth-century middle- and upper-class women dressed in sharp contrast to men of their economic position. If austerity was a component of feminine attire, its social message was sexual rather than economic. These were times when in the name of good taste, legs were referred to as "limbs" — if it was necessary to mention them at all. While men of wealth exuded the worldliness of the marketplace, women were the keepers of a higher morality, limited to the confines of the home. The sexual shame of "the Fall" was woman's to bear: a proper bourgeois wife and mother was covered from the nape of her neck to the tips of her toes; the display of skin was inappropriate. The ostensible morality of men in business was underwritten by the keepers of the home, untouched by the tarnished activities of commerce and isolated from an increasingly mobile and social world.

Within this bulwark of bourgeois morality, women were idealized icons, worshiped in a cult of purity and placed on a spiritual pedestal. If bourgeois men were actively consumed by the symbolism of industry, bourgeois women were symbols of virtue and decorum. This predominant social pattern, according to French historian Theodore Zeldin, effected an increasingly broad social distance between the realms of men and women. For women, "the cult of their purity made them inaccessible." Particularly, "pleasures in sexual intercourse could not in such circumstances be sought with them, who were dedicated to motherhood."[45] Childbearing defined the proper limits of married women's sexual horizon. Socially and emotionally, the

nineteenth-century institution of bourgeois marriage was a bar-
rier rather than a bond between men and women. For women,
the ideological baggage that informed this separation was nothing less than disastrous. By pious definition, women were unable
to fend for themselves. In the words of the feminist theoretician
Charlotte Perkins Gilman, women were imprisoned within a
"sexuo-economic" relation, one in which their moralistic and
child-rearing functions, their "home service," was exchanged for
economic survival, provided by men. Their femininity became
paramount as their social definition.[46]

This configuration, precisely as it claimed to elevate women
to a higher purity above worldly and carnal concerns, only
served to accentuate their carnality. To clarify this point, let us
take an example from another time and place. In China, over a
period of ten centuries and into the very recent past, the practice
of foot-binding was customarily enforced on women over a
broad range of social class. From an early age—usually about
seven years—little girls would have their toes pulled back under
the soles of their feet and bound in that position. Over years the
feet became deformed and misshapen. Effectively, foot-bound
women of China were systematically crippled by this custom. In
order to walk, they had to take slow, mincing steps, painfully
executed with the help of a walking stick.

Clearly, this example of hobbling, one of a variety of ornamental body practices that severely incapacitate the individual,
functioned to limit women's mobility in an environment that
designated women as a form of property. Yet within the context
of Chinese culture, foot-binding was not conceived of as restrictive. Rather it was considered as an aspect of eroticism. The
grossly transfigured foot was termed, poetically, "lily foot" or
"lotus foot." A broad liturgy of sexual practices focused on the
feet, and in its metamorphosis the foot became known as a sexual
organ, an additional genital. In addition to the use of botanical
terminology, the institution of foot-binding was founded on
horticultural theory. In plants, restricting the development of
one branch tends to accentuate the development of another.
Similarly, it was believed that by constricting the mobility of
women, their sexuality would flourish. As one student of the
foot has put it, by atrophying the foot, the genitals would under-

go hypertrophy. Our reason tells us that this is absurd and physiologically unfounded as a theory. Yet in certain ways, the theory became a self-fulfilling prophecy. By limiting the ability of
women to function in the broad range of human activities, foot-
binding did in effect accentuate the primacy of their sexual function. Sexuality became an expanded definition of womanhood,
as other definitions were culturally and physically eclipsed.[47]

The equivalent of the "lily foot" in nineteenth-century American and European middle-class culture was the commonly worn
corset, which restricted not only the mobility but even the
breathing of women who wore them. The romantic stereotype
of women continually fainting was a common occurrence, a result of the restriction and the debilitating pressure on internal organs from wearing corsets.[48] As a form of bodily restriction, the
corset accentuated carnal concerns precisely as its wearer was expected to transcend them. The very practice of restraining the
body of a woman implied that this model of chastity stood at the
frontiers of abandon. Along these lines, Havelock Ellis wrote
that corsets tended to make "breathing thoracic instead of abdominal, thereby keeping the bosom in a constant, and presumably sexually attractive, state of movement."[49]

At the same time, tight body lacing around the waist produced
what was idealized as a proper feminine bearing. The narrow
waist indicated minimal consumption of food, an imagistic
representation of self-denial. The broad expanses of bosom and
hip, accentuating the reproductive roles of women, provided an
image of bounty in childbearing and nurturance.

The bustle, a fixture of women's fashion for about twenty
years in the latter half of the nineteenth century, added to the
general broadness of the hips and to the imagery of reproductive
bounty. Bustles worn in conjunction with corsets effected the
posture known as the "Grecian bend," or the "S curve." With the
buttocks pushed up and back, and the back driven forward, the
bend approximated the posture of a female animal in heat, anticipating rear penetration by the male. In the midst of restrictive
purity, the implication was of a continual sexual readiness.

The question of women's wearing underpants is another example of this ambiguity and tension between chastity and carnality. Up until the 1850s, proper middle-class women wore no

underpants. Only those females who enjoyed some degree of mobility wore them. Little girls, up until the age of propriety, wore drawers under their skirts as a concession to the irrepressibility of youth. Upon maturation, drawers were abandoned, and the genital area remained uncovered save by the layers of skirts and underskirts. Occasionally, underskirts would be gartered around the knee, but the general convention presumed the combination of immobility and male protection. Oddly, underpants were perceived as male clothing, and the only women who wore them were those who enjoyed a greater degree of worldliness and mobility than proper wives and mothers—courtesans, coquettes, demimondaines. In a world of severely restricted womanhood, these were among the most visible models of a liberated womanhood, unifying sexuality and pleasure, worldliness, mobility, and education. Standing outside the highly delimiting kinship system of patrilineage, these women had rights and privileges unavailable to those of a "higher" morality and purpose. Wearing the pants of men, trimmed often with the lace reminiscent of the late-eighteenth-century French court, these women wore the garb of an erotic transvestism.

Good women, in their frail and housebound immobility, would never think of wearing underpants. Yet here too the signal of virtue is also one of continual availability. One's sexuality became paramount within an ethic that countenanced no sexuality. The restrictive foundation of a female bearing, accentuating the body at the cost of mobility and health, established the terms of feminine existence for many women. Insofar as fragile health was a mark of purity, social and dress restrictions resulted in a broad epidemic of female "troubles," specific to middle-class women. Corsetry produced a female population perpetually short of breath. Disease became part and parcel of the cult of proper womanhood. According to Paul Nystrom, "paleness, frequent fainting and ailing bodies were prized as desirable features of fashionable life. Medicine and therapy enjoyed an enormous boom. Patent medicines came into wide use." So general was this fetish of frailty that during the 1830s and 1840s in the United States, "customary greetings changed from 'Good morning' to 'How is your health?' "[50] This convention survives today in the form of "How are you?" Corsets also tended to cramp the stomach, thereby nullifying the appetite—consistent with the ideology of womanhood, which saw an appetite as vulgar. "It was much better to go into a decline," notes clothing historian Pearl Binder, "than to confess to an appetite for earthly food."[51]

While self-denial permeated the ornamentation of femininity, the resulting emotional and biological constraints produced a severe delicacy. By the latter part of the nineteenth century, the health of middle-class women was so debilitated that the corset became the target of increasing medical attack. In 1885 in Lyons, France, Dr. Frantz Gerard argued that corsets were "causing *enteroptose*, dropping of the female abdominal organs," in a number of women patients. So alarming was Gerard's assertion that the House of Worth, a leading fashion establishment in Paris, designed a corset specifically to correct this condition—one that pushed up instead of down. By 1904, however, the new design had taken its toll, reaching "so far in the opposite direction that it was pushing the bowels out of place upward instead of downward."[52] In 1904, another doctor, Arabella Kenealy, published a paper in London entitled "The Curse of Corsets." Based on experimental research, the article noted that if monkeys were put into corsets, so as to approximate the official posture of contemporaneous womanhood, they died within a matter of days. These were among a significant range of medical literature of the late nineteenth century calling for reform in women's dress.[53]

The enfeeblement of women was a crucial aspect of nineteenth-century middle-class fashion. The restrictive practices placed women on a pedestal, above concerns of trade and carnality, yet it produced generations of women whose concerns were mobilized around issues of the body. As the predominant ideology denied women any pleasures of the flesh, it simultaneously fixated on female flesh, molding it and restricting it. On the one hand women were the embodiment of spiritual purity; on the other, the purity was not intrinsic and had to be imposed. Like the foot-bound women of China, whose crippling was supposed to enhance their sexual role, the corseted women of the nineteenth century embodied the Victorian ideal: frail, self-denying, incapable of worldly pursuits, yet essentially carnal. Within the framework of dress restraint, women combined the reciprocal categories of purity and sin. Purity was, in effect, payment for sin. Physical restraint, essential to the structure of feminine attire, reenacted the biblical interpretation of the Fall. Because of Eve's transgression, humankind is destined to a life of work, a life of burden. In the bourgeois cosmology of the nineteenth century, man assumed the burden with a pious willingness, exploiting the marketplace with religious fervor. His clothing bore witness to his piety. Woman bore the guilt of sin while man pursued its world–historic implications. She was bound, restrained. The heights of her molded purity were only testimony to a sinfulness that demanded shaping and restraint. Among women, this restraint was monitored and enacted through the medium of clothing, the biblical mark of sin.

This imputation of female guilt through fashion continues today. Two recent ads supply us with a telling example. One is for women's lingerie (*Vogue*, October 1979). Three women, presumably prostitutes, are shown, backs against the wall in a police lineup. Dispensing with frills, these three stand in their underwear, bare and sexy: lace bras with deep *décolletage*, bikini underpants cut high on the thigh. The woman at the right stands with hand on hip, pelvis thrust forward, sporting a white lace garter belt and stockings. All three are in spiked heels and dripping with jewels; the accoutrements of "kept" women surround them. Even here, apprehended in the police station, their faces wear the complacent look of willful and casual seduction. They know that "sometimes innocence is no virtue." Beneath them, in the shadows, two men look up at them, inspecting the lineup. Which of them is guilty? All of them! "The new French Connection by Lily of France," says the caption. "Once you've worn it you can never plead innocent." The women appear in the filmy trappings of male pleasure; even as they await their punishment, it is men who get to enjoy their display. Yet while the pleasures they serve are those of men, it is men who make the judgment, women who wear the guilt. Adorned for the interests of men, these women bear the guilt of those interests, graphically reinforced in the context of a police station.

This ad is clearly not intended to promote garments of purity and virtue; these are clearly ladies of the world, blatantly sinful. Nevertheless, the same context of sin and judgment can be applied equally to demure fashions. An advertisement for Act I

dresses (*New York Times Magazine*, January 27, 1980) conforms
more closely to the nineteenth-century ideal of proper womanhood. Here again are three women, but they wear modest shifts,
and their pose betrays a girlish decorum and reticence. The
woman at the left assumes a posture of quiet retreat, while the
woman at the right pensively sucks her thumb. The woman in
the center strikes a somewhat more suggestive pose, but her

Act Romantic
Act Natural
Act Sensual
Act Guilty
Act Crazy
Act Smart
Act Darling
Act Sexy
Act Chic
Act Elusive
Act Dangerous
Act Glamourous
Act Devilish
Act Innocent
Act Sly
Act Lovable
Act Elegant
Act Silly
Act Haughty
Act Sophisticate
Act Casual
Act Worldly
Act Naughty
Act Happy
Act Vivacious
Act Coy
Act Cool
Act Sporty
Act Decadent
Act Luminous
Act Right
Act Mysterious
Act Precocious
Act Elegant...

POLICE DEPT.
145

toothsome smile assures us of a wholesome honesty. While in the lingerie ad the three women stood arrogantly, legs astride, these three stand knock-kneed with thighs held protectively closed. Yet here too these paragons of virtue stand in a police lineup. Even in innocence there is guilt. Under the assumption of purity lies the premise of judgment; the sin of Eve is a universal component of decorative womanhood, whether that decoration is openly seductive or passively restrained. Woman, in the logic of the ad, is essentially sinful. Innocence is but an act, and this is borne out in the accompanying text—a list of prescriptions for feminine behavior: "Act Romantic . . . Act Sensual . . . Act Sexy . . . Act Dangerous . . . Act Devilish . . . Act Innocent . . . Act Sly . . . Act Lovable . . . Act Elegant . . . Act Worldly . . . Act Naughty . . . Act Happy . . . Act Coy. . . Act Decadent . . . Act Right . . . Act Mysterious . . . Act Precocious." Amid this bevy of behavioral choices, "Act Innocent" is circled. It is a choice, along with the others, and as a choice for self-presentation it is marked by mendacity. Even innocence is a pose. As women conform to the cult of purity they receive the same judgment as those who assume "Naughty" or "Decadent." If men's clothing, in its sobriety and fit, reflects purposeful commitment, women's clothing, even in the display of virtue, demands judgment. Once again, women are apprehended. They assume the passivity of a restrictive sexual code, are policed by the eyes of men, yet their guilt is still unmitigated. Acceding to the terms of innocence, they continue to bear the burden of guilt. In the arena of masculine scrutiny, one's femininity, one's sexuality can never step down from the lineup. Whether flagrant or suppressed, sexuality perseveres as the primary acceptable social definition of womanhood.

If nineteenth-century middle-class women bore the guilt of sin, they also assumed the guilt of class, of wealth. The conventions of women's clothing were, to a large extent, the antithesis of men's. While men's clothing displayed an imagistic presentation of economy and purpose, women's fashions were the repository of bourgeois conspicuous consumption. If it was immoral for the capitalist man to adorn himself in the sumptuousness of wealth, there was still need to display prosperity and success, the visible results of his industrious and worldly efforts. Even as men dressed in the "plain style," the *ability* to consume stood as testimony to their commercial morality. Thus it is that within the bourgeois tradition, as it evolved in the nineteenth century, women became the visible evidence of this ability. Their dresses were full, spread out by numerous layers of skirts, or given a full appearance by crinolines and hoops. Here in women's clothing was the idiom of aristocracy that had been moralistically rejected in the fervor of bourgeois revolution. Women, and also servants, carried tangible proof of commercial success. They became, to use Veblen's terminology, "vicarious consumers" for men of wealth. Like the herd of cattle or the chests of gold in antiquity, women—through their fashions and forced exclusion from the productive world—entered the state as a generally understood form of social capital. For a man of property, a woman assumed the leisure and waste that only money and power could buy. As Quentin Bell has argued, "The demands of conspicuous consumption remain. Men might escape them, but women could not. Attached to each industrial breadwinner was his vicarious consumer; on all public and social occasions it was her task to demonstrate his ability to pay."[54]

Much of this demonstration was enacted on the level of the sheer expanse and weight of cloth. An 1891 medical study that sought to determine how much extra weight the "well-dressed" woman was required to carry "found that on the average . . . indoor clothing weighed seventeen pounds, while in many cases it far exceeded that amount." With outdoor clothing added, the average weight reached twenty-five to thirty pounds.[55] Clothing tended to consolidate the female body into bountiful masses, weighty and ponderous symbols of success. Breasts were unified, not separately defined, into what Bernard Rudofsky has termed the "monobosom."[56] Bustles exaggerated the storage of fat deposits in the rump, palpable evidence of a massive surplus. Within these garments, physical activity was not only proscribed, but virtually impossible. Women's clothing, insofar as it subscribed to fashion, was a representation of wealth, a bauble by which men could display their plunder without assuming any of the guilt associated with it. Once again, in a society that had designated the sumptuous practices of the nobility as marks of indolence and greed, the male cloak of morality was posed against the evidence of avarice, worn by the woman. To a large extent the life-styles and vestments of bourgeois womanhood became the imagistic repository of masculine, commercial transgressions. Men assumed the pose of virtue, while women bore the ornamentation of sin—even the commercial sin, which was the exclusive prerogative of men. It is not surprising that in the nineteenth century when the moral separation of gender enters the world of fashion to an extreme, we find that men begin to enter, and then dominate, the world of high-fashion design for women. The sins of wealth, like those of sexuality, were forged and articulated by men, as they were worn and displayed by women.[57] Once more, sexual politics ran true to the biblical inscription.

This tendency to define women as part of a male-controlled livestock is ancient, and continues today. While much of the extreme distinction between the morality of women's clothing versus that of men has receded, the construct that assumes a simple and austere man and a highly sumptuous woman still stands to underwrite masculine morality, feminine guilt. It is reenacted in the buying of furs and jewelry; excessive investments given by men, worn by women. An article about Ronald Reagan underwrites the perseverance of this logic. As reported by *Time* magazine, Reagan is presented as an archetype of capitalist ethics. Although he is worth "as much as $4 million," Reagan is a Protestant paragon. He "has simple tastes, carries little cash and doesn't like spending even that. Reagan once flew to Paris with only $5 in his pocket—and then was annoyed when he had to part with it for a tip." Yet this man of austere morality, we discover, "spends lavishly only on his wife. . . . Nancy Reagan wears $5,000 designer dresses, collects fine jewelry, paintings and antiques, and keeps her hairdresser and an interior decorator on call."[58] Reagan adorns himself in the garb of moral simplicity; his abilities for careful and sensible leadership are literally worn on his sleeve. All evidence of rapacity or self-aggrandizement is worn, conveniently, by his wife. Even the home in which Reagan lives, filled as it is with paintings and decorated with antiques, is her cross to bear. As Ronald Reagan takes on the visage of austere simplicity, Nancy Reagan undertakes the trappings of excess. A moral lesson is inscribed in the choreography of daily life: the man of wealth displays the rigors of thrift while his wife assumes the guilt of leisure, consumption, and the tangible symbols of an "upper class." The display of capitalist morality depended dearly upon those willing to bear the sumptuous evidence of guilt, of sin. For women, the enticing rewards of service were, and to some extent still are, the symbolic harness of elegance and the guilt that that entails. The cost of those rewards is to wear the signature of uncontrollable consumption and to be seen as one who bewitches and plays on the benevolent weaknesses of a man who—in terms of his own patterns of consumption—remains uncorrupted. To paraphrase a line from a recent song, *the very thing that makes her rich, makes him poor.*[59] The image is a continual fixture within our culture: women arrive home with vast quantities of department-store boxes, containing new dresses and outrageous hats; men wear the mantle of patient victimization and benevolent chagrin.

The dominant trend in bourgeois women's fashions of the nineteenth century perpetuated a moral defense of wealth through the delineation of gender. The spoils of power were borne most conspicuously by those who enjoyed little power themselves. Both ideologically and physiologically, the double burden of purity and elegance immobilized women within the idiom of guilt. Yet as we have seen before, fashion is not a phenomenon of historical stasis. Beyond providing a language of social caste and power, fashion is an arena in which social struggles are enacted and, perhaps, prefigured. While the predominant middle-class mode placed women in a position and symbolism of immobility and guilt, devoid of desires and appetites yet suffering for them, by the latter half of the nineteenth century women's fashions began to incorporate the language of transformation. Coinciding with the rise of a politics of female emancipation, two distinct trends emanated from the realm of feminine fashion that were expressions of a move toward greater mobility and worldliness, toward a goal of equal social possibilities for women.

To a large extent, these two trends offered a vestmental response to the idealized prescriptions of womanhood. If the proper Victorian was fragile and immobile, a stranger to the world and to pleasures of the flesh, these two developments — seemingly at odds with each other — provided a sartorial language of revolt. One development was the entry of certain styles of clothing — formerly associated with courtesans — into the fashionable attire of middle-class women in general. This development, emanating from the high-fashion houses of Paris, included the wearing of lace underwear, rouge, silk stockings, and the halting but increased display of flesh. By no means universal among middle-class women, this development was viewed by some as a mark of immorality and decadence. Yet so widespread was its impact that by the turn of the century, Edward Bok, editor of the *Ladies' Home Journal*, despaired that it was becoming difficult to tell the prostitute from the lady.[60] The interaction of prostitute and lady was enacted along the circuitous routes of fashion. Among Paris designers, great efforts were expended in dressing the demimondaines—the "half-worldly" courtesans with whom French gentlemen could engage in sensual and other worldly pleasures, unknown to their wives. Pictorial representations, fashion books and plates, and "fashion babies," pasteboard dolls dressed in the latest fashions, were shipped from France throughout Europe and America.[61] These sartorial images began to enter the vernacular of middle-class existence.

While these fashion influences may be seen as exploitative to women, insofar as they still countenanced the primacy of masculine concerns, they were also an emancipatory assault on the canons of Victorian womanhood. The conventions of proper womanhood had denied worldly access to those women whose offspring would assume the name and the inheritance of the father. Wives and mothers were, as we have seen, dressed in the attire of isolation and infirmity. On the other hand, even within the strict moral structures of the nineteenth-century bourgeois sexuality, there were some women who stood outside the confines of patriarchal lineage. Insofar as their offspring stood beyond the boundaries of inheritance, limitations on the mobility of these women were less severe; issues of paternity were of less significance. Thus while moral invocations placed the demimondaine in an inferior position to that of the proper middle-class woman, her reality was far freer and bore a broader range of worldly experience and possibility. Salons were not merely arenas of a sexuality that transcended the functional definitions of procreation, but were also establishments of culture. The courtesan was likely to be more educated and more worldly, more self-reliant than the wife. Degraded by moral sanction, she was at the same time more engaged and viable within the terms of society. The lace garters of the prostitute, standing as marks of Eve's unbridled passion, were also the trappings of a more active and less self-effacing womanhood.

If appetites were considered vulgar among women of the home, they were not only permissible, but encouraged, among women of the world. Erotic satisfaction, and power—albeit limited to arenas of sexuality—proscribed by propriety, found

fulfillment in the wombs of impropriety. Similarly, as demimondaine and gentleman shared a worldly sphere of commercial exchange, it is not unlikely that illicit relationships provided a more
fertile soil for equitable and textured involvements between men
and women than did the moral strictures of bourgeois marriage.

Clearly, this relative freedom must be understood within the
restrictive framework of patriarchy, but it was within that
framework that the proper wife was ensconced. The entry of
courtesanal influences in the realm of an "acceptable" fashion was
a suggestion of greater mobility, worldliness; an acknowledg-
ment of the possibility for erotic fulfillment for women. In an
evocative way, this shift of fashion was implicitly an attack on
the patriarchal ideal of a confined womanhood. The putting on
of such garments as panties was infused—given their connota-
tions—with a map of cultural meanings. In custom these were
the garments of prostitutes, and of women whose mobility presumed boundaries beyond the constant yoke of male protection.
Underpants on women sounded a strong erotic intonation—far
greater than the absence of them. According to Anne Hollander,
a historian of fashion and art, the French cancan was invented to
display the lacy drawers of the abandoned dancers, as a good deal
of Victorian pornography was fixated on displays of lace ornamentation.[62] This was an eroticism of female sexual power
and arrogance that stood as a thrilling and "perverse" counterpoint to the frail and lethargic dependency that marked the
horizons of wifely ethics.

The assumption of panties in the general realm of women's
fashion from the 1850s onward was no less than a statement of
desire for greater worldliness, a concession to the legitimacy of
the "temptations" and vestments of a female carnality and
pleasure.

There is an ahistorical temptation to understand the accoutrements of coquetry moralistically as flatly committed to the oppressive project of female objectification; to reject the devices of
allurement as the shackles of bondage. Yet the arrival of this
mode within the general theater of middle-class fashion carried
another facet of connotation. Breaking through the social imagery of confinement and passive weakness, this progression
empowered a larger population of women with the tools of

secular activity and pasionate love. Unquestionably, as is evident in the advertisement for Lily of France lingerie, the implication of guilt and sin was still judgmentally present, but now a woman might more justifiably enjoy pleasure and power within the ambit of her alleged transgressions. If carnality stood at the heart of the objective definition of bourgeois womanhood beforehand, now it was becoming a piece within a female subjectivity.

The vestments of passion and love provided one vector of resistance to the conventions of nineteenth-century middle-class life. An alternative vector was drawn from the masculine realm of moral diligence and work. Initiated not by Paris designers but by women who were attempting to escape what Jane Addams called "the snare of preparation," this second tactic of sartorial resistance found its roots in a small but strident move toward dress reform.

"Dress reform" had various embodiments, yet a common thread was the rejection of restrictive garments, often in favor of a more *mannish* costume. The simplicity of male tailoring provided a model for this development. From the rise of the bourgeois style, the evolution of men's suits had been a renunciation of conspicuous consumption and waste, a statement of motion and of industriousness of purpose. The "plain style" suggested a similar weapon to women, one by which they could break through the confined lethargies of middle-class feminine existence. If some women sought expanded social possibilities and activities, the clothing that relegated them to an immobile existence needed to be transcended. Insofar as it provided the most widely understood model of action and social purpose, the more comfortable "plain style" pointed the way for feminine dress reform. Consistent with the bourgeois-Protestant ethic of a purposeful "calling," these clothes were conceived within an earnest and programmatic appeal to "rational dress."

In the latter half of the nineteenth century in the United States, Germany, and England, proponents of dress reforms stood largely within circumscribed subcultures of social experimentation. Reform dress was a part of the experimental communalism of John Humphrey Noyes's Oneida Community, where plainly cut garments encouraged the group's commitment to a sexual politics—to greater equality between men and women in love and in work. Amelia Bloomer, an American feminist who in the 1850s promoted a costume consisting of a short, understated frock—with no petticoats—worn over billowing "Turkish" trousers, found support from Elizabeth Cady Standon and drew most of her comrades and adherents from among those active in the early movement for women's rights.

The taking on of clothing conventions previously defined as "male" challenged the basic social tenets of gender among the middle class. These had posited a rational piety and worldly engagement for men, while the feminine essence was understood to be dangerously passionate—to be restricted in the uniform of purity, or to be enjoyed away from home. Unlike the erotic inversion implied by the wearing of lace panties, this style broke from a fundamental equation of women with carnality. It sought to exemplify a more integrated, more totalistic vision of womanhood.

Insofar as the proponents of dress reform challenged the basic legacy of gender differentiation—essential to the physics of bourgeois morality—they were in large degree outcast and ridiculed, characterized and taunted as strange and fanatical. Yet their impulse toward a freer, less constricting garb evolved within a broader social environment that was pregnant with the possibilities of a burgeoning female mobility. By the last years of the nineteenth century, these tendencies had escaped the terminology of "reform" and entered the vocabulary of "fashion." Within that framework of propriety, they began to be adopted on an increasingly wide scale.

Beyond being ideological emblems of limited and sometimes idiosyncratic movements, mannish clothes prefigured the irreversible opening up of the public sphere to women that had been endemic to the rise of industrial capitalism. First and foremost, bourgeois gentlemen had demanded a virginal isolation for women of their own families. Yet against this stern demand stood an obvious and hypocritical double standard. Men, who insisted that one class of women conform to the social categories of a supposedly fragile and weaker sex, presided over an expanding industrial world that increasingly drew another class of women away from the confines of the home and into the degraded context of industrial production. Indeed, within the textile industry itself, the first factory force was drawn from farm girls of the New England countryside. For middle-class women, while confinement persevered as a basic principle within the cult of prescribed purity, the industrial era created contexts that made such confinement increasingly difficult to maintain. The modern city was a magnetic arena of motion and diverting display. Activity was its conspicuous spectacle, and the city made the insularity of the home ideal more and more anachronistic. Against the sensate allurements and attractions of urban pageantry, the notion of the home as an unsullied fortress became harder and harder to justify to its appointed keepers. Motion was the social language of a cosmopolitan tableau, and that language began to leave its explosive charge within female activity and dress. By the 1890s, the bicycle, for example, had become a vehicle of diversion and purpose for both men and women; altered styles of female adornment became not only statements of politics, but functionally requisite.

When the bicycle emerged as an acceptable device of female mobility, the weighty excessiveness of dress conventions had to be abandoned. Bicycles, and other mechanisms of urban transport, signaled a breakdown in the sartorial designations of gender. Massive skirts and their mountainous underpinnings of petticoats, crinolines, and bustles began to crumble in their aesthetic monopoly over ladylike propriety. As women entered the restless environs of urban desire and diversion—parks and kinetic boulevards—appropriate garments entered the borderland of fashion. Bicycles in particular required a simpler and lighter garb; trousers made a telling and prophetic incursion into the outposts of female respectability in the form of the divided skirt. Sports in general, which combined the conventional equation of middle-class *women* and *leisure* with the energetic choreography of city life, became a prime arena of transformation and synthesis. The "masculinization" of female clothing—the permissibility of trousers and other garments that allowed for the comforts of motion—made its first conquests of gentility in the garments of sport.

Increasingly, the allure of the social world stood at the gates of the bourgeois home, and this potent proximity imposed itself not only on the perceptions of women, but visibly on "the glass of fashion and the mould of form." Not all breaks from the nineteenth-century attire of confinement spelled liberation. Paul Poiret, the "King of Fashion" who took personal credit for leading Parisian designers in a war against the corset around 1910, replaced it with the "hobble skirt," which only altered the anatomy of constriction, tightly encircling the lower legs.[63] To a large extent, the move was toward an enhanced mobility for women of the middle class. The interplay between women and society, however, asserted itself not merely within the material presentation of self. For a growing number of women, the isolation of the home was rejected in favor of greater social engagement and commitment. Within this development, the mannish look made a dramatic leap from the particularity of sports clothing to the more general wardrobe. Throughout much of her active life, Jane Addams, who had learned the lessons of sartorial morality from her unwitting father on the way to Sunday school, wore the "plain style" as an emblem of honor and a statement of worldly dedication. "Dressed down" in austere threads, Addams pursued her earthly calling of social work, attempting, along the way, to shatter the mark of Eve, which had hobbled women of her estate throughout much of the nineteenth century.

The sartorial models of middle-class female emancipation derived from two distinct arenas: *honorable work* and *shameful love*. In distinctly different ways, the imagery of the Puritan and of the prostitute conspired to offer a way out of the ennui of "home service." Neither, unfortunately, offered the idiom for an integrated solution. One promised the possibilities of pleasure and of power, but confined both within a primarily sexual ghetto of self-definition. The other intoned the honors of worldly labors, often at the expense of acknowledging, openly, one's sensual self. In the name of purpose, one was forced—if one was a woman—to take flight from the pitfalls of the body. The mark of Eve presided over the terms of female existence, as it still does today; although lessened, the burdens of sexual inequality remained.

Social power and social transformation mark the history of bourgeois women's clothing in the nineteenth century, and much of today's fashion bears the imprint of this turmoil. Yet it would be misleading to assume that the roots of contemporary fashion can be understood only through the glass of nineteenth-century middle-class life. While conflicts and interactions of imagery are highly visible within the context of this existence, other forces were also at work. The clothing we have described was the province of an elite few, limited to those with access to the resources and skilled labor necessary to partake in the privilege of fashionability. To pursue the magnitude of fashion in our current world, we must look elsewhere, toward other changes that broadened and massified the social terms of fashion. These changes were experienced most dramatically, at first, not within the arena of the middle class, but of working-class life; it is to these general developments that we must turn.

Labor and Cloth

Today in the United States, as throughout much of the industrialized world, most people buy their clothing "off the rack." Like almost all of the goods by which we supply our needs, clothing comes to us ready-made. Through the prism of a consumer culture, these are the terms of survival; our experience within the world of merchandise is one where goods mysteriously appear. Their source is unknown. The people who produced them are unseen. Their presence in our lives, as a historical phenomenon, is generally unexamined. Fashion images abound, and their lure touches the lives of multitudes. What once was a concern of privilege is now known and consumed by almost everyone; it is the hallmark of a "democracy."

Yet the current ubiquity of ready-made clothing, and of fashion in general, has a relatively short history. Before the nineteenth century, ready-made was virtually unknown. For people of means, clothing was produced by skilled artisans of cloth: tailors and seamstresses. The opportunity to wear a skillfully crafted garment symbolized a status within society—the status of one able to afford the employment of those whose long labors and intricate touch could be mobilized to construct an appropriate public or private image.

For the majority of people, the wearing of clothes did not employ the capacities of seamstresses or tailors. Routinely, clothing was produced in the home and bore the functional mark of many of the products that—in a preindustrial world—were produced within the broad scope of household activity. Alexander Hamilton, in his *Report on Manufactures*, noted that in 1791, "two-thirds, three-fourths, and even four-fifths of all the clothing of the inhabitants" of many districts of the United States, "are made by themselves."[64] A government report issued twenty years later reaffirmed Hamilton's contention, indicating that "two-thirds of all garments worn by inhabitants of the United States" were made within the confines of the homes in which they lived. While men's tailored clothing and dresses sewn by seamstresses had a notable presence within the above percentages, for most people—particularly the poor—home production clearly predominated.

In the context of the late eighteenth and nineteenth centuries, the primacy of home-produced clothing was consistent with the more general terms of material life. The home was still a major center of production. The modern idea of a home as a receptacle of consumer goods was virtually unknown, unimaginable, save for those few whose wealth allowed them to attend to an aristocratic pursuit of luxury. Most of the accoutrements of life were produced by people for themselves. Self-sufficiency was not just a moral invocation; it was a necessity of survival. Women would take a wide spread of homespun "linsey-woolsey," lay it upon the family table, "mark it, and . . . cut out the article desired."[65] The cut of the resulting clothes was loose and often imprecise. Not elaborate in their conception, execution, or purpose, these clothes bore little trace of sumptuosness or elegance. If gracefully worked cloth was a mark of social exception, these simple clothes marked the common lot.

By the early twentieth century, clothing would undergo dramatic change in its production, distribution, and meaning. Clothes would increasingly be *bought*, not *made*, by the wearer. Moreover, fashion—long the symbolic preserve of wealth—would enter, more and more, the symbolic vernacular of common people. By 1913, home economist Bertha June Richardson noted that even poor shop girls of New York City, earning no more than five or six dollars a week, were able to dress "beyond their station." In tenement neighborhoods, she saw women with "plumes on their hats, a rustle of silk petticoats, everything about them in the latest style."[66]

In Robert and Helen Lynd's classic study *Middletown* (Muncie, Indiana) in the 1920s, an employer mused, "I used to be able to tell something of the background of the girl applying for a job" by the clothes that she wore. "Now," he complained, "I have to wait until she speaks, shows a gold tooth, or otherwise gives me a second clue."[67] Class distinctions remained, to be sure, but surface evidence pointed increasingly to a democracy of the image; a stylistic equality was unfolding.

The history of these developments is somewhat more complex than is generally conceded. The ideology of *progress* tends to encapsulate explanations for such evolutions within the framework of a triumphal, technological determinism. *Modernity brought science; science brought the machine; the machine brought a better life; it continues to do so!* So goes the argument. The historical rendition of the rise of mass fashion tends to follow this mechanical rationale: 1733 brought the flying shuttle, which allowed broad pieces of cloth to be woven at a quicker rate than ever before; 1764 brought the spinning jenny, improving production of yarn and thread. Late-eighteenth-century developments included the power loom — which replaced the old weaving frame — and the famous/infamous cotton gin, which separated cotton seeds from bolls at a rate that allowed for the mass production of cotton cloth. The list continues with only cursory mention of the Lowell system of factory production; the "dark Satanic mills" of Manchester in England; or the slave system of plantation labor that produced the vast quantities of raw material upon which the American industrial system of textiles and clothing was erected. We move to the first U.S. patented sewing machine in 1846; machinery for riveting boots and sewing leather, and so on. Late-nineteenth-century developments included lace-making machines, which made the *imago* of the eighteenth-century duchess and the nineteenth-century courtesan available to more and more women. With synthetic, chemically produced fabrics listed high among twentieth-century achievements, the look and texture of royalty — silk, velvet, fur — became replicable, available to almost anyone who had a yen for fashion. Each invention has its inventor, its "great man." Each has its corporate promoter, beneficently bringing "progress" as its "most important product," or "better living through chemistry."

Yet these technologies did not appear in a vacuum. The development of ready-to-wear clothes cannot be understood solely as an offshoot of technological advancement. The rise of the ready-made clothing industries found its roots, to a large extent, in new forms of social and economic life that were intrinsic to capitalist development and to the emergence of a world-market economy. The first markets for ready-to-wear clothing were among people who experienced the new mobile forms of social and economic life.

For the most part, ready-made clothes did not initially come about to serve the desires of an urban middle class with a taste for fashion. These people were still generally committed to handcrafting by tailors or seamstresses. The greatest part of early ready-to-wear clothing served a clientele who—caught within the historical maelstrom—were unable to supply clothing for themselves through customary home production. Ready-to-wear clothing came into being alongside the phenomena of increasing mobility, increasingly specialized forms of labor, and the evolution of an individualistic mode of life. Its roots were crude and functional. Rather than signs of egalitarianism, these clothes stood testimony to the broad chasm between laboring and propertied lives in the nineteenth century. They were a piece of the oppression that shaped working-class existence, and outrage.

The first ready-made establishments, mostly situated on streets adjoining wharves, appeared around the turn of the nineteenth century in Boston, New York, Philadelphia, Baltimore, and in smaller cities with whaling or fishing trades. In Boston, the first of these shops appeared on Fish and Ann streets; later, on North. New York's first clothing shops were on Water and Front streets; then on Cherry Street and Maiden Lane. Philadelphia's ready-made shops were on Front Street; Baltimore's could be found on Calvert and Water streets.[68]

The initial customers were sailors who required clothing when they came into port. Ready-to-wear emerged as a service industry, supplying the needs of a work force in the varied seabound trades. Clothing sold in these shops stood in stark contrast to the tailored garments of gentlemen; it was woefully crude in terms of both workmanship and materials used. Clothing was generally produced in only one size, to be tied, tucked, or cut by its wearer to achieve the approximation of comfort, if not of "fit." From the early 1800s, when the first such shop opened its doors in New Bedford, Massachusetts, until the 1870s, when industrial clothing began to undergo significant changes, ready-to-wear establishments were known simply as "slop shops." The clothing they sold was called "slop clothes."[69] Like the "slops" for animals from which they got their name, these clothes denoted degraded and minimal terms of subsistence. Their presence was hardly glamorous. It served the functional requirements of clothing a work force that—due to the force of circumstance—was unable to produce clothing for itself, much less afford to have clothing tailored to order. One of America's most illustrious haberdasheries, Brooks Brothers, began as a "slop shop" around 1810.

Slop shops would purchase rough material—often of English or East Indian origin—to cut on the premises. Cut cloth would then be sent out to women who, working at home, would hand-sew the "slops." Most of these were farm women, living in regions adjacent to big coastal cities. Long winter evenings were spent by the fire, bringing cash into the realm of the farm, dispensing goods for a merchantile trade.[70] This is worth mentioning, not merely as another fact within the history of ready-made clothing, but to indicate that the lives of women were, from the beginning of the industrial era, deeply affected and transformed. Farm girls had provided America's first factory force within New England's incipient textile industry, only later to be displaced by entire families of immigrants. Far more than is evidenced among women adhering to the doctrines of the middle class, these early industrial women's lives reveal—even as they sat beside the home fire of the farm—the inexorable tendency of the tendrils of capitalist enterprise to draw increasing numbers of people into the marketplace. With the taking in of slop work, the very meaning of home production was immeasurably altered.

Sailors ambled along portside alleys and streets wearing the fruit of these women's home enterprises. New patterns of production were linked to embryonic contours of consumption, the beginnings of a mass-produced clothing industry, geared to the needs of anonymous consumers—initially produced to clothe laboring men, a configuration that would continue throughout much of the nineteenth century. Fashion imagery was not discernible, nor was it an issue. Functional uniformity was the paramount characteristic of slop clothing.

The factory production of clothing proceeded hesitantly in the 1830s, turning out a humble product for wearers at the bottom levels of society. Then, following the gold rush in 1849, the market for ready-to-wear moved west. Dealers on the East Coast and in the Mississippi Valley responded to the demand for large amounts of ready-made, shipping goods westward. Such manufacturing and merchandising pioneers as Levi Strauss and John H. Browning began producing ready-mades in San Francisco to outfit hordes of gold diggers, miners, and lumbermen arriving in search of work or fortune. Again, the market for ready-made was built on the foundation of a mobile labor force, separated from the customary arenas of home production. Overalls and trousers, made from hearty sailcloth or the somewhat lighter—but still rugged—blue denim, were designed for long and continuous wear.[71] Against the sweat of a hard laboring existence, the primary demand upon clothing was durability. The adoption of rivets from horse blankets and the multiple stitching along seams were not elements of style, but tactics of construction. While today Levi Strauss advertising may claim that "a legend doesn't come apart at the seams," legendary considerations were the last things on the minds of western miners as they pulled on their dungarees. The seams didn't contain legends, but tired bodies whose meager wages ruled out products that were ornately sewn, or had to be cared for or frequently replaced.

Aside from sailors and forty-niners, the biggest early market for ready-made clothing—the market that dramatically expanded the scope of the industry—was provided by the Southern system of plantation slavery. In many ways, the idea of "ready-to-wear" as an "intrinsic outcome"—to borrow a phrase from Raymond Williams—of capitalist development is illustrated most graphically here. The archetype for the modern industrial labor system, slaves were a population of forced, migrant labor. With the rise of the British textile industry, and then that of New England, cotton was a lucrative source of America's merchant and landed wealth. A cash crop of burgeoning magnitude, cotton—particularly in the middle states of the Deep South—mobilized black labor in increasingly large-scale patterns of production. While some plantations continued to produce their own supplies, employing a small number of slaves to produce clothing for the general population, the period 1840–60 brought profound changes. As cotton production grew to the exclusion of other plantation activity, a large sector of the American ready-to-wear clothing industry took up the slack, and "the business of supplying rough working clothing for the slave laborers of the South grew to large proportions."[72] Trade routes between an incipient garment industry in New York and other Eastern cities and the port of New Orleans were established, supplying the clothing needs of large plantations. Among British ready-made exports as well, "a good portion of the shipments went under the heading of 'slops and Negro clothing.' " Dealers in New Orleans, such as Folger and Blake Company of Magazine Street, advertised to planters that they would "find it greatly to their advantage to purchase their clothing ready-made" for slaves.[73] Drawing the greatest part of their fortunes from cotton sold to industries in the North and in Britain, Southern planters welcomed the opportunity of purchasing cheap, mass-produced provisions, rather than divert valuable slave labor toward these unprofitable handicraft activities.

Slavery thus was a prime impetus to the U.S. garment industry. Numerous firms in New York were organized specifically around the production of what was designated as "Negro clothing." These clothes were made of cheap, coarse fabric. Despite the low price these firms received for their goods, oppressive conditions of high productivity and low pay for factory or home workers maintained high levels of profit. Even technology was geared to the task. In the 1850s, the I. M. Singer (sewing machine) Company advertised the development of a "new, improved sewing machine especially adapted to the making up of Negro clothing."[74]

Even outside New York, a garment industry grew to cash in on the plantation market. The Louisiana Plantation Clothing

Manufactory produced clothing on a large scale during the 1850s, "with ready-made Negro clothing" offered at low cost.[75] In Cincinnati, Ohio, "the growing demand for cheap clothing to supply farm hands and Negro Slaves" was cited by the Commissioner of Statistics as the prime reason for the development of the clothing industry in that city.[76]

Throughout the South, stores advertised "slop clothing" for black slaves, in the pattern such clothing was marketed to "free" labor forces of the Eastern seaboard and the West Coast. Developments in large-scale production (industrial and agricultural) and in trade brought about new demands for a clothing industry to supply those laboring within the expanding social orbit of slavery and capitalism. By the time of the Civil War, the idea of clothing produced for an impersonal audience of wearers was beginning to take hold as an American institution; within a few decades, hand tailoring and the work of seamstresses would be eclipsed.

With the advent of the Civil War, the ready-made clothing industry suffered somewhat on a localized level. The end of economic relations between North and South proved calamitous to several companies whose viability depended on open routes of trade, and over a period of time, some bankruptcies were filed.[77] Overall, however, the Civil War provided boom conditions for the garment industry, primarily in New York. Another form of mobile activity provided a new market for mass-produced clothes — military uniforms — and the ready-made industry grew, sprouting important refinements in production and distribution. Whereas "slop clothes" had been produced with no regard for the size or shape of the wearer, the military market gave rise to the development of size standards and distributions. Conscripts were measured, and a range of sizes was established. A broad variety of physiques could now be clothed in a manner approximating "reasonable fit."[78] The Grim Reaper now fetched his crop from among a more regular bunch of irregulars than ever before: an industrially fitted army. A key aspect of a modern, mass-produced clothing industry — diverse sizing — was established adjacent to the field of battle. Later the Spanish-American War and then the First World War provided sanguine opportunities for additional refinement and clarity in the designation of fit.

By the end of the 1860s, the sizing of garments — if not splendidly accurate in each individual's case — was generally adopted in the production of ready-to-wear. The human body was submitted to a mechanical/industrial categorization, subdivided into species of standardized body types. Civilian ready-made clothing, and even paper patterns for homemade clothing, followed the military initiative. The production and design of shoes was likewise refined and industrialized in the years of battle.

The Civil War provided an explosive catalyst for a general industrial development. In its aftermath, American industry grew to monumental proportions; vast armies of laborers made the journey into industrial cities; robber barons and finance capitalists reaped incomprehensible fortunes and amassed the tools of modern political power. Though "free" in the years following the war, labor enjoyed little freedom. "Wage slavery," it was called, and it meant long and hard toil and miserable dependency. The urban industrial poor became a massive market for clothes poor in quality, cheap in price. Coming out of the war, the industry grew by leaps and bounds, a massive supply industry for those who had no choice but to consume its wares.

While today's ready-made clothing industry is enveloped by the propaganda of aesthetic transcendence, its roots were neither aesthetic nor transcendent, but a part of the banal misery of nineteenth-century working-class life.

Images of Democracy

While the industrialization of America deepened the divisions of caste and class, other developments in the mechanical age offered a new, leveling language of democracy and social promise. If the machine represented a modern basis for misery and domination, it also contained an ability to reproduce — on a massive scale — the images and symbols of luxury and abundance, of privilege and franchise. Things previously limited to the province of an upper class now became reproducible, if only as surface images.

This capability had been prefigured in the development of printing four hundred years before. While the printing press presented new modes of establishing power and authority, it was also intrinsically democratic. Little by little, over centuries, the written word spread to the masses, and reading and writing became aspirations of common folk. The very existence of a mechanically reproduced text, multiplying what had previously been a hand-inscribed treasure, was a palpably democratizing development. For those intent on maintaining or protecting their traditional prerogatives and power, this trend was viewed— rightly, from their vantage point—with foreboding. Censorship was established to assert control over what had, before printing, been controlled by virtue of its rarity and the small number of those with access to its cipher. In England, as a mobile working class emerged out of a landed peasantry, print and literacy became symbols of common aspirations, of democratic goals. During the Puritan revolution of the 1640s, mobile masses of Englishmen carried printing presses to the field of battle, asserting in pamphlets and proclamations their "freeborn" rights.[79] Printing was democratic not only for what it could say, but for *what it was.* Given a common memory of exclusion from *the word,* the very presence of a machinery that spread the word embodied the promise of a "world turned upside down."

By the mid-nineteenth century, in the United States, the horizons of printed matter were wide. A mass-circulation, commercial press, read by factory operatives and mechanics, stood as evidence of an American democracy, even as its editorial pages defended the privileges of landed or monied wealth. Literacy and social possibility went hand in hand, and the press pointed to itself as a democratic institution, regardless of its outlook.

Within this proliferation of printed matter, there was a particularly significant development, perhaps as significant as the development of printing itself. *This was the enhanced ability, from the 1840s onward, to mass-produce not only words, but images.* The elegant tokens of wealth and high culture now became reproducible. The impact of this enterprise was staggering.

Previously, most artistic imagery was a guarded possession, limited to those few who could afford it. Original oil paintings, most prominently, were a holding of wealth; moreover, they were—as they are today—a *form* of wealth. John Berger has argued that the European tradition of oil painting evolved "in order to express a particular view of life," a view predicated on possession. As landed wealth gave way to the abstraction of money, *representations* became—little by little—the accoutrements of wealth and power. If money represented the ability to buy, oil paintings represented what could be bought. To the art collector, paintings "show him sights: sights of what he may possess." Oil painting, according to Berger, was particularly suited to this task of representing things to be possessed.

> What distinguishes oil painting from any other form of painting is its special ability to render the tangibility, the texture, the lustre, the solidity of what it depicts. It defines the real as that which you can put your hands on. Although its painted images are two-dimensional, its potential of illusionism is far greater than that of sculpture, for it can suggest objects possessing colour, texture and temperature, filling a space and, by implication, filling the entire world.[80]

Within the framework of the bourgeois epoch, oil paintings, like luxurious clothing, were designations of status: of wealth and social power. Their absence from the lives of common people was part of the fact of class, as much as was their presence on the walls of those who displayed them as property. Access to the image was limited to those able to enjoy what Berger calls "the special relation between oil painting and property."[81]

These patterns, regarding images, conveyed a social language—one that divided rich from poor, the haves from the have-nots. A power relation was embedded in the history of the painting, and of its possession. When, beginning in the 1840s, printers—mostly German immigrants—began producing "chromolithographs" in the United States, the monopoly over the image began to crumble. While original oil paintings continued as an expensive investment and diversion of the wealthy, the new technique of chromolithography was able to capture and replicate much of their aura. The image was concrete and lustrous—and available. The symbolic province of the image had been invaded.

Between 1840 and 1900, a mass market in imagery developed. "Original paintings were being reproduced lithographically in color and sold in America by the millions." What came to be "the public's voracious hunger for images in color" was "marked by a faith in fine art, a belief in the power of art to enrich the life of anyone."[82] If art was an enjoyment of privilege and abundance, its dissemination was perceived as the spread not only of rare images, but of the social conditions those images invoked. The market in "chromos" was broad and expansive; they were merchandised by mail, through advertising, and as premiums, as well as being sold in galleries. Amid the gray din of industrial development, here was a tangible rupture in the customary inequities of class. Chromos were a dramatic display of democracy; their spread broke through the symbolic boundaries of an old and hierarchical order.

Many chromolithographs were brilliant reproductions of paintings, previously unknown and unseen by their now-broad audience. In addition, chromos spurred an evocative impetus to the embryonic field of advertising. Billboards reached out to command the attention of passersby; advertising cards gave the goods of the industrial age the aura of sumptuosness and the magic of allegory. Goods and alluring images were linked, forging one of the most basic and prophetic alliances of contemporary capitalist culture. A world of symbolic promise was emerging; the mass dissemination of this promise made for a conspicuous and mesmerizing gesture toward a more equitable world.

The printers who produced these wonders saw themselves as the authors of a new and democratic world, and, to a limited extent, they were right. Chromos represented a flourishing democracy of the image as it had never before existed. Few chromolithographers were native born; most came from European societies, schooled by hierarchies of class and opportunity. Lithographically produced images were understood as emblems of privilege; their dissemination throughout American society appeared as nothing less than a social revolution of giant consequence. By 1893, a spokesman for the National Lithographers' Association hailed the rise of chromolithography as a monument to improved and egalitarian social conditions:

> Within a few decades, public taste has been lifted out of the sluggish disregard for the beautiful . . . and now seeks to adopt the decorative accessories, which beneficent enterprise has so cheapened as to place them within reach of all, to the ornamentation of its homes. . . . The

depressing monotony of plain walls are [*sic*] now relieved by bright
touches of color . . . awakening in some degree, however faint, the in-
nate love of beauty which marks the scale of aspiration in the human
soul. There is no place, high or low, where pictures are not now seen,
for the campaign of popular education in art has been carried to the very
utmost boundaries of ignorance, and the cost of reaping its advantages is
next to nothing.[83]

It was argued that life now could be enhanced by a "beneficent
enterprise," an industrialism of image production, offsetting the
"depressing monotony" of industrial life, spreading the surface
impression of a better life at a relatively low cost. While the disparities of society remained, and industrial conditions worsened,
a democracy of surfaces was being born.

For people coming out of a history of deprivation, the power
of these images cannot be underestimated. European immigrants, coming to labor in America, confronted a free flow of
words and images unimaginable in the Old World. Brightly colored labels, an offspring of chromolithography, transformed industrial swill into icons of a better life. Images, deriving their
power by association with the historical freedoms of upper-class
life, proliferated in America by the end of the nineteenth century.
Cruel capitalism was assuming a generous face, countering the
scorn and rebelliousness of working people. Urban life was now
graced by the imagery of nature and bounty, even if these only
colored its facade. The chromo took the lustrous symbols of
privilege and generalized them across the visible skin of industrial society.

Frederick Douglass saw the spread of chromos as a tangible
transcendence of oppression. Coming out of the harsh and un-
adorned experience of slavery, he interpreted the dispersal of
beautiful images as proof of concrete, material improvement of
social conditions. Speaking particularly of the availability of
chromos to black Americans, Douglass placed these bright images against the grim backdrop of slavery:

Heretofore, colored Americans have thought little of adorning their
parlors with pictures. . . . Pictures come not with slavery and oppression and destitution, but with liberty, fair play, leisure, and refinement.
These conditions are now possible to colored American citizens, and I

think the walls of their houses will soon begin to bear evidence of their altered relations to the people about them.[84]

By the turn of the twentieth century, these images could be widely seen in the homes of the urban poor. Social worker Elsa G. Herzfeld, whose *Family Monographs* surveyed the tenement homes of New York City in 1905, noted the presence of chromos in abundance. Chromos would be given as cheap but luminous presents for weddings and other occasions. Peddlers sold them throughout tenement districts; they were distributed as cigar coupons and premiums; Sunday papers occasionally included them as a bonus. Offering themes of sentiment, heroism, drama, and religion, these were the graven images of American industrialism. Soap coupons presented devotional pictures of American presidents: Lincoln, Washington, and a recent "martyr," William McKinley. The female characterization of "Liberty" was likewise available as a soap coupon. Chromos comprised part of the political education of immigrants into Americanization. Buying soap was tantamount to a patriotic experience; an American past was here available to all, in brilliant color, to be consumed. A heritage, a culture was being erected, in the form of cheap and consumable merchandise.[85]

Protectors of "culture," as an elite province, spoke disparagingly of the newly emergent "chromo-civilization." To it they attributed a decline in morality, in commerce, in political life. Edwin Godkin, editor of *Nation* magazine, expressed the feeling that chromos brought art to those who were unable to appreciate it. Within this democratization, he felt, lay grave dangers:

> A society of ignoramuses who know they are ignoramuses, might lead a tolerably happy and useful existence, but a society of ignoramuses each of whom thinks he is a Solon, would be an approach to Bedlam let loose. . . . The result is a kind of mental and moral chaos.[86]

Yet in the imagination of those entrepreneurs who produced and disseminated them, chromos appeared more as a social palliative than as something that would engender chaos and class upheaval. Amid the widespread hostility to the social conditions of capitalist America, chromos could help achieve a harmonious peace. Understanding fantasy and inner desire as a realm to be exploited by enterprise, a writer in the *Lithographer's Journal* (September 1893) noted chromos' ability to turn the mind away from immediate conditions:

> The love for the beautiful . . . acts upon the individual and forces him to unconsciously idealize the scenes of his daily life. So habitual does this become . . . that new avenues of refinement and true culture are continually being opened by its unseen activity. The individual thus becomes an added power to the nation.[87]

Slowly, desperately, perhaps unconsciously, a social strategy was beginning to coalesce. While the basic relations of social power would remain intact, the "democracy" of the image would act as a fundamental prop of capitalist American society. Beneficence and opportunity were being codified, not in an expansion of social power and rights, but in the widely extended availability of images *associated* with the prerogatives of power. If mounting working-class demands expressed the imperative of an industrial democracy, chromos and other images offered a superficial alternative to genuine democracy. Broadened access to lustrous imagery was an inexpensive, purchasable response; a lucrative response to potentially subversive demands for a better life.

As chromolithography made deep inroads into popular consciousness, the spread of the image took many additional forms. Photography, stereopticons, public expositions, and a popular press all contributed their visionary output to the popular perception of the world. Greater access to the material world, if only through pictures, expanded the sensual parameters of popular experience. A consumer culture, in which apparitions of a better life were appended to the surface of manufactured goods, was assuming a primitive yet premonitory form.

Concomitant with the rise of popular images, an important change took place in the second wave of ready-made clothing after the Civil War. Goods that had, in the first wave of their production, expressed the modern terms of social stigma and degradation—first as "slops," then as "standardized" military garb[88]—now in the second wave took on the *look* of improved conditions. Insofar as fashion had existed for centuries as a franchise of wealth, the mass production of clothing implied a rising egalitarianism within American industrial society, paralleling the proliferation of chromolithographs. By the 1920s, this development had left its mark on the surface of American culture. Social critic Stuart Chase, writing in 1929, mused that "the function of clothing as a protection against the weather is certainly declining for both men and women." Noting the cohabitation of social inequality and egalitarian symbolism, Chase commented on the cunning capacities of fashion.

> The function of clothes as a badge of social rank is enormously expanding over all classes in America for both sexes, but particularly for women. Only a connoisseur can distinguish Miss Astorbilt on Fifth Avenue from her father's stenographer or secretary. An immigrant arriving on the Avenue from the Polish plain described all American women as countesses. So eager are the lower income groups to dress as well in style, if not in quality, as their economic superiors, that class distinctions have all but disappeared. To the casual observer all American women dress alike. The movement to cut down the margin of class distinction . . . has made great headway since [World War I].[89]

This ability to erect a unity of opposites, social and economic disparity along with a mask of parity, is part of the genius and achievement of American capitalism.

As early as the 1900s, poverty and finery no longer inhabited entirely separate worlds. The look of fashion was everywhere: on Fifth Avenue and Orchard Street, among "swells" and slum dwellers simultaneously. Layered cloth, once worn primarily for warmth by the poor, now conveyed some of the symbolism historically preserved for the rich. Layers were cut, slashed, and tucked, even in mass-produced garments, diminishing their "value as insulation" but implying a "conspicuously expensive character . . . cut away so as to show how many things are being worn and what expensive things they are."[90] What fashion merchandising expert Paul Nystrom referred to as the "effective and cheap reproduction of style goods" gave impetus to the spread of fashion, and the concern for fashion, among an ever-broadening swatch of the American social fabric.[91]

With the rise of mass fashion, the language of elegance and luxury entered the common vernacular of perception and expression. The garment industry, initially a supplier of clothes designed explicitly for workers, and *for work*, now began to dress its public in wares that suggested the common accessibility of prosperity and leisure. The infrastructure of a consumer democracy was taking hold; demands and desires for equality, self-determination, and individual diversity amid standardized tedium were being codified within the range of industrially produced goods.

In the garment industry, the first step in this direction was taken in the arena of men's clothes. Factories originally producing uniforms for the Civil War began producing men's suits at low prices. Wholesalers (such as Julius Rosenwald, who eventually became president of Sears, Roebuck & Company) were middlemen who ordered suits from sweatshop owners, focusing most of their energies on marketing and distribution. Tailor-made was replicated, at some cost to quality and fit, and reproduced on a grand scale.[92] The display of linen, once a prerogative of gentlemen in daycoats and vests, was now available to all. A generation whose first encounter with "ready-made" came on the battlefield gave to their sons and grandsons the legacy of civilian uniformity: the suit.

During the 1880s, as the men's garment industry expanded its product, labor force, and market, women's clothing also began to be mass-produced. The rise of a large-scale women's garment industry meant more than a new and decorative product; it signaled a profound alteration in the daily lives of women. As the rise of "ready-made" clothing had had its early origins in the provision of a primarily masculine, mobile work force, the mass production of "ladies' garments" was a response to the increased mobility of women in an urban, industrial world. Ironically, if women's moving out of the home established them as consumers of mass-produced fashions, they were likely to be working within the garment industry itself. As home producers became garment workers, they also became a market for the fruit of their new labor.

It began with cloaks, modeled after those worn by European women of rank, emanating from factories and sweatshops in New York and Chicago. Within a decade, bustles, corsets, crinolines, and other tributes to the delicacy of Victorian upper- and middle-class women were being sold cheaply to the millions. Elaborate dresses, with flounced skirts and decorative folds, were topped off by ornamented hats, turbans, and bonnets, once

exclusive signs of upper-class majesty. Even as women's clothing evolved in response to conditions of greater mobility, such
styles as the popular shirtwaist of the early 1900s were fronted
by folds of lace and ruffles. Marks of "distinction" were appended to the garb of mobile labor.

While for two decades into the twentieth century, the stockings and undergarments of common girls were made from cotton lisle, in the 1920s silk began gracing the thighs of more and
more women. If late-nineteenth-century women of wealth had
sought the mobility of "shameful love" by embracing the silken
sensuality of courtesans, by the 1920s this mark of independence
was broadly marketed. Women increasingly moved from the
dreary utilitarianism of cotton underwear toward the implied
glossy leisure of silk. With the development of rayon, a lower-
priced imitation of silk, the trend spread. Legs, also, were increasingly displayed through sleek transparency. A sartorial idiom, once the risqué accent of class distinction, was entering the
common parlance.[93]

In the sphere of cosmetics, certain "society" women had, by
the late nineteenth century, taken on the "unrespectable" practice
of making up their faces with powders, paints, and rouge. Borrowing once again from the theatrical world of the demimondaine, such women were chided by *true* Victorians as "painted ladies," seduced from nature by "artificiality," shamefully "blind of
the spectacle they present to the world." Similar to the proliferation of silk (later, rayon) stockings and drawers, this "tawdry"
presentation of female independence was widely available across
store counters and from mail-order catalogs by 1905. David
Cohn, a historian of Sears, Roebuck and a former Sears em-
ployee, wrote that "by 1905, rouge in limited quantities was
demanded and used by simple housewives throughout the country," sold to them as "Rouge de Théâtre." Such a designation indicated the mass appeal of the demimondaine motif: "To say, in
1905, that rouge, a then morally dubious product, is being used
by the theatrical profession, a then morally dubious profession,
is the equivalent of recommending a bed today because it is the
kind used in some bawdyhouse."[94]

Today, although clothing and cosmetics are marked by clear
distinctions of quality, style, and pricing, the impact of these de-

velopments is unmistakable. Clothes consciousness and the attention to fashion constitute near-universal elements within American culture; their lure and mystique are worldwide. Beginning in the 1880s, the look of fashion attached to industrially produced clothing did more than alter the character of economic life. It offered an essential channel of popular desire, which has left its mark on the world ever since. The tracks still had two sides, but they were linked by a mesmerizing, symbolic bridge. This bridge asserted itself as visible evidence of increased social equality; for people who over millennia had lived beneath the symbols of its absence, its appeal should not be underestimated. The idea of "democracy" was assuming its modern, consumerist dimensions. Writing in 1925, a social prognosticator, Allen Devere, articulated this development in strident ideological terms:

> Progress toward democracy has made amazing strides in this matter of personal decoration. Formerly it was the ladies of the court who used it most. Today it is the serious concern and dearest pastime of all three estates. . . . And nowadays no one can tell . . . whether a given person lives on Riverside Drive or East 4th Street.[95]

Devere's proclamation is certainly an overstatement. It cannot be assumed that personal decoration was not an element in the home production of poor people's clothes. While little evidence remains as to the dress of common people in preindustrial times, it may be assumed that homespun crafts evinced a popular, sartorial vernacular, marked surely by the limits of scarcity yet embroidered by desire as well. Neither can we accept Devere's claims about the leveling capacities of fashion uncritically. Despite his literary linkage between the avenues of wealth and the alleys of deprivation—a device common in writing about clothing from the 1920s—there were sharp gradations in quality and fit, as there are today. The hidden secret of fashion democracy was the class dimensions, demarcating differences between hand-sewn originals and the cavalry of often shoddy copies that followed with varying degrees of loyalty—pregnant blind spots in his statement.

Be that as it may, the most telling point within Devere's rhapsody is the existence of a marketplace that gave some support to his claims. Clothing was emerging as a vehicle of presentability,

of self-realization, of distinction for an increasingly large purchasing public. For more and more people, "fashion" was now
available as a device of outward appearance.

Yet surface features are—by definition—potentially deceptive. Social history cannot be divined merely by looking at its
objects. To understand the development of mass fashion, we
must look more closely at the fateful interaction between it and
its public. The labor process by which these potent channels of
desire were produced—and are still, for the most part, produced
—laid bare the painful contradictions of an industrial culture itself: economic exploitation; monotony and boredom; crowded
and miserable working conditions; "work and work without
end"; all within a machinery of "plenty."

The fashion industry, in its genesis, offers a revealing lens for
examining some of the cultural collisions of modern life.
Through it can be seen both the bold promise of social transformation, of "freedom," and the conditions of purgatory to which
that promise addressed itself so loudly, as *a way out*. In purgatory
we find not only those whose laboring lives were spent inside the
machinery of fashion, but also those who were among its most
conspicuous early consumers.

The Backrooms of Fashion

It was in the decades following the Civil War, beginning with
the production of men's suits, that the mass production of
fashionable goods began to take hold. By the 1880s women's
clothing was also entering the modern networks of production
and distribution. Organized initially by German-Jewish immigrants, the mass market in styled clothing represented a dual,
often-contradictory reality. While the market offered goods that
broke through the class monopoly on fashionable imagery, so
too did it breed conditions that exacerbated the sting of social
disparity.

The rise of fashion goods was led by German Jews who had
entered the men's clothing industry during the 1850s. The
Rosenwald family offers us an illustrative example. The father,

Samuel Rosenwald, came to the United States in 1854, an immigrant from Bünde, Westphalia, in Germany. Beginning here as a peddler — first on foot, then by horse and wagon — the elder Rosenwald was, by 1856, employed by the Hammerslough brothers' Baltimore clothing firm. Marrying into the family, Samuel migrated to Springfield, Illinois, to run the family outlet there. During the Civil War his business grew, selling large shipments of uniforms to the Union.[96]

The son, Julius Rosenwald (born in 1862), carried his father's trade into the civilian market. With a cousin, Julius Weil, the younger Rosenwald built a successful business, selling men's ready-made suits. After early troubles in New York, the business moved to Chicago with much success. So effective was Julius Rosenwald in the wholesale men's garment industry that his father soon sold the business in Springfield and joined his son's firm in Chicago. During a period of general economic difficulty and of depression (1893), Rosenwald and Weil flourished, wholesaling the first generation of inexpensive, ready-to-wear men's suits. Business boomed as Rosenwald and Weil began to sell suits to the new and promising mail-order firm of Sears, Roebuck & Company. By the turn of the century, Rosenwald had moved into management at Sears itself, beginning with the clothing department, later becoming president of the company.[97] Within a period of three decades, this family had moved from peddler, to the selling of military uniforms ("shoddy" clothes), to large-scale men's fashion merchandising.

Like most of his generation of clothiers, Julius Rosenwald conformed to a pattern within the industry. He was not a producer of merchandise, nor was he a factory owner. He was a *jobber*. Selling clothes at wholesale, jobbers would farm production out to people who ran sweatshops, employing immigrant workers at low wages.

Dramatically divorcing clothing production from its domestic traditions, fashion jobbers altered patterns of work, and of dress as well. Before the 1870s, for example, "women's cloaks and jackets were little known in the United States. Shawls were worn by the masses. What few cloaks were seen were on women of means and fashion . . . imported from Germany."[98] With the massive migration of Russian Jews beginning early in the

1880s, a labor force was mobilized that gave a tremendous impetus to the American women's cloak business. Jobbers organized this development.

Copying and counterfeiting the look of fashion, jobbers sent patterns out for production. Insofar as the business was dominated by these wholesale merchandisers and distributors, sweatshop owners and labor contractors competed for their patronage. Jobbers sought to farm out production as cheaply as possible. Factory owners and subcontractors were pushed to drive their own costs down, in order to meet the demands of competition. For workers, the result was devastating. As fashion merchandising grew, the domination of jobbers over subcontractors was firmly implanted in the garment industry; patterns of low pay and fragmentation of the work force became the norm.

Amid this structure, the American garment trades grew dramatically. Between 1880 and 1889 alone, the value of the product increased from thirty-two to sixty-eight million dollars; capital investment grew from eight million to over twenty-one million dollars. The number of manufacturers increased from 562 to 1,224, and the number of workers employed in the trades increased from 25,192 to 39,149. Of these latter, 23,030 lived and worked in New York City.[99]

> Immigrants unused to industrial conditions would work fragmentarily in
> their homes. They bought sewing machines and supplied the foot power
> to run them. Contractors organized immigrant labor, maintaining their
> isolation, extracting labor from them in their tenement homes.[100]

Securing a dominant position within the garment industries, jobbers took on the role of fashion enterprisers. By 1920 women's fashion comprised 76 percent of the product of the industry, and was produced according to established seasonal patterns. Two times each year, jobbers would map out merchandising plans for the coming season. Designs were developed according to an emerging "market for styles"; fashions were derived from a variety of places: copying, "self-design," and purchase of precut patterns. After buying cloth from mills, the jobber would then farm out its manufacture. "The method is that of consignment. The jobber sells his materials on consignment to the sub-manufacturer and buys back the finished goods."[101] Within this apparatus, labor exploitation was virtually ensured. Louis Levine, in his classic study of the International Ladies' Garment Workers' Union, explained the characteristic burden carried by laborers in the trade:

> It is to the advantage of the jobber to increase the number of sub-manufacturers in order to pit one against another. But the sub-manufacturer cannot carry on production without transmitting the pressure of the jobber. Having "figured" the cost of a garment of a certain style, the sub-manufacturer is anxious to produce the garment at that cost. If he finds that the standards and wage rates fixed by the union will not permit this, he tries in every way open to him to evade union restrictions. If he cannot succeed in that and maintain a fair shop, he removes to a less desirable district and decreases the size of his shop.[102]

This general situation, described by Levine in the early 1920s, has continued, attested to by the subsequent migration of garment production to the nonunion South, and then to Hong Kong, South Korea, and elsewhere.

This was the structure of an industry that through its mass selling, its appropriation of imagery, and its national advertising was promoting dreams and propounding misery as well. As handcrafted clothing was displaced by a garment industry, the home made a transition from self-production to contracted labor. Shops grew up in tenement buildings. Inside them, investigators such as Jacob Riis found "men and women bending over their machines or ironing clothes at the window, half naked." Riding the Second Avenue elevated train through the "sweaters' district" of New York City, one was flanked by a perpetual row of tenement sweatshops. "The road is like a big gangway through an endless workroom where vast multitudes are forever laboring. Morning, noon, or night, it makes no difference; the scene is always the same."[103] In the mid-1880s, as sweatshop labor multiplied in New York and Chicago, sixty- to eighty-four-hour work weeks were common, and even after this, many workers took "material home and worked until two and three o'clock in the morning."[104] Wages were meager and days were consumed in dark and filthy quarters.

During the 1890s, tenement sweatshops came under attack by reformers and by legislation. The general tenor of legislation was to develop a clearer separation between work districts and residential areas. In the aftermath, after 1900, production began to migrate to a "more distinctly manufacturing district." Foot power was replaced, to some extent, by steam and electricity. New machinery "such as the braiding machine, the cording machine, the seaming and binding machine" came into shops, as did more advanced tools for cutting and pressing. With these developments, eastern European Jews were joined by Italian immigrants as laborers in the industry. Despite all this, Levine concludes, "the general condition of the trade and of the vast majority of workers showed little improvement."[105]

Between the 1880s and 1920, a large proportion of the people working in garment production were women. The necessity of industrial labor among vast numbers of immigrant women cut deep into traditional patterns of home production, and on the most basic level forced women not only into the production of industrial goods, but into their consumption as well. Mass-produced clothes were a necessity, increasingly, among women whose lives were circumscribed by long hours of wage labor or piecework. Against the backdrop of a middle-class morality that inscribed women with delicacy and home service, the industrial city drew women of poor immigrant families into the complex tendrils of the marketplace. Women found themselves in circumstances that defined them more and more as consumers, a basic category of industrial life.

The backrooms of "fashion" were scenes of extreme exploitation and monotony. While the garment industry drew women into the social world, it was a socialization that was marked by the repetitions and futility of the shop. At the very moment that the garment industry was giving shape to an important archetype of industrial oppression, so too was it creating social and psychological conditions that inspired widespread demands for social change. This happened in other early-twentieth-century industries as well, and by 1909 the United States was gripped by widespread labor agitation. Caught in a wave of anticapitalist feeling, much of this agitation looked beyond immediate economic issues and evoked visions of a better world, often reflecting tenets of anarchism, socialism, syndicalism: economic equality and industrial democracy.

Within the garment industry, in response to its daily humiliations, labor activity was conspicuous and often militant. As early as 1885, the Knights of Labor made inroads into the garment trades of New York and Chicago. In August of that year, "the entire cloak trade of New York was thrown into a 'general strike' which lasted two weeks." Strikes followed in Chicago, also under the banner of the Knights of Labor.[106] Pushing for unionization in 1902–3, the youthful ILGWU encouraged and orchestrated boycotts of goods not bearing the union label.[107]

Deeply influenced by radical ideas, and receptive to the socialist and anarchist perspectives voiced by many immigrant intellectuals, the militancy and vision of garment workers grew amidst an interchange and climate of "worker education."[108] From 1905 to 1909, when many shops were closed down by their owners, the Industrial Workers of the World gained a presence in some shops, "advocating 'the abolition of capitalism,' by means of 'class struggle.' "[109]

A massive strike of shirtwaist makers in New York in 1909 and 1910 lasted nearly three months. It involved twenty to thirty thousand women, most of them young women of sixteen to twenty-five.[110] In 1910, sixty thousand cloakmakers walked off the job over wages and conditions. In that same year, forty thousand tailors struck Hart, Schaffner and Marx in Chicago.[111]

Industrial conditions were wretched and inflammatory in the garment industry and elsewhere. The demand for industrial democracy, for greater social equality, was in the minds and on the lips of countless working people. A wave of industrial warfare shook the nation.

Yet in this climate, labor struggle was not the only avenue of change that was presenting itself. Ironically, the very garment industry that existed as a site of misery and exploitation was also generating a provocative array of goods that sounded their own trumpets for social equality and industrial democracy. Sidestepping the fundamental issues of social power and the distribution of wealth, fashion posed a spectacle of change. Despite the limits of the spectacle, its lure was powerful, even among those whose labor produced it. If garment production provided an arena of social discontent, there were other elements of urban industrial life that encouraged an immigrant, laboring population to embrace the promise of mass fashion. While sweatshop labor dampened the hopes of many who had sought a land of freedom, there were other, provocative elements of urban America that encouraged one to "dress for success." Forsaken in the promised land, working people saw mass-produced fashion as one key to the mastery of a new world. The terms of that world can be reduced to a single word: *appearance.*

Beyond coping with the specific terms of their employment, migrants to industrial cities found themselves embedded in the unfamiliar terms of a swelling urban culture. If mobility had brought immigrants into the city, it was also a powerful component within the urban choreography. People, en masse, were constantly on the move; the city was a rush of mobile people, mobile wealth, mobile ideals. Likewise, if customary existence was one in which the people you confronted on a day-to-day basis were familiar to you, the metropolis was a society of strangers; unknown faces were commonplace. The concentration of people in streets, in manufacturing districts, and in dance halls and other urban entertainments, confronted people with an unremitting parade of strangers. These were, and still are, the terms of mass life. Within it, one was continually forced to make silent, often-unconscious decisions, based on outward appearances. There was no time, no possibility, to get to "know everyone." Judging and presenting appearances became stocks in trade.

Within such a context, appearances entered the rhythm of existence at almost every turn. They were essential to a sense of security as one turned a corner. They became a vehicle of employment. In a strange environment, they separated the "greenhorns" from those who knew their way around. As personal life became increasingly mobile and private, one donned appearances as a prelude to public expeditions.

The increased accessibility of fashion fit the terms of urban life like a glove. In a theater of perpetual quick judgment, one was encouraged to assemble an effective response to the judgments of others. The city, a flourishing seat of commercial activity, set the terms for the commercialization of the self. In her 1929 study of the psychology of dress, Elizabeth Hurlock put it this way:

> No one likes to be considered mediocre, or to be so like every one else
> that he is passed over unnoticed. From the cradle to the grave, no one is
> totally free from regard for the opinion of others. . . . One of the chief
> values of clothing is that it enables people to advertise themselves in a
> way that will win the attention and admiration of others. Many who
> lack any ability and could not hope to rise above the "average" on their
> merits alone, find a satisfactory outlet for this desire for recognition
> through the medium of dress.[112]

Clothes filled a vacuum, provided an effective medium of exchange, in a milieu where the density of population, the jaggedness of time made careful scrutiny less and less possible.

The atmosphere of the city itself reinforced this. It was a jungle of display, an unrelenting spectacle, a circus of facade. Signs and lights shouted for attention. Window displays cried "Look and see!" It wasn't just a "habitat," it was, by its form, a self-promoter. With electricity, the promotion grew and became magical in its captivation. It was forbidden fruit . . . asking to be eaten. To be a part of this amphitheater, one imbibed its principle of display. Under its lights, within its motion, fashionable clothing became an imperative medium of engagement.

The urban stage not only offered a continual spectacle, it also generated continual opportunities for people to see themselves as part of the cityscape. As the metropolis took on its modern dimensions, it became a collection of glass and mirrored surfaces, unavoidable occasions for seeing oneself as a sight. Anne Hollander, looking at the relationship between clothing and images, has said that the mirror "is the personal link between the human subject and its representation." In front of it, or as we catch a glimpse of ourselves as we pass by a shop window, we engage in "the imaginative act of making art out of facts: the aim is to mold the reflection into an acceptable picture, instantaneously and repeatedly, with no other means than the eyes themselves. . . . Behind the reflecting surface is something waiting to be born."[113] If the "facts" of life for many among the urban population were constituted by endless toil and the anonymity of the streets, fashion provided a symbolic medium of escape. It offered a way of molding reflections, of making art out of facts, of transcending the forces of circumstance by embracing the tools of display. In a world of strangers, such devices entered the realm of common sense.

Avenues of Display

The city provided a fertile soil within which mass fashion took root. As a mobile and personalized form of display, fashion was particularly suited to a society characterized, more and more, by mobile individuals. It played a major part in the ensemble of outer features that has come to be known as "personality."

The emergence of mass fashion, however, was not an idiosyncratic development. As it shared complementary capacities with chromolithography, and as it reflected and transmitted the priorities of urban existence, it was an integral component within a symphony of social developments. It was an important feature of an industrial, consumer culture that was taking hold across the American landscape. It contributed to tangible social change. It also reflected the change. Yet its propagation was dependent upon a broad range of other institutions, which were part and parcel of a consumerist mode of life. As the imagery of fashionability moved through cities, then on into small-town and rural America, it did so upon pathways cut by other, new vehicles of display.

Within the city, an essential publicizer of fashion was the department store. Itself a child of industrial merchandising, its presence gave testimony to the journey from itinerant peddler to palaces of consumption that had taken place in the area of retailing across the nineteenth century. In the mid-nineteenth century, department stores had begun to appear, simultaneously, in Paris, London, and New York, led by Frenchman Aristide Boucicaut, who established the renowned Bon Marché in Paris in 1852.[114]

The American department store was the offspring of numerous patriarchs: A. T. Stewart, Rowland H. Macy, and B. Altman in New York; John Wanamaker in Philadelphia; Marshall Field in Chicago; William Filene, first in Lynn and then in Boston, Massachusetts.[115] For the most part, department stores were founded by immigrants from Britain; Jewish émigrés from Germany and then eastern Europe; and by "descendants of Quaker families settled in New England in the seventeenth century."[116]

From their beginnings, these establishments were purveyors of clothing. Some dated back to the era of "slops." The chain of Browning, King & Company got its start supplying clothes to forty-niners in California.[117] Relatively soon, however, these stores became purveyors of more fashionable goods. Selling clothes in a range of prices to a corresponding range of customers, department stores provided a dazzling atmosphere for their wares.

If ready-made clothing became increasingly ornamental over the latter part of the nineteenth century, the principle of department-store design was similarly elegant. The engagement was reciprocal, reinforcing each other. Ready-made clothing put the imitative symbolism of wealth in reach of more and more people, to be worn as an emblem of achievement. Similarly, the department store created an architectural environment that was palatial, a mimicry of space and style that was, by custom, a prerogative of opulence. New York's first department store, predating the age of mass fashion, was A. T. Stewart's "Marble Dry-Goods Palace" at Broadway and Chambers Street. Fifteen years later, Stewart's erected a new store, utilizing a cast-iron building facade, a cheaper, lighter mode of display, which was painted to approximate the weight and substance of stone. A democracy of surfaces was being erected through architectural innovation.[118]

Internally, these "palaces of consumption" were true to the principles of appearance and display. In 1853, Lord and Taylor built a store at Grand and Chrystie streets that defied the crowded terms of urban space. Built before the introduction of electric lighting, the illumination of such a structure was always a problem. Gaslights, though bright, were extremely dangerous, particularly in an establishment where crowds would risk the sudden apocalypse of fire and explosion. The Lord and Taylor store introduced a pattern that was replicated elsewhere. "The new store incorporated a large central rotunda with glass dome which allowed daylight and air to penetrate into the building."[119] The resulting structure provided a dramatic diversion from the crowdedness of urban life that was generally experienced by its clientele. The rotunda design created a spectacle of air, space, and light that provided a symbolic retreat from the terms of an increasingly congested city life. Such innovations of structure and display provided a seductive and promising context for the retailing of industrial wares. Within such an arena, the din of the sweatshop, the filth of the factory, and the monotony of work were masked. The buying environment complemented the claims and conceits of the goods themselves, often defying experience.

These temples of Mammon were particularly effective places for the display of industrial "plenty." They reiterated its optimism and, at least symbolically, avoided its costs. As ready-made garments became conspicuous vehicles of style, they found a suitable home within the big stores. Making their first appearances in the latter decades of the nineteenth century, by 1915 ready-to-wear departments were entrenched as features within the stores. The distribution of these goods was further aided by the founding of the United Parcel Service in 1907, a basic metropolitan delivery service.[120]

While department stores took hold in cities in the 1880s, most Americans still lived in the country. In 1880 the United States was still mainly rural; agriculture was still the predominant area of employment and production. Yet these farm areas and people were inoculated by the spectacle of industrial goods as well. A dynamic medium of urban images and goods was the mail-order catalog. Beginning in 1869 with E. C. Allen's "People's Literary Companion," a catalog displaying a diversity of items, the mail-order approach to merchandising was perfected by Aaron Montgomery Ward, who became the official supplier to the Grange, an organization of farmers. Rural social networks were becoming an infrastructure for the establishment of industrial merchandising networks. Ward's success was followed by that of Sears, Roebuck & Company whose catalog ws dubbed, simultaneously, "The Farmer's Friend" and "America's Dream Book." The pages of Sears's catalog were glutted with pictures and print. For an audience used to open spaces, these pages offered a crowded representation of city life; Chicago was the home base of Sears, Roebuck. Yet if the experienced crowdedness of the city was often marked by deprivation, the pages of the catalog were cornucopian.

Richard Sears and Julius Rosenwald combined an understanding of rural, preconsumerist social values with an expertise in mass retailing. The catalog posed an inviting advertisement for this combination; sympathetic to the hesitancy of farm folk to deal in distant markets, ostentatious in its proselytizing for consumer goods. With Rosenwald as the curator of Sears's fashion display and manager of its immense corporate structure, clothing stood prominently within the catalog. If in turn-of-the-century catalogs timepieces were featured first within its pages, by the 1920s fashion goods for women held that honored spot. Read and reread throughout the American countryside, Sears, Roebuck catalogs carried the imagistic message of the garment center into the outer reaches of the society.[121] It offered the wherewithal and the definition of modernity: *ready-made*.

Mail-order catalogs were just one of the ways by which ready-to-wear was spread through printed literature and images. The growing institution of mass-circulation newspapers also carried the tidings of fashion. From the late nineteenth century onward, advertising for ready-made clothing became a part of the printed vernacular of the city. Advertising methods adhered to the principle of display. Beyond being an originator in department stores themselves, Rowland Macy was also innovative in the area of journalistic advertising. His store utilized an advertising mode that broke many of the conventions of printing, and grabbed the attention of its viewers. Departing from "the usual straight lines of letterpress," Macy instead opted "for an arrangement of words into patterns and the use of repetition of short, incisive phrases — all to catch the reader's eye."[122] Such verbal techniques were enhanced, increasingly, by pictorial displays. In addition to showing readers what a garment looked like, pictures afforded the occasion to place the garments within a setting, offering occasions and atmospheres that linked the product with privilege and leisure, whether available to the consumer or not. Beyond newspapers, such mass magazines as Edward Bok's *Ladies' Home Journal* promoted the ideals of fashion and gave fashion advice to a growing audience of readers. Slick pages enhanced the glamor of pictorial display.

Techniques developed by chromolithographers figured heavily in the graphic broadcasting of fashion. As chromos could approximate the rich density of oil paints, so too could they enhance the look and textures of cloth. A cultural system of cross-referencing was established in the array of artistically rendered reproductions; on paper, in cloth. One of the most interesting uses of chromolithography in relation to fashion was in the printing and selling of paper dolls, which expanded around the turn of the century.

Fashion miniatures had a long history. Early in the nineteenth century, and before, American women of wealth purchased "fashion babies" from Europe. These were dolls, produced on the Continent, wearing fashions as models for imitation by dressmakers. They were accoutrements to the spread of fashion among the rich. Later on, these costly models were replaced by "pantines," pasteboard dolls that served a similar purpose: providing models for imitation by seamstresses.[123] These items were part of a tradition that equated fashion with class privilege.

By 1900, with the spread of fashionable ready-to-wear, "fashion babies" experienced a similar democratization. While early examples had been exclusive models and dressmakers' aids, chromolithographed paper cutout dolls were children's toys. Cheaply produced yet elaborately colored, paper cutouts spread the imagery of fashion to little girls of different backgrounds and circumstances. The generational implications are suggestive. Even if older generation rural or immigrant parents adhered to austere traditions in dress, paper dolls introduced fashion to their little girls at an early age, setting the desires of impressionable youth against the resistant conventions of age.

For people living in certain American cities, a wave of large public expositions provided another spectacular arena of display. These elaborate fairs, offering a utopian panorama of industrial and artistic achievement, were themselves facades of "monumental grandeur." Their architectural motifs were testimony to the principle of superficial display. One of the grandest was the Columbian Exposition, held in Chicago in 1893. At an estimated cost of forty-six million dollars, Chicago businessmen attempted to construct an environment that mirrored the distinction of European neoclassical design. Mimicking the perpetuity of

Renaissance ideals, a mule team of architects put up a city that was primarily surface, true to the priorities of the age. Historian John F. Kasson has described the telling combination of classical ideals and temporary construction:

> The Columbian Exposition offered architects, artists, and patrons an opportunity to construct an ideal that would purify the gross materialism of American culture, order its chaotic energies, and uplift its taste and character. Out of their united efforts, they aimed to create a monumental White City, an image of Venice purified and reborn. As an ideal, the White City would be a Dream City, rising in less than two and a half years out of the Chicago mire to flourish for a few seasons, and then in 1896 to be dismantled.

The exposition, like the fashions it propagandized, reflected a characteristic discovery of consumer capitalism: turning sows' ears into silk purses. "On closer inspection," Kasson points out, "the gleaming white marble of the Exposition buildings turned out to be staff, a compound of plaster and fibrous binding, clothing wood and steel" as an armature.[124] The vistas of privilege were produced for a sight-seeing public, and then disposed of. This disposable environment, beyond its adherence to the principles of appearance and display, was also a testimony to the logic of consumption, so essential to the industrial system that spawned it. In the world of ever-changing fashion, in particular, the consumerist ethic—continually using things up—was an intrinsic component.

Within the halls of expositions, fashion was an important exhibit. At the Centennial Exhibition in Philadelphia (1876), the propagation of style was part of the show. Particularly for visitors from the West, what they saw was filled with new and unfamiliar goods: "finer things in fabrics, apparel, furniture, home furnishings and other lines of goods used in the arts of living, goods that had formed but a small part of their thought up to that time."[125] Likewise, the Columbian Exposition promoted new trends in fashion among a large mob of visitors.

In their form and in their content, expositions interacted with the products of the garment industry and reinforced their aura. Display, as a notable element of urban existence, was magnified and utopianized in the shadowless dazzle of the White Cities.

By 1920, the most powerful agencies of mass impression, the

movies, were playing their part in the rise of fashion. Shown in movie palaces, which—like department stores and expositions— were grand monuments to elaborate facades, films riveted the imagination. In their study of Middletown, Helen and Robert Lynd noted that by the midtwenties, among high-school-age youths, the "sharp figures on the silver screen are always authoritatively present with their gay and confident designs for living."[126] Anne Hollander elaborates:

> Movies taught everyone how ways of walking and dancing, of using the hands and moving the head and shoulders, could be incorporated into the conscious ways of wearing clothes.

Hollander continues, implying that film, in its magnification of motion, contributed to the diminution of cloth in women's fashion following the First World War:

> After about 1920 the fact that women's clothes showed such a reduction in overall volume was undoubtedly partly due to the visual need for the completely clothed body to be satisfactorily seen *in motion*.
>   The still body that is nevertheless perceived as ideally in motion seems to present a blurred image—a perpetual suggestion of all the other possible moments at which it might be seen. It seems to have a dynamic, expanding outline.[127] (Emphasis added.)

As a basic source of Americanization, film provided a visual manual to urban and rural people. It magnified ideals of consumption, of motion, of beauty, and of dress. Writing in 1929, fashion analyst Elizabeth Hurlock commented on the impact of film over the preceding decade:

> In recent years the popularity of the cinema and its far- reaching effects have made screen stars more powerful in the determination of present-day fashions than the actors and actresses of the legitimate state. The nation-wide publicity which is given to them, has made them the popular heroes and heroines of the day. What they do, say, think, eat, or wear serves as a model for their devoted followers.[128]

If screen stars were thin and mobile, so too would be their imitators. The 1920s became an era of dieting and thin, skimpy styles. If the screen images were luminescent white and black, fashions likewise moved toward black and white; "color drained out of elegance, and was replaced by the whole black and white spectrum" during the twenties.[129] The silver screen brought fashion imagery to everyone, and set it before them in terms larger than life. A pattern of interaction between screen stars and popular desires was taking hold. In baroque palaces sculpted of plaster and horsehair, in a flood of publicity and fan magazines, people confronted stars as models for sexual fantasy, excitement in life, consumption. Fashion stood at the surface of this confrontation.

By the 1920s, there was a massive interaction of fashion display. Countless new institutions carried the message and repeated each other's chants. Yet the rise of mass fashion was not the result of a series of discrete avenues of display. It came amid a broad and general development that encompassed the flowering of mass production and mass consumption. Within this general development, mass fashion went beyond the reproduction of styles, adapted from the modes of nineteenth-century wealth. A reciprocity, an interaction began to develop, between fashion and the industrial structure that was propagating it on a mass scale. If mass production affected the construction of clothing, it also left its imprint on design. Approaching the 1920s, fashionable clothing was already marked by the new, mobile terms of a mass industrial society.

New Patterns

From the time of the Civil War, the connective tissue between fashion and industrialism spread the look of finery beyond its formerly insular sanctums. As mass production appropriated the imagery of fashion, the imagery of fashion itself was irrevocably affected by that intercourse. By 1863, mechanical reproduction had made its mark even on the handcraft traditions of home-produced clothing and dressmaking. Where beforehand each garment was patterned and cut individually, now printed paper patterns were commercially available. Developed by a New England tailor named Butterick, the principles of standardization had insinuated themselves into the home. Such patterns were also employed in factories, establishing a link between public and private spheres of production.[130] As in so many other areas of life, the conceptualization of a product was gravitating from the imagination of the producer to the designs of commerce.

By the early decades of the twentieth century, the proliferation of ready-to-wear clothing began to coincide with dramatic changes in the silhouette of fashion itself. Patterns of sumptuousness and conspicuous consumption of cloth were costly both in terms of the amount of cloth and the labor they required. Textile yardage decreased as simpler, less fulsome styles began to appear. In a world of mass fashion, questions of cost increasingly invaded the realm of design. In 1913 an average women's outfit required 19 yards of fabric in its production. By 1928, with more and more women donning fashionable products from the garment center, the average outfit consumed only 7 yards of cloth.[131]

While the diminishing amount of cloth may be partly explained as attempts to minimize productive costs, other aspects of industrial society also left their imprint on style. As fashion became a staple among women who entered into the outer world of work, designs that were predicated on docility and enforced leisure became patently restrictive. Among rich women, sport and city life denoted a need for more mobile styles. Among poor women it was wage labor. If the first generations of ready-to-wear had provided working-class women the opportunity to emulate the fashions of the rich, by the 1920s fashion had begun to emulate the logic of industrialism. The fashion ideal for women increasingly became that of "the young, agile, long-limbed girl, whose naturally shaped body is well suited to the working requirements and mobility of the modern world. Her well-proportioned figure is easily clothed by a standardized manufactured garment."[132] Among fashion designers, it was the "King of Fashion," Paul Poiret, whose Parisian workshop legitimized and advocated simple and comfortable dress. Avoiding any link between fashion and social utility, however, Poiret asserted that he was merely expressing an "Oriental influence."[133]

Despite such disclaimers, the connection between simple dress and the terms of twentieth-century life is clear. The increasing worldliness and mobility of women, and their engagement in wage labor, were accommodated and symbolized by a style of dress that forswore the sedentary ideas of Victorianism. Style reflected a kinetic potential: lean, taut, with emphasis on the legs. Reverberating against the staunch sexual dualism of the nineteenth century, the entry of woman into the world of work, or the world of public life in general, was seen as her masculinization. Fashion reflected this metamorphosis of gender, dramatically. Where nineteenth-century corsetry had molded women to emphasize their reproductive functions, styles moving toward the 1920s were productive in orientation. The idiom of action and of masculinity bagan to transform the ideals of young womanhood. Industrial ideals of youth and physical endurance infected the terms of beauty. If film and entertainment were vehicles of fashion ideals in the public consciousness, they were also ideals of mobile industrialism and efficiency. In a memoir on fashion, Cecil Beaton waxes eloquent on the beauty of Irene Castle, a star of the years around 1915. As a feminine ideal, dancer Castle was a repudiation of the delicate uselessness of Victorianism:

> Irene Castle's appearance was unlike anyone else's, yet overnight people accepted it and emulated her wherever possible. The primary effect that she created was one of an exquisite grace combined with an extraordinarily boyish youthfulness. There was something terrifically healthy and clean about her. In her whiplike and taut bearing she hinted at the wonderful play of muscles beneath the surface, as a fine-bred horse betrays its beauty by a ripple. There was something bladelike and steely about her muscles and her limbs. She used her hands with such a bold grace that one had the notion that she gesticulated rather than gestured. . . . She walked with very long strides, with no daintiness, swinging along with wonderful, live, big gestures. She invented a whole balance of movement, with the pelvis thrust forward and the body leaning backwards. . . . It was as if a gyroscope were inside her, always stabilizing the body's framework no-matter on which tangent it moved off.[134]

Beaton's imagery is that of the mobile, engaged woman of the industrial age. The cushioned, parlorbound woman of the past was now described in metallic and mechanical terms. Still an object of masculine passion, that passion was now evoked by the power of motion and of strength. Unencumbered by trails of ringlets from her head, she now was capped by a short, boyish haircut, known by those who copied the style as the "Castle bob." In the turbulent motion of mass industrialism, fashionable women were increasingly attuned to its demands. Lean and sinewy, the flapper style of the 1920s provided a unified principle of work and leisure. Whether dancing or wage earning, the flapper was a model of endurance.

While hardly scanty, men's clothing after the turn of the century also reflected the primacy of endurance. If the cloak of morality, denoting entrepreneurial austerity, had informed the construction of men's suits throughout much of the nineteenth century, the masculine ideal underwent certain changes in the years after 1900 as well. Describing the shift, Paul Nystrom spoke of how "the styles of clothing for men seemed to aim at emphasizing size and physical strength. Men in the clothing of the period from 1900–1905 looked like giant athletes."[135] If women's clothing intimated strength and motion, the steel-worker physique inculcated in the imagery of men's fashion also had a symbolic intimacy with the priorities and proximity of labor. The magnetism of fashion, born in the consumption patterns of a leisure class, had now evolved to reflect the life patterns of its latest practitioners: working-class women and men.

Insofar as fashion took on the imprint of industrial modernity, it reflected a variety of influences. Work and mobility were major factors in the delineation of new styles, but there are also myriad elusive aspects to the wiles of fashion. Some questions are suggested but unanswerable. The entry of vertical lines and geometric patterns evokes the translation of the body into the architectural forms of the urban edifice. The thin and taut ideal, while linked to mobility and action, may also engage the anxieties and anomies of modern existence. It is hard to be conclusive, but important to speculate on such parallels of meaning. The conspicuous consumption of cloth, now joined by the conspicuous consumption of human energy as a fashion ideal, however, was clearly an outcome of industrial modernity. As Henry Adams once observed, the virgin is replaced by the dynamo as a sensuous ideal.

Not all interactions between fashion and industrialism were symbolic in their origin. During the First World War, for example, concrete social and material priorities had a direct impact on style. The war that drew legions of men onto the fields of battle also drew unprecedented numbers of women into factory work.

Within such a development, the move toward more mobile fashions was expanded as a necessity among women. In addition, as war production demanded the channeling of essential materials toward military ends, the War Industries Board established a series of regulations regarding clothing:

> Shoes for both men and women were made with shorter tops, the limit allowed being eight inches, and no leather linings. Coats for men were shortened and the cuffs removed from their trousers as a means of conserving woolen material. The steel, formerly used for women's corsets, was needed for wire cables to hoist guns and munitions over the peaks in the Alps, and the result was that corset manufacturers were summoned to Washington where they were told that a decrease of one-fourth in the amount of wire used for stays must be made at once.

The war created social and material demands that gave further impetus to trends begun beforehand, dramatizing the symbiosis between fashion and material life.

In the early decades of this century, as social life and structures of survival took on a new shape, patterns of sartorial meaning were altered. While earlier mass fashion had mimicked the displays of elites, now the idiom of display took on the trappings of common life. Industrial labor and production made inroads into the visual language of fashion. An emulation of the proletarian lot now joined the emulation of elites within the patterns and energies of style. The democratization of access to fashion had now injected fashion with a more democratic ethos, setting the stage for a time when the once-scorned clothing of miners would carry the labels of couturiers.

The Sirens of Style

"Why did I choose to come to America?" begins the father, a Roumanian immigrant, in Mike Gold's classic *Jews without Money.* "I will tell you why," he continues, "it was because of envy. . . . " The envy was a product of tales told in his native village, but it also had roots in pictures he had seen in the window of a show that sold Singer sewing machines. Here, in the pictures, were representations of a world that transformed the inequities of experience. Presumably, this world was made possible by sewing machines.

> One picture had in it the tallest building I had ever seen. It was called a
> skyscraper. At the bottom of it walked the proud Americans. The men
> wore derby hats and had fine mustaches and gold watch chains. The
> women wore silks and satins, and had proud faces like queens. Not a
> single poor man or woman was there; every one was rich.

For Mike Gold's father, clothing was decisive in a vision of opportunity that stood, far away, in America. Clothing told him that in this distant land, "the poorest ragpicker lived better than a Roumanian millionaire."

"In America," he believed, "people did little work, but had fun all day." The democracy of the image presented an inviting promise, and he embarked upon his pilgrimage, his mind reeling with the expectation that now he too might "wear a derby hat."[136]

While Mike Gold's tale is ultimately one of painful disenchantment, the availability of fashion mesmerized immigrants upon their arrival in America. Its apparent power seemed to overturn the conventions of ages. It offered the possibility to assume the bearing and carriage of people who, in the old country, had had an exclusive claim on sartorial grace. Mass fashion afforded immigrants the possibility to "be somebody" in a new world, rejecting the indignities of the past and accommodating themselves to the world of display in which they sought their future.

For Italian immigrants in New York, donning ready-to-wear broke ancient taboos. As peasants from the southern tier, they had learned that certain lines should not be crossed: "No woman of the poorer classes," for example, "dared put on a hat. She would have been the laughing stock of her community if she did. To don a hat was the privilege of the signora [woman of the landowning gentry], or the whores."[137] In America, a war broke out over such customs. While older women held to the conventions of the past, wearing scarves over their heads and shawls over their shoulders, young Italian women eagerly ate of the formerly forbidden fruit. These were the accoutrements of the New World. Not only were they the means of survival for those who made them; they were a symbolic ascendancy to the level of the signora; or, perhaps, to the freedom from family constraints represented, once more, by the finery of "shameful love." If work was long and tedious and housing decrepit, clothing afforded the illusion of stepping out of one's circumstances. Those who held to the lure of the past looked askance at those who adopted the idiom of fashionable democracy. Among one Sicilian community on New York's Lower East Side, women who learned the vernacular of ready-made were chided:

> In the old country she used to carry baskets of tomatoes on her head and now she carries a hat on it . . . look at the daughter of so and so. In Cinisi [a village in Sicily] she worked in the field and the sun burnt her black. Here she dares to carry a parasol.[138]

For an older generation schooled in the indignities of sumptuary law, fashion was proscribed from desire. For their children, it represented a transcendent escape. It was one of the few areas in which the promises of industrial plenty could, at least superficially, be met.

The promise of industrial democracy had early been expressed in terms of clothing. Clothing had long been a device in the elevation of classes. For the bourgeoisie, fashion had been an important emblem of their arrival; for laboring people the expectation was similar. As New England farm girls made their first forays into the cotton mills of Lowell, Massachusetts, they were seduced by a "hoisting of false colors." Labor recruiters, scouting rural Vermont and New Hampshire, promised girls that they would tend their machinery dressed in silks, and would work at a leisurely enough rate so as to "spend half their time reading."[139] Some girls did in fact return to family farms, arrayed with "new silk dresses"—an effective advertisement to those girls who would come next to work in the factories.

By the turn of the century, with the deluge of ready-to-wear, the lure held out many decades before to the Lowell mill girls was a visible claim made across the broad tawdry horizon of a developing consumer culture.

For people "caught between a longing for love and the struggle for the legal tender,"[140] cheap, evocative ready-made clothing fed the hungry fires of social wish and personal desire. It made the often tough journey into the modern industrial world seem all the more promising. For hardworking, ill-housed immigrants, despised by the middle-class "natives," clothing offered one of the few avenues by which people could assume a sense of belonging. In a world of strangers, the ability to construct appearances, a disguise, was one of the most essential lessons. It could be observed as one moved from tenement district to tenement district; from wretched ghetto to screaming tenderloin. The abundance of cheap ready-to-wear was one of the first acquisitions of the urban poor, often procured before some things more necessary, but less visible.

In the 1890s, the area of New York City between Twenty-seventh and Fortieth streets at Seventh Avenue was known as "African Broadway," the quarter in which a large number of the city's black residents lived. Most had recently arrived from the South, what W. E. B. Du Bois called "country bred." These were the children of slaves, refugees from a land in which plantation aristocrats dressed in the style of conspicuous elegance, while blacks — like all poor rural folk — wore overalls and other "slops." Yet there on African Broadway, the availability of mass fashion was widely evident:

> Always and invariably on "dress parade" is the new quarter (reported by the *New York Tribune*, October of 1895). . . . The younger women, arrayed in gowns that are wonderfully good imitations of the fashions, though heaven knows how they can afford them, walk in pairs and trios up and down Seventh Avenue. . . . The people . . . are poor, with only a dollar or two standing between them and starvation most of the time. . . . [Nonetheless, one sees a] daily promenade of gayly dressed girls and *sprig* [sic] young colored men. Yellow is the prime tint of the young colored girls' clothes. The favorite dress of the young men "in style" is a glossy silk hat, patent leathers, a black suit with a sack coat of remarkable shortness, and a figured waistcoat. Paste diamonds are *de rigueur*.[141]

In a world of degraded housing, racism, and general economic deprivation, clothing afforded these recent migrants from the South one of the few avenues by which a selfhood could be publicly expressed, one consistent with principles of appearance and display.

The power of the lure of finery is heard in the lament of

Mamie Craven, a laundress quoted in Ruth True's study of New York's poor West Side in 1914: "Oh . . . you don't know *how* I want a chinchilla coat." This from a young woman not content to see her earnings eaten up by rent, food, fuel.[142]

The immigrants' desire for fine clothing was the object of ridicule and moralizing by the middle class. Unable to appreciate the meaning of clothes to those who were denied nearly all else, they would refer to these fashionable poor, walking up the avenue, as a "Monkey's Parade." What they condemned were the "shop apprentices, the young work girls, the boy clerks, and so forth, stirred by mysterious intimations, spending their first-earned money upon collars and ties, chiffon hats, smart lace collars, walking-sticks, sunshades . . . "[143]

Bertha June Richardson, in her 1913 study of "the woman who spends," explained the impulse toward finery among immigrant girls in city settlement houses. Speaking to a middle-class audience concerned with "uplifting" these "misbegottens," she says:

> Did you ever go down to one of our city settlements full of the desire to help and lift up the poor shop girl? . . . There must be some mistake, you thought. These could not be poor girls, earning five or six dollars a week. They looked better dressed than you did! Plumes on their hats, a rustle of silk petticoats, everything about them in the latest style. You went home thoughtful about those girls who wasted their hard-earned money on cheap imitation, who dressed beyond their station, and you failed to see what enjoyment they got out of it. In time you learned that it was only an attempt "to bridge the difference" between themselves and those with larger opportunities by imitating all they could see.[144]

Thorstein Veblen once argued that emulation was the fuel that energized fashion. For an urban poor, raised in the traditions of sumptuary law and dazzled by the expanding array of mass-produced imagery, the tools of emulation were now increasingly available. Middle-class women who worked in the social-work movement of the early twentieth century were often perplexed at the vigor with which poor immigrant girls picked up these tools. Social workers often came from affluent backgrounds; their lives did not so require the erection of appearances. Like Jane Addams, such a person "may afford to be very simple, or even shabby as to her clothes, if she likes." As many of these women were carrying on their own battles against the constraints of Victorianism, a simple approach to dress was not uncommon among them. But Addams understood the imperative of dress among working girls:

> But the working girl, whose family lives in a tenement, or moves from one small apartment to another, who has little social standing and has to make her own place, knows full well how much habit and style of dress has to do with her position. Her income goes into her clothing, out of all proportion to the amount which she spends upon other things. But, if social advancement is her aim, it is the most sensible thing she can do. She is judged largely by her clothes. Her house furnishing, with its pitiful little decorations, her scanty supply of books, are never seen by the people whose social opinions she most values. Her clothes are her background, and from them she is largely judged.[145]

The same impulse was noted by Stuart Chase later on, in 1929:

> Not long ago I walked along New York's East Side where the more poorly paid workers live. The buildings were old, slatternly, ugly and depressing beyond description. Yet out of a ramshackle doorway would come a child in a brand-new overcoat; a girl in silk stockings and furs. The contrast struck one between the eyes. It serves to typify the whole uneven, lateral development of American living standards.[146]

Emerging was a basic pattern of American consumer culture. Produced in a variety of price lines but imitating the look of affluence, mass fashion provided a means by which poor people could develop an appearance of upward mobility, construct a presentable, public self by which that mobility might in fact be actualized. The remarkable success of the fashion industry was built on such aspirations, which by the late 1920s enveloped the lives of almost everyone. Writing in 1929, Elizabeth Hurlock proclaimed:

> Never in history has fashion held such power as it does today. Never have fashions been so varied and so fleeting. Never has fashion's sway been so universal that to be out of fashion might literally be interpreted to be "out of the world."[147]

Hurlock's last phrase reveals the tyranny of fashion. If clothing presented people with the possibility of concealing their origins and if fashion was a tool of outer display for more and more people, it was also true that the new world *demanded* the "Americanization" of the self. Fashion and presentability were, increasingly, categories imposed upon modern industrial citizens. To turn away from the pull of fashion was to remain alien and different, to stand "outside the gates." To embrace fashion was to move ahead with society. Leonard Covello, an immigrant from Italy, described his sartorial Americanization with an ironic sense of contradiction:

> My long European trousers had been replaced by the short knickers of the time, and I wore black ribbed stockings and new, American shoes. To all outward appearances I was an American, except that I did not speak a word of English.[148]

Bertha June Richardson argued that the tyranny of fashion, among middle- as well as working-class people, undercut the principles of *nature*, substituting individual consumption for the common good. To Richardson, the elaborate structure of fashion set people against one another in a ritual of "purposeless imitation." The ritual wove itself through the classes of society, elevating personal gain above social needs:

> The shops imitate each other and dictate to the woman just the line of imitation she shall follow, without a thought for her needs. The Fourth Avenue shop says to the Fourth Avenue buyer: "Behold my clever imitation. For less than you could pay in a Fifth Avenue shop, I can give you a perfect imitation. You would not be behind the styles, I know. I can make you look like the real peacock, so buy here." The Third Avenue shop . . . say(s) the same to its customers. The First Avenue shop has a still cheaper imitation, and in Hester Street, on the pushcarts, ghosts of the real are "Going, going, going" for thirty-nine cents.

In Richardson's estimation, this journey of the imitation downward merely turned people's minds to the worship of worthless things, while essential needs were overlooked. Invoking *nature* against the dominion of style, Richardson cautioned that "*She will teach you to struggle for and to imitate those things which make for life, the highest life, the best life, not for yourself alone, but for all to whom you are bound by the common ties of life*"[149] (emphasis added). For all its utilitarian moralism and stuffy contempt, Richardson's was a potent insight. If fashion was a powerful device, requisite to modern life, it was also an element in the social process by which common bonds of community and commitment were subverted by the individualism of a consumer society. Mass fashion was providing more and more people with the idiom of sartorial expression, but it was a vernacular punctuated by the lingo of social competition.

Other critics of mass fashion spoke from the platform of the old elite monopoly. Cecil Beaton argued that images that were once unique and mysterious were now being "reduced to journalistic commonplaces." Fashion imagery greeted everyone at breakfast, in the morning paper. To Beaton, the traditional magic of fashion had been based on its rarity, its spontaneity. "Without mystery," he bemoaned, "magic disappears. . . . If distance lends enchantment, then there is little distance in our contemporary world." Celebrities, carrying fashion into the public domain of popular consciousness, had, for Beaton, robbed fashion of its imagination.[150]

In line with this, Karlyne Anspach reported that as late as 1967, elite New York department store Bergdorf Goodman expected its employees to avoid looking overly stylish. Committed to upholding an air of mystery, magic, and originality for its clientele, Bergdorf's instructed its employees: "We don't want our sales people mistaken for customers."[151] The availability of mass fashion made it all the more important for purveyors of elite fashion to hold on to the apparent province of uniqueness.

Another source of concern over the homogenization of style was the elite fashion designers themselves, who saw ready-to-wear as the Waterloo of the imagination. Paris designer Paul Poiret felt that the trend to mass fashion was ultimately a fetish for labels:

> Another thing which the American traders appeared to me to practise was to pack mediocre merchandise under a distinguished label. In that country they will have labels, and as they have no understanding of the value of objects, they go by labels only. To sell common merchandise under the name of Poiret seems to them a happy and fortunate notion.[152]

The current mode of "designer jeans" is the ultimate expression of fetishization Poiret decried. To him, American garment manufacturers were servile copyists; "their absolute lack of imagination prevents them from conceiving the unforeseen and the hypothetical."[153] His heir in the leadership of Paris fashion, Christian Dior, put it somewhat more delicately during the 1950s:

> [Americans'] clothes, hair, nails and shoes are all impeccable. This is true of all classes of society from the millionaire down to the elevator operator . . . but I must at the same time admit that in the end there was something uniform about it.[154]

Though these criticisms sprang from the self-interest of elites, they contained more than a grain of truth. If fashion gave more and more people access to a language of individual expression, its mass production tended toward the opposite: mass expression. Rooted in the production of industrial and military uniform, the ready-made fashion industry also created a mode of uniformity, though touched by the elegance of style.

Defenders of mass fashion, during the decisive period of the 1920s, described it as a force of great political and social magnitude. Paul Nystrom, an architect of modern fashion merchandising, waxed eloquent on the imprint of fashion on the popular sensibility.

> Once the pursuit of the wealthy and aristocratic few, [it] is now followed by the masses. . . . Fashion is one of the greatest forces in present-day life. It determines both the character and the direction of consumption. Fashion makes men shave every day, grow moustaches, cut their hair in certain ways, wear certain colors in hats, clothing and shoes, certain shapes in collars, four-in-hand neck-ties, trousers creased, and low shoes all the year round. For women it changes the tint of the face powder, the odor of the perfume, the wave of the hair, the position of the waist line, the length of the skirt, the color of the clothes, and the height of the heels. . . . Fashion causes all of these changes and, at the same time, makes people like it.[155]

To Elizabeth Hurlock, fashion liberated people from the burdens of the past:

> It has prompted nations to advance at a pace never apparent in those bound by rigid custom. It stimulates industry and inventiveness. It tends to break down the barriers between classes, lessens the feeling of national differences, and decreases the tendency toward national superiority, which is apt to develop when nations are differently clothed.[156]

For Hurlock, the homogenizing influence would be a predicator of international understanding; common goals and aspirations, common bonds of commodities would allow people to transcend ethnic identities and social economic differences. Fashion, it was argued, offered the promise of equality. It created a common aesthetic symbolism, which if at first provided an idiom of class identity, would increasingly provide an idiom of national and then international identity, transcending class.

Clearly, fashion did not deliver the same goods to everyone. Depending on who one was and where one shopped, fashions came in a variety of prices and qualities. The ready-made fashions that greeted immigrants to America, early in the century, were usually of "the cheapest and poorest quality. . . . The clothes wore badly and had frequently to be replaced."[157] But in a society presumed to embody a variety of experiences and possibilities, the institution of mass fashion helped to construct what Anspach had termed "a common subjective life."[158]

Despite fashion's promise of equality, the structure of the industry itself pointed up the inherent contradictions of the promise. Ready-to-wear fashions appeared in a variety of forms and prices reflecting concrete economic inequities of society. Yet the common element, established within the variety, was its most visible element: its surface, its style.

The proliferation of these symbolic surfaces, in a variety of prices and qualities, was structured—formally and informally—within the developing garment industry. Counterfeiting and "style piracy" are as old as mass fashion. They are an "underworld" without which mass fashion would not have come about. In the twenties Paul Nystrom exclaimed, "The copyist is everywhere," conceding that it was unavoidable. "Almost every one deplores design copying in principle, but, lacking any legal check, copying continues openly and brazenly as a dominant fact in our economic life."[159] For designers of originals, it was very difficult to protect against the piracy of styles. One of the few mechanisms of protection was the elevation of the label, the registered trademark, to an element of style itself. This tendency is widespread today, where many fashions are conspicuously marked by labels. Even here piracy is possible, although legally more risky. When one steps into a pair of fifty-dollar Calvin

Klein jeans, there is always the possibility that they are coun-
terfeits.

Beyond style copying, the proliferation and gradation of varieties of fashion have heavily depended upon the development of
synthetic fabrics. Beginning with rayon, the ability to capture
the look of luxurious fabrics and to reproduce it on a mass scale
with the use of chemicals has been a key to the egalitarianism of
the image.

If piracy and copying were the early means to the spread of
mass fashion, by the late 1940s the high-fashion houses themselves were joining in the proliferation of fashion. In 1947 Christian Dior entered into a partnership with Marcel Boussac, a
French manufacturer of cotton textiles, to produce a line of
mass-produced clothing offering various levels of quality. Thus,
they countered style piracy by creating an institutional amalgam
of original design and mass production:

> Dior and Boussac did not stop at top fashion; they founded a whole in-
> dustry around it. . . . The main business of Christian Dior commences
> with the selling of models at the fashion shows twice a year. Sometimes
> a model is sold one hundred times. . . . A buyer from overseas can do
> one of three things: he can buy a paper pattern of the model, but he
> may not label it Christian Dior; or he can buy a canvas copy and change
> it to suit his purposes naming it "Original-Christian-Dior-Copy"; or he
> can buy the original model in material which is the most expensive and
> is permitted to label it "Christian Dior." The more the buyer buys, the
> greater the discount he receives from Dior. Crowds of busily sewing
> midinettes are responsible for the quick finishing of garments so that the
> buyer can soon travel home with his new models safely in his suitcase.
> Exact drawings and reproductions of the new fashions are first allowed
> to appear a month after the fashion shows.[160]

The structure revolutionized *haute couture* and established
pathways by which the imprimatur of designers could, in a variety of forms, reach a range of markets. For American, French,
and Italian designers today, the pattern set by Dior is the basis
of their success. The pattern has been refined and has evolved,
but the principle continues. Today's designers give their franchise, their label, to manufacturers of garments whose factories
may be in Southeast Asia and whose customers feel blessed to
have acquired something above the common cut. If the bourgeois tradition in clothing began at a time when the wearing of

finery, after the French Revolution, was a risky business, today's fashion industry owes its existence to the fact that the wearing of finery became a right of citizenship.

From the period of 1917 to the present, a stock criticism of "Communist" countries has been the absence of finery: "drab," "dull," "unimaginative!" While socialist movements proclaimed struggle against social and economic inequity in the name of the people, capitalist enterprises were developing their own curiously appealing respite from inequity by denying its existence and backing this up with a democracy of images and universal fashion. The success of this phenomenon is irrefutable; the allure of fashion crosses the boundaries of social system and political ideology.

Youth, more than any other segment of the society, was caught by the windy voice of fashion. It was a language young people listened to, one that cajoled them at every turn, and one they learned to speak for themselves. By 1922, as shown in a survey taken among readers of the movie fan magazine *Photoplay*, teenage girls were assuming an increasingly decisive and autonomous role in the selection of clothing. Patterns of family budgeting were now subjected to the preferences and demands of adolescents. Of the girls surveyed by *Photoplay*, about half of them shopped for clothing alone, "without any guidance or aid from their parents." Personal tastes and the desire to attract the interests of young men were seen as the main considerations in the purchase of clothes. New principles of appearance and display had implanted themselves in family life. This trend marked a stark contrast to patterns that had predominated only a short time before; practices by which "women of mature years and experience"—mothers—had done most family shopping for clothing. Such a transformation had only altered family patterns of consumption; it was of enormous marketing significance to the clothing industry itself. By 1922, nearly all categories of garments found their primary markets among people under thirty years of age:

55 percent of the buyers of "dress goods" were under thirty;
53 percent of the buyers of ready-to-wear were under thirty;

61 percent of the buyers of underwear were under thirty;

65 percent of the buyers of hoisery were under thirty.[161]

Clothing manufacturers responded to and reinforced these trends, aiming merchandise primarily "to capture the interest of the younger generation." To those in the business of marketing mass fashion, daughters were far more receptive to the rhythms of the market than their mothers, whose impulses were more likely budgetary. Youth, embroiled in the "free market" courting practices of modernity, was perceived as a market whose "most absorbing problem is that of personal adornment." Merchants and manufacturers of the twenties fostered youthful, fashionable ideals, geared toward people for whom the "practical has little appeal." "Youth," it was perceived, "lives in today and allows tomorrow to take care of itself."[162]

Such a definition of "youth" cast the young as ideal consumers, unconcerned with questions of profligacy or waste; committed to an understanding of needs that placed them within the confines of a continually changing marketplace. As the older generation was often attuned to a different logic, issues of clothing and consumption occasioned considerable family conflict, then as now. Whereas in *customary* society elders taught the young, the consumer society reversed this physics, encouraging elders to look to youth for guidance. The marketplace reinforced this, needless to say, through advertising and goods, so that by the 1920s Elizabeth Hurlock noted that it was not uncommon for the young woman of between eighteen and thirty to influence the selections made by her mother.

Among immigrants, where parents held fast to tradition, this trend placed children in the role of Americanizers, instructing their parents in the ways and means of modern life. Antonio Mangano, in his autobiography *Sons of Italy*, tells of the time when his sister finally convinced his mother to abandon the dress practices of her past: "What a triumph it was when she succeeded in persuading her to wear a hat instead of a scarf over her head, and to put away her old shawl and wear an American coat."[163]

The finger-knowledge of the future was the province of youth, and only by following the dictates of the young could parents hope to be anything but mired in the past. In the wisdom of the garment industry, "youth was extremely suggestive and easily led."[164] What better group to serve as fashion leaders for the rest of society? The implicit logic, which extended beyond clothing to almost all areas of life, was that the "first duty of the citizen is to be a good consumer." This was the modern patriotic wisdom of David Cohn, a former Sears executive and a chronicler of "morals and manners" in the consumer age. It was a patriotic wisdom that assumed the triumph of youth over age, of the *new* over the *durable*.

Even during the Depression years, "commercial pressure for 'correct' clothing impaled the imaginations of the young." As the Lynds looked at "Middletown" again during the 1930s, they discovered that while fewer people could afford to buy new clothes, the high school was still a scene of driven fashion consciousness, of unrelenting "social pace."[165]

Seen in retrospect, the interaction between fashion and youth has been a double-edged sword. Learning the idiom of fashion may make one more susceptible to imagistic propaganda of the fashion industry, but one may also employ the vernacular of dress in one's own terms. This is a sidelight of fashion consciousness. If youth was wishfully described as suggestible, it was also true that youth employed and has continued to employ clothing as a form of rebellion. The fervor that accompanied the uses of fashion as a wedge against the ancient customs of family life has likewise been unleashed against the dictates of contemporary life.

In instructing manufacturers and designers on the intricacies of merchandising, Paul Nystrom was keenly aware of young people's capacity to *set* styles:

> The conflict of youth with convention grows out of the difficulty of learning the rules of society as set down by custom. . . . In the field of dress, as well as popular thinking and government, changes and new styles are generally sponsored by youth, and even in dress these new styles are often offered with all the ardor of revolution. The new fashion is promoted by appeals to freedom.[166]

The tendency of youth in revolt to appropriate the social language of dress has been an important feature of the past hundred years. It played a role in the dismantling of traditional social bonds, but also within social movements, both cultural and political. It is a part of the modern political sensibility, a visible statement of resistance.

The visibility of the statement, however, contributes to its ambiguity. While it serves the energies of resistance, it also can feed the smolderings of consent: as a reproducible surface, it can itself be merchandised; its meaning, changed. As this happens, freedom becomes something to be bought, alone. Collective origins of the image are hidden. While much of today's fashions still emulate upper-class styles, the emulation of the rebellious, self-motivated uses of the fashion vernacular is also widespread. As clothing is employed, spontaneously, to burst through the confines of convention, it can also be magnified by the channels of mass production, by the modern instruments of communication. It then becomes part of a new consensus. A voice of outrage and self-determination becomes a whimper of docile uniformity. When this process takes place, and objections are raised, the industry shrugs its shoulders and says: "The people set the styles." Most often, when this happens, the price goes up: the final insult.

The Commerce of Choice

The major accomplishment of the mass-fashion industry was its ability to plumb the wells of popular desire. Against a backdrop of historical denial, its dazzling array of wares offered the symbolism of a world turned upside down. As it became increasingly available, it was embraced with energetic fervor.

Fashion, once the prerogative of those who enjoyed leisure and economic privilege, became the insignia of freedom, available to all. Yet fashion was really an odd admixture. As it intertwined with the instruments of mass production and consumption, its "freedom" was underlined by uniformity. The success of the industry was in its capacity to produce and distribute standardized goods, laced with the lingo of individual choice and self-expression.

The contradictions that lay within the institution of mass fashion did not escape the critical eye of Paul Poiret, a designer of the old elite school of couturiers. Poiret believed fashion design to be an art, its aura dependent upon originality and spontaneity. Mass production, he contended, robbed it of its meaning. As Walter Benjamin noted in his essay "The Work of Art in the Age of Mechanical Reproduction," when a piece of art is reproduced its commercial potential may be enhanced, but it loses some of its aura. As originals are mass-produced, Benjamin argued, the elite lose their hold on a traditional province of imagistic power.

Visiting the United States in the early years of the century, Poiret was disturbed by the translation of fashion into terms of mass consumption. While respectful of America's ability to produce goods en masse, he saw the society as lacking in "artistic spirit." The women of America, embroiled as they were in the lure of mass fashion, seemed to lack "personality."

To Poiret, these failings were unavoidable. Massive in size and population—unlike the "little land of France"—the United States was not amenable to the "licence or libertarian customs" that were necessary to artistic creativity. America was best at display of energy and endurance—"sport and business"—but lacking in "poets, musicians, or painters."

Looking over American society and its institution of mass fashion, Poiret concluded that there was a suppression of "feelings," a tendency toward "control."

> Its population must be canalized into rigidly straight channels, like the roads there, and protected from all risk of meeting with accident. . . . Let them not say that they expect in the future a generation of aesthetes and lovers of art.[167]

While the development of mass fashion was predicated on the coexistence of spontaneity and uniformity, this combination escaped Poiret's sensibility. Poiret's experiences as he traveled across the country, a celebrity of fashion, only reinforced his cynicism.

Visiting a school in Chickasha, Oklahoma, Poiret was enlisted to address a group of three thousand girls on matters of color coordination. When he found that the girls had difficulty understanding his advice, he was forced to perform personal consultations for half of the audience.

> The girls' Directress gave permission to the pupils of the senior class to parade past me in order to learn from my own mouth which was the

color that each ought to adopt. Thus, I saw file by in front of me 1,500
virgins, into whose eyes I stared to discover the color of their irises, and
I had to say immediately, like a seer, the tone that suited them. I said:
"Blue, green, garnet," and the young ladies withdrew content.[168]

The tale evokes the unity of the assembly line and the promise
of individual choice implicit in the ideology of mass fashion.
From the vantage point of the girls, they were receiving the tools
of individuality; for Poiret they were a parade of barely indistinguishable numbers, demanding discipline and regulation.

By the 1920s, the merchandising of individuated styles had
gone beyond Poiret's parade of virgins. Fashion was increasingly
promulgated by more sophisticated marketing and merchandising techniques. Insofar as "the people" had a voice in the delineation of fashion, that voice was increasingly monitored and studied to promote more effective retailing. The reconciliation of
individuality and standardization demanded an elaborate and
imaginative structure. Concerns like those raised by Poiret had
little place within it.

As clothing was an important arena of popular expression—
often a self-defined voice—the fashion industry depended on access to that expression. Access often began with the development of fashion research departments within clothing concerns.
These departments, utilizing the methods of style-consulting
committees, boards, or juries, kept watch on new designs before
they went into production.[169] "Trends of taste" were examined,
and were employed more and more in the design of goods.

Fashion, perhaps more than any other area of consumption,
was a piece of the marketplace that displayed an interaction between spontaneous choice and mass-produced goods. The process by which social desire was translated into commodified
forms was more present within the realm of fashion—on the surface of things—than anywhere else in the unfolding consumer
society. This is why the term "manipulation" is inadequate to describe fashion merchandising, although the corporate profit motive certainly plays its part in the drama. The capitalist process
of producing fashion on a mass scale, rather, was a fusion of expressed, popular desire and the powerful ability to replicate that
materialization in a mass-produced, mass-marketed form.

Beyond monitoring popular innovations in style, the analysis of consumer patterns took on the shape of modern consumer survey research. Past sales records were screened; sales tests and direct inquiries were pursued in the form of personal calls and field studies. There was a general development of modern retailing techniques: stock controls; inventories; customer and sales counts; unsuccessful sales studies; store-by-store customer-control studies—all were ways of attempting to measure changing tastes.[170]

While these methods may be seen as ways of trying to "paralyze the critical powers of an individual with the result that he or she follows the lead, whatever that lead may be," fashion merchandisers attempted to surround the actual sales process with an aura of individuality.[171] "One of the most important points in selling fashion goods is the necessity of individualizing every sale and of avoiding any attempt to handle either merchandise or customers in a mass way," warned Paul Nystrom.[172] Many retailers—particularly chain and department stores—ignored Nystrom's dictum, but more recently his approach has been adopted enthusiastically. Even in large department stores, serving vast herds of customers, the trend has been toward a "boutique" style of merchandising, creating the aura of a small shop within an arena of mass selling. If clothing is a symbolic route to individual freedom, all connections to the mass are best denied.

Concerned with developing responsive markets, fashion merchandisers of the twenties began to develop a more refined consumer typology. If the first clothing typology was rooted in sizing, the new typology plumbed the diversity of psyches. Attitudes and approaches to life were sorted out into a manageable bunch of personality types; each was then correlated to a fashion type.

Bullock's Department Store in Los Angeles "devised a list of personality types which [was] . . . fairly representative of the work done in this line."[173] The store developed six categories of customers, and divided women's fashion sales among them. The six were

1. Romantic—slender, youthful;
2. Statuesque—tall, remote, blonde;
3. Artistic—enigmatic, suggestive of the "foreign";

4. Picturesque—soft outline;

5. Modern;

6. Conventional—older, stouter, economical.

While definitions of types varied, all were geared toward the routinization of sales, unifying the vagaries of desire with the conformity of the marketplace. A new way of understanding oneself, in relation to society, was emerging. Linked to matters of personal decoration, it broke from a past in which *who you were* in society was a matter of social and economic class. The new structure was more superficially defined, and one's classification was, ostensibly, a matter of choice. Some might choose "romantic," others "artistic." Social identity, according to the schema, was there on the racks, to be bought.

Consumer types were often correlated to an appeal to intrinsic human motives and instincts, much as the advertising industry of the twenties was attempting to sell a broad variety of goods by appeal to instinct, impulse, and fundamental hungers.[174] As they developed, these "hungers" were linked to a historical tradition. Fashion, as in the bourgeois tradition of the nineteenth century, was primarily defined in terms of women. Types, styles, and colors proliferated in women's clothes, while men's clothing continued to be relatively sedate, a "cloak of morality." Along with mass fashion, women were sold a moral code of family life. Even if poor women were forced by circumstance to work outside the home, the fashion ideal was one of docility and uselessness. Women, as they bought a wardrobe and were coached to follow the lead of ever-changing fashion, became family symbols of success. Like the wives of nineteenth-century bourgeois before them, they carried the wealth, or more precisely in their case the *look* of wealth, of the family. Clothing was an objective representation, for each woman, of her husband's ability to provide for her. Mass fashion made such a display all the more possible, if, at the same time, all the less meaningful.

To Paul Nystrom, fashion represented a ray of light, a seasonal panorama of promise and change, in what was otherwise an often-dismal present. Separated from customary bonds, the hunger for meaning weighed heavily over the lives of modern Americans. They were, he felt, subjects of an existential philosophy of "futility"; the burdensome reverie of mass, industrial existence. It was this condition, he argued, that made fashion-merchandising techniques so successful. The engineered individuality and aesthetics of mass fashion were, if thoughtfully merchandised, a vitalizing tonic to the "fatigue and boredom" that plagued the mass of people, caught as they were, questioning "the purpose of life itself."[175]

While Poiret had decried American mass fashion as a failure of imagination, the garment industry erected a market based on the stifled imaginations of its clientele. Within such a context, mass fashion developed as a primary channel of expression and desire. Methods of selling and of gauging the market, though predicated on productive uniformity, were geared to responding to the cries of individual and social need. As Nystrom said, evaluating the appeal of fashion:

> It is not easy to jump out of oneself, but in the effort to make such changes as are possible, it is easy enough, particularly for people who have the means, to change one's dress, and the mental effects of change of clothing are quite remarkable. . . . The desire for new sensations and the spirit of adventure . . . are powerful forces.[176]

Where it might be argued that the desire for change would be more meaningfully pursued in the realms of concerted social action, fashion offered a continually changing outlet that located personal fulfillment, a sense of self, alongside the canals of social conformity.

History and Clothes Consciousness

Within the fashion codes of nineteenth-century bourgeois life, it was a woman's role to display the economic and social success of her husband's virtue and enterprise. Though relegated to the status of a passive emblem, she was also a clarion of the moral order, proclaiming its legitimacy and its historical mission.

In the twentieth century, amid a growing challenge from socialism, the florescence of a fashionably dressed working class has served a similar function. Where working people had once looked as poor as they were, now they were able to take on the appearance of abundance. Not only did the evolution of ready-to-wear fashions appeal to the ancient desires of people schooled by scarcity; it also became one of the most splendid and cited examples of capitalist society's claim to deliver the goods, to respond to human needs. Even in the midst of dire poverty, the iconography of fashion is ubiquitous and casts its spell. Clothing has become—for more and more people—an arena of social dialogue in which desires are expressed, and symbolically met. Within the expansive parameters of fashion, questions of *class*; *sexuality* and *gender*; and conflicting vectors of *resistance* and *conformity* have played themselves out visibly and dramatically. In a consumer society, the language and meaning of objects are fused with those of the marketplace.

The unlikely interaction between the images of freedom and spontaneity and the uniformity of mass production and merchandising stands at the heart of this development and is the dynamic of mass fashion. But beyond this, the interaction raises fundamental questions about the industrial culture in which we live, its achievements and its contradictions. The tensions between spontaneity and uniformity speak to the issue of what it means to be a person, living in the shadows of commercial enterprise, striving for the democratic objective of self-determination for all. Adjacent to the world of fashion lies a turbulent society in conflict. Fashion bears the imprint of its dissonance and outrage, but it also temporizes.

Over the past five decades, discord and social clash have been evident upon the landscape of fashion, as they have in American culture as a whole. The 1950s in the United States was a period lit by the radioactive afterglow of war. If the fact of the atomic bomb made for a new sense of horror in the general consciousness, it was also—with its unfathomable expression of energy and waste—a decisive metaphor for a mature consumer culture. Insofar as *consumerism* represented the principles of conspicuous waste and the domination over nature, the atom was a potent symbol for the new way of life that was unfolding. Under the immeasurable weight of *impending doom*, a consolidation of commercial power and the growth of consumer industries gave shape to a way of life.

Fueled by the postwar economic boom, an "American way of

life," permeated by the democracy of images, took hold for un-precedented numbers of people. Material circumstances changed; the architecture of daily life assumed new forms; new and uniform symbols moved beyond marks of prosperity, to be-ing marks of *loyalty*.

Many of these new circumstances and symbols centered on the rise of suburbia. Swiftly populated by a migration of mil-lions, the suburbs were seen as a refuge of family life away from the exigencies of urban existence. These new developments placed people, particularly women and children, away from the centers of production and commerce. The initial attraction of suburban living was that it responded to the deeply felt needs of the population—desires for autonomy and space. Against the noise, dirt, and multitude of the industrial cityscape, the suburbs claimed to elevate "family life" as a safe and private reserve, im-munized from the corruption of the metropolis. Once the ideal of wealthy Victorians, "family service" was canonized as the universal feminine ideal, responsive to trends in the labor force, which were pushing women out of jobs they had assumed dur-ing the war years. Suburban plots offered a miniaturized, mass-marketed mimicry of the estates of a landed gentry. Suburban homes were standardized parodies of independence, of leisure, and, most important of all, of the property that made the first two possible. The American ideal, in the era of postwar growth, was that of the *landed consumer*. "Castles" were offered in a variety of models, each tied to a romantic, preindustrial motif: *ranch*, *colonial*, and so forth.

Yet the independence and escape offered by suburban ideolo-gy never took one very far from the scrutiny of one's neighbors. The vertical configuration of the city was made horizontal, but the seclusion of the land was illusory. Consistent with the world of appearance and display, images were deceptive. Predicated on the notion of individualism, yet erected as a parade of repetition, the search for a community of individuals was overwhelmed by the imperative of display once again. "Keeping up with the Joneses" became a cliché of suburban living. Entrenched in a commitment to prosperous leisure, suburban families became a spawning ground for fierce social competition. "Presentability" imposed its tyranny on manicured lawns, and, more and more, on manicured people. Presentation of self was an essential activity, displayed through the "picture windows" of new "developments."

Within this new theater of appearance and display, and in the lives of its inhabitants, clothing played an important part. Americans were expected to dress a certain way, and the avalanche of commercial imagery that accompanied the postwar boom — magazines; film; advertisements; and the new "Information Bomb," television — supplied constant reminders. Doris Day, *Father Knows Best*, Betty Furness, *Ronald Reagan for General Electric* — these were the voices and imagistic role models of suburbanization.

As the appearances of land and housing were supposed to be romantic replicas of the estates and ranches of a nineteenth-century landed class, clothing followed suit. The world of home and the world of work were dramatically cleaved from each other. This was echoed in the sartorial separation of women and men. Women's clothing ideals in the fifties, as materialized by the garment industry, struck close to the spirit, if not the specific prescriptions of Victorian womanhood. Leisure, delicacy, and at times the preponderance of cloth were marks of suburban womanhood. For "knocking around," Bermuda shorts, sports shirts, and the like provided the beginnings of a massive leisure-wear industry. Dressing up, women drew from Victorian prescriptions more specifically. Skirts flowed over stiff under-layers of crinoline; pastel colors provided a symbolic immunity from the proximity of grime and work, as they also did from the exotic hues of *shameful* sensuality. Even at wifely "chores" — rarely referred to as "work" — women turned to the ambiguous symbolism of the "frilly apron." Sweaters, push-up bras, and girdles conspired together, focusing their effects on the reproductive components of a woman's body, not unlike the declaration made by nineteenth-century corsetry. For leisure, women wore "sneakers," like the kids. Otherwise, high-heeled shoes — to the extreme — added to the hobbled presentation of American womanhood. Amid an ideology of unsullied chastity, women were reduced to a primarily sexual identity, or to the identity of a child. Makeup, deodorants, and other visual and olfactory barriers were set up to protect womanhood from personhood. Identity was, by prescription, no more than the assembling of a "self."

Insofar as a woman held to the prescribed ideal, she became an advertisement for her own inadequacies in the world of paid work, concurrently advertising her husband's adequacy as a provider. True to the sexual ethics of Victorianism, she was delicate, childlike, unsuited for worldly engagement, the bearer of her man's (and her nation's) economic success. At the same time she was a patriotic symbol; fashion and modern appliances shared the spotlight with automobiles in the theater of national destiny.

In the emanations of the mass culture, the suburban wife was also characterized as the bearer of the guilt of sin. While the culture encouraged her to buy and assemble a fashionable veneer, her commitments to the marketplace were simultaneously ridiculed as wasteful and frivolous. Situation comedies of the time were populated by a parade of women whose primary identity was that of "mad shopper." Hobbled, decorated, infantilized, isolated, and scorned, she was ensnared in a trap not unlike that against which Jane Addams and other expatriates from Victorianism had rebelled. Within the "snare of preparation" of suburban womanhood, women were at best the receptacles of male adoration; at worst, the targets of male frustration.

The masculine ideal was also true to nineteenth-century bourgeois patterns of attitude and dress. Wearing a cloak of morality, the man went off to work in the enervating whirl of the city, giving of himself to sustain the suburban dream. The austerity of the business suit—gray flannel, pin-striped, and so on—expressed a uniform commitment to hard work, dedication to family and society, and explicitly denied spontaneity. For men, war and prosperity were intertwined by recent memory, and their sense of "duty" and economic pursuit coalesced into a style. To defend the rights of the folks at home "against the Communist threat," men were expected to submit to the terms of uniformity right down to the crew cut that was fashionable in the period. Unswerving loyalty to nation, to home, to place of work, and to the principles of consumerism was the sartorial message. So unimaginative, unemotional, indistinguishable, so bland was this masculine ideal that by the late fifties, the men's clothing industry embarked on a special campaign to sell more goods, to expand masculine interest in fashion. As the masculine ideal had been permeated by an ethic of denial, marketing strategy attempted to reach men through women: "Mothers, wives, girl friends, and secretaries," reasoned Pierre Martineau, "can do a tremendous job of exerting pressure on a man to make him dress right." The men's apparel businesses, unhappy with the economic implications of the suburban ethic, sought to mold men into a "seasonal, volatile, style-conscious class."[177]

Children in the 1950s were expected to emulate their parents, and did. The successful and popular suburban girl was a "clotheshorse"; each day at school she would show her envious classmates that her closets were bulging with an endless supply of color-coordinated outfits and accessories. Boys had somewhat more latitude, since rough-and-tumble was a rite of passage on the route to the austere responsibilities of manhood. Colors were muted; cut was simple, double-reinforced at the knees; sensible; "clean-cut." If the display of cloth and decoration was requisite among girls, it was not the case for boys. An eighth-grader in 1957 made the mistake of going to school one day in a pair of red pants, bought for him by a mother unschooled in sartorial logic. As he entered his first-period math class, his pants caused an immediate commotion among classmates. His teacher was so outraged by the transgression, and so committed to the role of disciplinarian, that the boy had five points immediately subtracted from his average. At midday the boy was sent home for causing a disruption. Needless to add, he never wore his red pants again. Schools underwrote the dictates of propriety by enforcing unwritten dress codes, maintaining the standards of fashionable decorum, of social order.

On the surfaces of suburban life and in its panoply of imagery, the imprimature of purchasable "leisure" was in force everywhere. Here was a world far from the corruptions of the city and the scarcities of a rural past. True to the patterns of Victorianism, home was a retreat from "the real world." Mass fashion adapted to this suburban motif, under the rubric of "leisure wear." All could now aspire to the symbolic language of affluence, and the postwar consumer industries were standardizing a symbolically charged mode of life that fulfilled aspirations on the monthly installment plan. "Landed" consumers had little of the social wealth or power of those whom they emulated, but they could wear the emblems of wealth and power. These emblems formed the panoply of a new suburban conformity, beacons that illuminated an unfolding definition of American prosperity. Suburbs were an abundant theater of commodities and display.

Fortune magazine, in a marketing profile of the suburbs in 1953, noted that residents were "sharply sensitive to group opinion"; had a "large and growing 'discretionary' income" with which to buy a wide variety of consumer goods; and were psychologically "preoccupied with spending problems . . . particularly with expenditures on items that are not necessities."[178] Increasingly, argued *Fortune*, suburbs would be "the clue to the future, as far as marketing went. Here was the "average American group," which national merchandisers should target for their goods. In clothing, in automobiles, in appliances and home furnishings, suburbia provided an ideological template for the shaping of a uniform, national market. The "mythical individual" at whom businesses were encouraged to aim their products was the *suburbanite*. In a period of rapid economic growth and the intense political suspicion of McCarthyism, suburbia provided a tyranically strident and uniform measure of who *belonged* and who didn't.

Yet, ironically, as the suburban life-style was promoted over and over, its limits became increasingly manifest. Here was the language of "individualism," carved out of slavish conformity. "Happiness" was ghettoized in the shopping centers of regimented acquisition. In many ways, the leisure-time motif of the suburbs amounted to a philosophical statement of the contradictions of twentieth-century American development.

The suburbs were a watershed in the unfolding of Americanization and consumption. They were the "intrinsic outcome" of a society of "mobile individuals," living in an environment where production and consumption were—to all appearances —unconnected, shorn of their past, existing only for the present. Suburbia canonized an industrial system in which goods were invested with potent symbolic meaning by the marketers and promoters, a symbolism that totally obscured their source of origin. The suburban lifestyle was one in which consumption was a patriotic duty, encouraged with no hint of the social or environmental costs involved. Separated from the world of work, suburbs were islands whose inhabitants were virtually blind to the reality of the surrounding seas. Suburbia existed for itself. The rest of the world had no other function than to feed its appetite for goods.

It was this lack of vision, this insularity, that ignited a massive disaffection from the conformity of suburban existence. While the suburbs offered a consumable apparition of leisure, they did not easily allow for an understanding of that which lay beyond its codes. Both urban and rural existence, in spite of their shortcomings, had made a broad world available. Their inhabitants understood much about what was inscrutable in the suburbs. Rural Americans, and migrants from rural pasts elsewhere, had understood the ecological laws of survival. Living off the land, depending directly upon it for their continuity, they shared a respect for the earth, for the nature, which bound them to the millennia of human experience.

The cities provided a reference from this sensibility and functioned to enlarge a worldview in other ways. Cities did not hide the world, but gave it new dimensions, in the flow of migrations, in a mosaic of cultures, languages and skin tones that reverberated in the streets. Sexual possibilities were expanded by the very proximity of bodies. Different worlds were always in contact and collision, as work and life commingled, inexorably intertwined. Both the country and the city, in their own ways, brought people in touch with the world, its breadth of cultures, its primordial drives, its terms of survival.

The suburbs were divorced from the understandings of either. The great claim of suburban living was escape — from work, cultural multiplicity, passion — and it set itself against the notion of land as a resource necessary to survival. In the suburbs, land itself had entered the realm of total display. Suburbia perpetrated a vision of the world according to the narrow categories of consumerism; it was an arena of appearance, of spending, of retreat.

As the preeminent cultural ideal of the fifties, suburbia came increasingly under attack from those beyond its margins of concern. Its conformism ate away at many who lived, desperately and discreetly, within. The lack of vision; the mindless spending for its own sake; the merchandised conformism began to alienate suburban youth by the end of the fifties.

Insofar as suburbia was elevated — commercially, culturally, politically — as the embodiment of "typical" America, its limits came to be seen as America's limits, and people began crying out against America. Voices banished, suppressed, or ignored in the pacific motifs of the leisure-time dream were being heard articulating an increasingly provocative critique and alternatives. The land of consumer plenty was being characterized, more and more, as one of spiritual impoverishment, sexlessness, of "one-dimensionality." Image was attacked by rhythm. Hidden cultures emerged. Music, poetry, political chants heralded the coming of resistance.

"America," wailed poet Allen Ginsberg, in a poem dated January 17, 1956, "I've given you all and now I'm nothing." To Ginsberg, and other voices of artistic opposition, America was the thief of passion and compassion; the robber of personhood, of freedom.

> *I can't stand my own mind.*
> *America when will we end the human war?*
> *Go fuck yourself with your atom bomb.*
> *I don't feel good don't bother me. . . .*
>
> *America when will you be angelic?*
> *When will you take off your clothes? . . .*
>
> *America why are your libraries full of tears?*
> *America when will you send your eggs to India?*
> *I'm sick of your insane demands.*
> *When can I go into the supermarket and buy*
> *   what I need with my good looks? . . .*
>
> *Your machinery is too much for me.*[179]

As clothing had been central to the elaboration of a suburban uniformity, it was also central to its undoing. As "Beat" poet and playwright Michael McClure explained his art, it was a vital resistance, against the backdrop of a forbidden climate of conformism.

It was like being on an elevator containing a lot of people with crew cuts and pin-striped suits. As I looked around them, I realized that I couldn't get off the elevator unless I discovered some alchemical or superhuman way of doing it. The way to escape was to create poems that were living creatures. My hope was that my poems might become alive, become living organisms through the energy that I threw into them. I wanted poems to grow their own eyes, ears, noses, legs, and teeth.

My poetry was not the expression of the ideas that I'd been taught by the culture, but the expression of the fleshy facts of myself that I'd discovered in spite of the culture. And I think that's what all of us were doing—we were in the act of discovering ourselves, not what we had been instructed to discover by the culture.[180]

Mass life and suburban existence were seen as straitjackets; sartorial codes especially put the mind in uniform. Adjacent to the Beat revolt and to its powerful musical counterpart—rock 'n' roll—a new style of dress was adopted. Spontaneous choices asserted themselves against the uniformity of national symbols. Pastel sports shirts were answered by denim pants and black turtlenecks, as suburbia was answered by the underworlds of work and bohemianism. Antifashion became a conspicuous weapon of outrage.

Others raised a jagged edge against the smooth informality of suburbanism. The struggle of blacks to overturn the burdens of racism and oppression was heard as a dissonant rumble against the contented quietude of suburbia. As this rumble mounted to a roar, the culture of black America shook the underpinnings of the *mainstream*. First the flashy finery of the "tenderloin," worn by such entertainers as Little Richard, then Afros, dashikis— symbols of the roots of African-Americans—expanded the sartorial revolt. Through music, politics, through the geyser of the *countercultural* refusal, passions suppressed or obfuscated by the consumerist conformity of the fifties erupted into the field of vision. By the midsixties, the world at large was battling the suburban sensibility. Peasants of Asia and Latin America, Africans, shaking the chains of colonialism, dissonant and disaffected young Americans and Europeans were collaborators in a rhythmic panorama of revolt against the values enshrined in the suburbs of the United States.

The clothes that played such an important role in this revolt were assembled from the assorted cultural battlefields upon which the process of Americanization had been fought. Self-consciously nonconformist, uniforms of work and alienation, of distant cultures and angry underworlds came together as a symbolic rejection of the bland consumerism of "typical" Americanism. Blue jeans, peasant blouses and frocks, and army surplus collaborated to repudiate the standardized "democracy" of images in a return of repressed realities, worn as conspicuously as possible. These were drawn from the countless worlds scorned by the enforced compact of leisure and abundance. Labor, war, and the neglected cultures and subcultures of America (Native American, hipster, ethnic, nudist, juvenile delinquent) inspired a revolt of sartorial sensibility. In a society predicated on the marketing of images, images became a weapon of resistance.

In the 1960s, young people appropriated outrageous admixtures of clothing as a popular form of expression. The most potent, the most sensual, the most theatrical idioms of design erupted in spontaneity and diversity along with the worlds from which they came. Almost overnight, the consumer industries of mass fashion were out of step, "out of fashion." Where fashion industries did make waves, it was on the crest of the wave of social movement. The miniskirt was an outrageous expression of rejection, aimed at the prim niceties of suburbia and fueled by an impassioned popular mood. Yet it too was part of a fashion cycle that aimed at achieving a regularity, a conformity in the market. The counterculture made such regularity elusive and unmanageable. Diana Vreeland, noted fashion expert, described the breakdown of the fashion mainstream during the sixties:

> A youthquake was starting. High society had disintegrated incredibly . . . suddenly it seemed everyone had gravitated to his own private world and the center was lost. Meanwhile, the young did things their way without regard to the old world. And anyone who wasn't with them made no difference at all.[181]

The fashion industry, successful for decades in dictating the sartorial definitions of democracy on a seasonable basis, was now chasing the public from behind. Fashion, or antifashion, was riding the crest of popular initiative. Images and meanings were actively constructed; clothing was increasingly an exercise in imagination, in unpredictability. A proliferation of new and powerful surfaces represented a shift of creative initiative, from the design rooms of industry to the emancipated intuition of people in search of autonomy and personhood.

Yet if it appeared for a time that mass fashion had been overturned by this outpouring of popular expression, the sixties was *rather* a period in which the machinery of mass fashion was forced to confront its limits, to adjust itself.

The culture of the fifties was built on the ability to fabricate images and meanings and to distribute them en masse. A uniform and mass-produced culture was inoculated by the imagery of casual leisure, sold as a national product. Yet the superficiality of suburban identity made it eminently vulnerable. Piercing through the veneers of suburban life, many people confronted the general discontent, the cultural price paid by people in an industrial, consumer culture: standardization, monotony, the eradication of social bonds and understandings, a "philosophy of futility."

If the power of surface imagery sustained the development of the suburban landscape, it also contributed to its undoing. The ability to assume surfaces of meaning provided radical youth in the sixties with an essential tool of revolt. The revolt established alternative imagery, alternative information, alternative meaning as the conspicuous agents of political and cultural display.

Clothing was a prime vehicle of repudiation. If the mainstream imagery propagated a sharp demarcation of gender and the insularity of a nuclear family, alternative imagery challenged notions of gender and raised the question of communalism to the fore. If the dominant culture clothed gray industrialism in the Dacron pastels of suburbia, the counterculture examined the principle of play in the cotton garments of work. If the fifties was a time when to be "un-American" was to be immediately suspect, the sixties assumed the vestments of unassimilated ethnicity, particularly of the Third World. If the fifties had promoted the nobility of the cowboy and his expansionist violence, the clothing of the sixties spoke up for the Indian with beads and headbands. The staunch sexual divisions of suburban life were answered by motifs that made gender increasingly ambiguous. The olive drab of war was turned against itself, becoming a uniform of pacifism. The capacity to give images and meanings to objects, so exploited by the vernacular of the consumer society, was turned against itself with a vengeance. Clothing of revolt became all the more possible among people schooled by a world in which meanings and images were infinitely manipulable. The consumer society, with its heavy implantation of imagery, had supplied its opposition with the visual terminology of revolt.

The phenomenon of mass fashion had begun nearly one hundred years before, at a time when capitalism was under widespread attack as a social system. For laboring people, squalor and exploitation had marked the emergence of the industrial system. "Wage slavery" and vast chasms of possibility shaped their experiences. Slowly the modern ready-to-wear garment industry emerged, sharing a potent image-making capacity with other emerging industries of mass impression. A democracy of images, compelling and promising, began to define the landscape of a new industrial, consumer culture.

Rising from a world in which formal and informal sumptuary laws had predominated, mass fashion appropriated the symbolic codes of status and made them available on a mass scale. For people nurtured by denial and living in a world increasingly defined by the principles of appearance and display, mass fashion served as a powerful lens of expectation. The democracy of images came together, promising to fill the thirsty wells of hope, of long-standing desires.

By the 1950s the tradition of mass fashion was deeply entrenched. The ability to standardize the imagos of leisure and status had been refined, reaching a point where these had become the clichés of a mass-produced existence. The lure of mass fashion, heralded in the twenties as the apotheosis of an industrial capitalist democracy, was now under assault as a desert of perpetual sameness.

The 1960s, in a cultural insurgence, redefined the terms of opposition, of challenge to industrial life. Where mass fashion had once appealed to the hungers of new, industrial citizens, now it evoked a sense of cultural famine. The sartorial radicalism of the sixties posed an articulate statement of alienation from the confines of suburbanism, establishing new sartorial idioms. These reflected, far more than the uniform fabrications of the fifties, the wishes and desires, the concerns and aspirations, of Americans coming of age during the post-World War II era. Donning blue jeans offered an egalitarian repulsion against the symbolic luxuries of imitation. Putting on a dashiki was a turning away from the Western European aesthetic, which had motivated fashion and dominated the marketplace. Peasant blouses celebrated the simplicity of rural life above the artifices of modernity. Responding to Ginsberg's wail, when America took off its clothes, it repudiated the conventional promises of mass fashion. Sartorial revolt provided a brilliant imagistic rendering of social demands and popular expressions.

Within this context, fashion merchandising evolved a response, attempting to appropriate and reproduce its visual language of resistance. As mass fashion in the nineteenth century had engaged the hopes of an industrial population, the marketers of the 1970s engaged, more and more, the critique of industrial uniformity. A mass fashion has emerged, over the past ten years, that draws its style and structure from the questions of the sixties. Images of refusal, autonomy, and cultural diversity, permeated by patterns of sexual liberation and working-class culture, are the warp and woof of recent fashion marketing. The language of diversity and revolt, born in an outrage against a merchandised reality, has entered the parlance of merchandising. The genius of a consumer society, to translate popular aspirations into the terms of the marketplace, has asserted itself once again.

The sartorial revolt of the 1960s was not merely a presentation of different clothing styles. It was also a voice of people whose lives could not be lived within the constrictions of the fifties' cultural conservatism. The radicalism was, to a large extent, a statement by people of who they were, who they had become, how the terms of American society had made the dictates of suburbanism impossible for them. In assuming a new way of dressing, people were saying much about who they were.

Though the voices are quiet today, the visual and conspicuous statement of sixties radicalism provided a wide range of industries with a powerful lesson in marketing, in diversification. If within the clothing styles of the sixties lay new and critical understandings of family life, sexual life, notions about work and consumption, and questions of cultural identity, the fashion industry from the early seventies onward has produced goods that are, largely, a response to this challenge. The sartorial mode of resistance produced the pattern by which the clothes of the present are cut and sold. T-shirts; jeans; pantsuits for women; peasant, gypsy, western and outlaw styles; the embroideries of non-Western ideals; the influence of homosexual culture within the styles worn in the culture at large: all of these trends have been drawn from the critical repository of the sixties.

A look across the pages of fashion magazines reinforces the pattern. Today there is no fashion; there are only *fashions*. The diversity of revolt has been translated into a diversity of markets. The entire historical and cultural panorama of clothing is available. Blue jeans are high fashion; emblems of egalitarianism become weapons of social competition and sexual struggle. Discos enforce sumptuary laws, requiring clientele to be dressed in the now elevated finery of "designer jeans"; laws of exclusivity persist, turned on their heads. Original meanings are lost or rearranged, as designer Calvin Klein proclaims: "Jeans are sexual. Why do you think people buy jeans?" Alongside designer jeans, the delicate armors of Victorian womanhood can be purchased. With women increasingly entering the work force, mannish clothing becomes the garb of employability, shorn of its earlier rebellious meaning. Even the styles of the "Ivy League" fifties have made a comeback in the pseudo-tongue-in-cheek form of the "Preppie look."

Elsewhere are the notorious garments of "shameful love." Sold boldly from shop windows, such items are also available at suburban buying parties, not unlike those formerly reserved for such domesticated items as Tupperware. Against the sharp challenge of cultural and political diversity posed in the 1960s, recent developments in fashion have seen an unfolding of market diversity. The images come from everywhere. The history of fashion, in all its contradiction, has imprinted itself, in symphony, upon the surfaces of the marketplace. Its multiplicity of display dazzles — a break from the convention of standardized ideals — while the objective terms of daily life become increasingly dull, decreasingly promising.

Today's fashions are completely impregnated by the claim that they too make war against uniformity; they enhance one's

ability to "do one's own thing." Matched ensembles, once a garment-industry staple, have given way increasingly to interchangeable components. In fashion pages, women are encouraged to blaze a "personal path through the plethora of
current fashion" in assembling the styles that fit their lives.[182]

Looking back to a time when fashion codes were inviolable,
Enid Nemy writes that the old rules no longer stick. "The old
signals aren't working, and there aren't any new decipherable
ones. . . . Women now are wearing what they like, not what
they're told to like."[183] In a flourish of libertarian lingo, fashion
writers inform readers that "all of the old rules for what to wear,
when to wear it and where, have been tossed out."[184] Such statements come in magazines, flanked by ads that likewise promise
freedom, independence, uniqueness, status.

No rules, only choices is the current claim; selling goods is still
the game. The parameters of freedom are circumscribed, once
again, by a renovated strategy of the market. Learning a lesson
from the outbreak of sartorial autonomy that characterized the
fashion vernacular in the sixties, today's fashions offer the
weapons of resistance and compliance in one, ready to wear. Image and information, recast and readapted to the machinery of
fashion marketing, to the politics of culture, assert a revolt
against conformity once again. A multiplicity of imagery
abounds; meaning is lost. The sartorial tools of social revolt provide the fashions and surfaces of a society gripped by quietude.
Next to them, on the shelves, lie the sartorial tools of constriction, the cloaks of morality. It is all there. Everyone can be
anyone.

In fashion, as in much of the imagery of a mass culture, we
confront the echoes of our own desires. The history of mass
fashion is one of a powerful conjuration, implanting the idiom
of people's longings upon the outer textures of corporate enterprise; beneath the surface lies a continuity of frustration, a
squelching of initiative. A perpetual vernacular of critical, popular expression—torn from the confines of the marketplace—is
the only alternative to the echo of mass fashion, to the claims
made by a democracy of images.

5

Shadows on the Wall

Cynicism, whatever finery it is dressed up with, is a capitulation to things as they are. It is diametrically opposed to my impulse, which is carefully ironic. Irony begins with an attempt to see things as they really are, but reserves a part of the imagination for the kind of world we might have — or, more accurately, could and should have.

— Brian Fawcett, *Public Eye:*
An Investigation into the Disappearance of the World (1990)

Secure the shadow ere the substance fade

— Advertising slogan for a photographer's studio (1840s)

T HE TENSION between the "real" world, and the ways people perceive it has been a problem that has confounded Western culture since antiquity. This question stands at the heart of Plato's often-cited "parable of the cave," which appears in *The Republic*. In the parable, Plato describes human life as if it were lived "in a sort of underground den." Inside the den, people's eyes are averted from the mouth of the cave, turned toward its innermost wall. Their perception of the world outside is perpetually indirect, limited to the shadows that play upon the wall. Though only a mediation of the actual world, to the person inside the den these shadows constitute "reality."

The inability to know the world, except through its representations, has continued to plague philosophy into the modern era. This dilemma posed a pivotal issue for Immanuel Kant in his *Critique of Pure Reason*. While Hegel, and then Marx, envisioned a future in which *concept* and *reality* would come together in the unfolding of human history, the twentieth century, once again, has

189

witnessed the resuscitation of this persistent paradox. The spell that *the image* casts upon the human imagination has reemerged as a preoccupation of contemporary existence.

There is something about twentieth-century life that dramatizes the division between the material world and its aspect, between form and substance. In large part it stems from the exponential growth of a modern media system, a profound apparatus of representation that has come to permeate nearly all facets of life. In an increasingly global market society, the chasm between immediate experience, and mediations of a "world at large" grows greater. Life is lived deeper and deeper within the cave, while the shadows cast by the media grow more numerous, more authoritative, more alluring. It is little wonder that historians and cultural analysts have, in the past twenty-five years, zeroed in on "the problem of representation" as the cardinal issue of our time.

The modern foundations of this concern can be traced to the early nineteenth century when, alongside the advance of machine-produced goods, came the high-speed mechanical reproduction of words and images; the flowering of early mass media. The impact of these media on popular consciousness was almost immediately seen. An example can be drawn from the *New York Sun*, one of the first mass-readership commercial newspapers in the United States.

In 1835 a prophetic event occurred. In late August of that year, the *Sun* began publishing a series of articles about Sir John Herschel's telescopic explorations of the moon from his observatory at the Cape of Good Hope, in Southern Africa.

The first article in the series described the telescope he was using in great technological detail. The machine was a hybrid of science and magic. Its lens was twenty-four feet in diameter, and weighed nearly eight tons. Its estimated power of magnification was forty-two thousand times. Herschel, the *Sun* reported, believed that his instrument would make him a pioneer in an epoch of technological discovery. It would allow him "to study even the entomology of the moon, in case she contained insects upon her surface."

The installments that followed were a temptation in the religion we call "progress." Readers were provided with an itemized description of the lunar surface and of the shady vegetation that flourished there. Then, in a wooded valley, the scientist "beheld continuous herds of brown quadrupeds, having all the external characteristics of the bison."

The articles were the work of Richard Adams Locke, a relation of John Locke, and star reporter for the *Sun*. Needless to say, the articles were a hoax. The alleged source for the articles, the Edinburgh *Journal of Science*, was — at the time — defunct. Herschel continued his work in Africa, altogether ignorant of the stories' appearance. As he sat there on the Cape of Good Hope, the stories of his discoveries were taking on the character of *fact* in New York City. Despite the fictional roots of the articles, the most important thing about them was their *facticity*. People believed them. A burgeoning network of mass-circulation newspapers spread the word further. Whatever doubts there were were expressed cautiously. Academics sought out the printed accounts in the spirit of inquiry. A modern media audience was being assembled around a linchpin of sensationalism.

By the time that silken, copper-colored humanoids appeared, the whole world was watching. Unlike the busy, urban, industrializing people who were reading about them, these moon creatures glided on diaphanous membranes linking hand and foot; they were "winged creatures" who, far from being "engaged in any work of industry or art . . . spent their happy hours in collecting various fruits in the woods, in eating, flying, bathing, and loitering about upon the summits of precipices." At the far end of mechanical science — it might have been argued — lay paradise.[1]

What was it about this fantastic world, standing beyond the edges of common sense, that made it so believable? Clearly, the answer to this question is historical. It is connected to the emergence of the media of communication, and to common patterns of perception that have developed since the beginnings of the industrial revolution. It is also wedded to a market society in which worlds beyond the orbit of immediate experience were of increasing relevance to people's lives.

The media provided a powerful lens through which this broader universe might be seen and interpreted. As we have seen, the ability to communicate a persuasive rendition of reality was an early capacity of print. This capacity has been constantly enlarged by new devices for collecting, maintaining, and disseminating information. As *the word* or *the image* is reproduced, again and again, it becomes *fact*, known simultaneously by strangers, a common, if sometimes deceptive, bond. It is the lifeblood of a mobile world-system employing standardized meanings and requiring uniform understandings. *Fact!* is seen, over and over again, repeated by itself, repeated by others. When it is stored, it becomes *a history*, a common heritage. Against the random and irretrievable quality of daily life lies the tangible evidence of the printed word, of the graven image, of the fact. Its presence is awesome, and the tale of Richard Adams Locke's "moon hoax" reveals this power at a prescient moment of discovery.

In published histories of the mass media, incidents like the "moon hoax" tend to survive as anecdotes with an amusing edge. They are more significant than that. Within our kind of world, they can provide a road map of the modern contours of knowledge and information. Fantasy is often processed as the raw material of what becomes *truth*. The hopes and the terrors of the imagination are channeled by the positivity of the evident fact; reinforced by reproducible certainty.

In 1922, Walter Lippmann argued that these reproducible certainties had become a cognitive fabric out of which "public opinion" was being sewn. If eighteenth-century revolutionaries, like Thomas Paine, understood democracy as the work of citizens engaged in shaping their social environment, Lippmann contended that modern citizens lived lives of disengagement from the world as it is, informed, primarily, by "the pictures in our heads."[2]

In the nineteenth century, the newspaper had been the dominant agency of truth. The twentieth had seen the evolution of new structures of communication that were even more persuasive. The cinema and photography, Lippmann maintained, "have the kind of authority over the imagination to-day, which the printed word had yesterday, and the spoken word before that." He continued:

They seem utterly real. They come, we imagine, directly to us without human meddling, and they are the most effortless food for the mind conceivable. Any description in words, or even any inert picture, requires an effort of memory before a picture exists in the mind. But on the screen the whole process of observing, describing, reporting, and then imagining, has been accomplished for you. Without more trouble than is needed to stay awake the result which imagination is always aiming at is reeled off on the screen.[3]

Lippmann's analysis suggested that more than being vehicles of particular messages and visions, the modern media of communication provided a "pseudo-environment" within which an all-encompassing perspective was contained. While, to a greater or lesser degree, that "pseudo-environment" might be connected to the actual world, its ability to create palpable shadows of reality was even more pronounced. For people living in their shade, he argued, these shadows—with their distortions, assumptions, biases, and blind spots—*become* reality.

Today, "the pictures in our heads" have only multiplied. Television has taken the power of the screen and inserted it into the intimacies of daily life. Beyond that, in the decades since the twenties, vast industries have emerged whose primary intent is the packaging of image and information for the purpose of influencing attitudes and behavior. In merchandising, in finance, in politics, in everyday life, the primacy of representation has escalated; the ability to shape perception has become the bottom line. Even in entertainment, ostensibly a respite from the workaday world, the durability of an image or an idea is inseparable from its ability to garner a "significant" market share.

Together, these developments convene to offer a detailed portrait of the world. At the same time, it must be noted, it is a portrait that is perpetually shifting. In a society where novelty and disposability make up the backbone of the market, images and ideas fall into disuse as soon as new ones enter the scene. Yet within the ephemera there is, perhaps, a logic. Our shadows on the wall are projected by the social, cultural, economic, and political currents that mark our time. In the remaining sections of this essay, we will attempt to look at some of the prominent shadows that have constituted "reality" in the United States in recent years. Yet beyond offering a catalog of media images, it is important to approach this subject with a critical eye. If the shadows present a rendition of the world, it is necessary to evaluate their underlying assumptions and priorities, to look at them as a language to be deciphered.

What follows is not all-inclusive. For the purpose of clarity, we have chosen to focus on three prevalent and interconnected arenas of imagery that, ensemble, reveal much about the cultural soil in which they have grown. The first of these arenas is one that projects American society as encompassing a *culture of choice*. The second, which draws its materials from media of fact and fiction, provides a look at America as a *culture of violence*. Last, and perhaps most disturbing, we will examine those shadows that constitute the political arena, which render a picture of democracy that depends increasingly upon a *culture of ignorance*.

The Culture of Choice

A recent TV commercial for Canon cameras shows tennis pro Andre Agassi leaping out of a sports car and onto the court. Rejecting the uniformity of "tennis whites," he is adorned in flashy, multihued spandex. The scene is defined by the screaming logo: *"REBEL!"* Heavy metal blares in the background as the tennis court dissolves to a frantic, digitized cityscape. At the moment of climax, Agassi turns away from the highly produced commotion and ejaculates: *"Image is everything!"*

Elsewhere a more sedate advertisement for Macy's men's sportswear portrays men in a medley of athletic embarrassments. One falls off a horse; another chips a golf ball into a water trap; bumbling outdoorsmen capsize their fishing dinghies and struggle under collapsing tents. Even where star performance fails, the commercial tutors, no need to worry. *"At Macy's we understand it's just as important how you look as how you play."* In the sacraments of merchandising, the athlete and the schlepp taste from the same wafer. For both, "image is everything," the overwhelming yardstick for success.

While the circulation of mass-produced, commercial images dates to the middle of the nineteenth century in the United

States, the past couple of decades have witnessed a dramatic acceleration of this trend. In every imaginable venue, and employing instruments that would have staggered Walter Lippmann, visual salesmanship has become a boundless feature of life.

Just twenty years ago, if you were asked to list the commercial media, you would have responded with a discrete catalog of organs and institutions: newspapers, magazines, movies, radio, and television. A boundary between media and society still appeared to exist. Today that boundary is evaporating. Every moment of human perception is viewed, by marketers, as a potential media opportunity, a point of contact for advertising. The phone rings and a prerecorded, computer-dialed message tries to sell you a vacation home in rural Pennsylvania. Calls like this are now made two-and-a-half billion times a year. Figures on "junk mail" are incalculable. Thanks to Whittle Communications, public school "homeroom" periods are now sponsored by those advertisers who run commercials on Whittle's "Channel One," a video infotainment-news program adopted by school districts in exchange for much-needed equipment. Soon doctors' waiting rooms will be presenting "health information" videos, thinly veiled drug company ads, to captive and vulnerable audiences.

For people with particular preoccupations, "900" telephone numbers offer a range of services, including shopping services, confessional services, sexual services, and electronic healing. The charge per minute can be astronomical. Now, just appearing, supermarket shopping carts are being outfitted with liquid crystal display screens in the place where children used to sit. These monitors receive short-distance infrared signals from the ceiling of the store which assure that as you pass through a particular aisle, you receive a commercial for products within close reach.

The commercial and the noncommercial mingle together so seamlessly that we hardly notice the difference. Breaking down a history of "consumer resistance" that has plagued the advertising industry since the 1920s, MTV has pioneered a form of advertising—music videos—that people watch for pure "entertainment" value, often unaware that they are watching an advertisement. Paid-for "product placements" insert familiar consumer goods into the settings and story lines of Hollywood films. Testifying before a congressional committee on the Iran-

Contra scandal, Oliver North affected a boyish innocence, conspicuously sipping from a red-and-white can of Coca-Cola.
General Norman Schwarzkopf's press conference, announcing a
cease-fire in the Persian Gulf War, was lent an air of congeniality
as he hoisted a can of Diet Pepsi, repeatedly, to his lips.

On the streets of America, and around the world, people wear
the exploding paraphernalia of the marketplace on their backs,
their fronts, their heads. Madonna, Teenage Mutant Ninja Tur-
tles, Air Jordan, Nike, Bud Man, Golden Arches, Fight the Power!: all contend for the public eye, all stand for products to be
purchased, all project an image of personal and group identity.
Within the alluring whir of images, where the commercial media
end, and life begins, is indeterminate.

At the heart of this engaging pageant of images, however, lies
sweet confusion, what Walter Benjamin called a "continual state
of distraction." A sense of groundedness and a connection to customary patterns of existence still have a hold on people's sense
of meaning, but this is increasingly challenged by history, and by
dancing shadows. To some extent the textures and tensions of
this challenge can be felt in the ways that social scientists sometimes describe the dilemmas of contemporary social life. Writing
in *Society* magazine in 1985, for example, David Goslin noted
that "years ago options were fewer." He goes on:

> A person went to school, got a job, married for better or worse — and
> raised children. A woman's place was in the home, and the home, for
> the most part, was not far from where one was raised. Widely accepted
> standards of morality and conduct governed much of our behavior.
> During the last twenty years much of that has changed. Now we must
> make real choices; to marry or not to marry; to stay married or not; to
> remarry or not; to have children or not; to work or not; to live near our
> family or not.[4]

In large measure, Goslin's description is a caricature of something real. Most of the changes he enumerates are not simply
choices that people make, but rather the ways in which history
and circumstance impact upon their lives. The decision for a
woman "to work," for example, is trivialized when seen merely
as a *choice*. Such a description supposes that women, unlike men,
are immune from necessity. Similar objections could be raised
about the other *options* he describes. What is interesting, howev-

er, is the particular language by which the author *chooses* to interpret these developments, and the way that his *choices*, too, bear
the footprints of history. In adopting the language of *choice*, Goslin submits the lived terms of life to the propaganda of the marketplace. In the process, the historical circumstances, the am-
bivalences, and the social restrictions that affect all people's
biographies are neglected. Life becomes "life-style," a thing, out
there on the market, to be consumed. Amid the diffusion of possible life-styles—each with its own identifiable array of purchasable images—comes the appearance of choice. This concept of
electable life-styles cannot be separated from the historical
swelling of a media-merchandising environment, one in which
the play of images often obscures underlying realities.

The commercial traffic in images—each with a sale to make—
has become a central force of culture, delineating ideals of behavior and social life, ideas of morality and conduct. In this play
of enticing visuals, a key element of its charisma is the implicit
and ritual claim that it offers an inexhaustible spectrum of
choices, simply to be made. More and more, as the "free market"
has been elevated to the status of a religious icon, unregulated
capitalism is openly trumpeted as the fountain out of which all
choice and possibility flow. The only acknowledged limit is the
failure of individual backbone, an unwillingness to make (purchase) the right choice.

Built into the equation of consumption and choice, however,
lies a decidedly undemocratic assumption. If consumption is
choice, then choice is inevitably dependent upon one's ability to
consume. At a moment when, for many, basic economic survival
is becoming difficult, this equation spells mass disenfranchise-
ment. If choice is limited to the marketplace, those priced out
have no voice.

Amid the celebration of unfettered options, however, there
are a number of social, economic, and anthropological issues that
fester beneath the spectacle of consumable freedom. Residing
within this apparent panoply of alternatives is a contradiction
that is marked within those institutions that serve as prime
proselytizers of choice: the commercial mass media. On the surface of things—as evidenced by cable television or the array of
magazines at any newsstand—it would appear that more and

more media are available, simultaneously answering the purchasing needs of an increasingly inclusive audience while, at the
same time, responding to its diverse and specialized tastes.

If American mass culture was once dominated by three television networks and a few general national magazines, today—
according to many media business observers—there is no "mass
culture" any longer, no "mass market." Instead, it is commonly
argued, there are *many* markets, responding to the wills of myriad groups of people. *Consumer sovereignty reigns.*

Missing from this fairy tale, however, are a number of critical
developments. First, the move toward "market segmentation"
that defines media and other industries today, is not merely a response to the democratic will of the people. If anything, it is an
attempt to make what was formerly a rigid conception of marketing more efficient, and more profitable. The shift began in the
late sixties and early seventies, during a period of social turmoil.
Marketing professionals were concerned that many sectors of
the population were either not being effectively reached by or
were resistant to, the appeals encoded in advertising and product
design. A broad, relatively undifferentiated approach to marketing had spurred economic growth during the 1920s and then,
impressively, in the 1950s. By the end of the 1960s, however,
that growth had begun to stagnate. Even more alarming was the
conspicuous emergence of local and subcultural forms of expression. Many of these explored the possibility of a mode of life, and
of a material culture, that looked beyond the gargantuan system
of production, distribution, and merchandising that had defined
the American Way of Life since the 1920s.

Reacting to these indigenous popular trends, new-age marketers began to rely more heavily on an anthropological analysis
of the heterogeneous American populace. Taking into account
variations of ethnicity, gender, economic class, and sociopolitical
attitude, the American population was divided into a variety of
instrumentally conceived segments, each defined by its "life-
style." Each "life-style" was projected according to the ways that
its attitudes or circumstances suggested particular marketing
techniques.[5] What—at a grass roots level—was marked by imagination, self-expression, and self-activity, was now being
transformed into economically functional categories designed to

influence behavior, expand markets, and maximize profits. Issues of choice were being recast as issues of *consumer choice*. Social ideas, ecological concerns, the search for meaningful identity; these became new raw materials of merchandising. This move toward consumption-defined "life-styles" is particularly evident when one analyzes the subject matter that defines much of the media diversity we find today. While it is true that there are more and more magazines on the newsstand, their orientation is becoming increasingly uniform. Whether they are addressing audiences of tennis enthusiasts, career women, new parents, audiophiles, dirt bikers, or computer users, the consumption of products provides a focal point for most of these publishing ventures. Advertising and editorial content melt together. Meanwhile, general-interest journalism—defined by interests apart from consumption—is dying.

In back of the curtain of choice, it must be added, lies a planetary consolidation of economic power that puts the lie to the notion that it is individual consumers who determine the offerings of the market. This consolidation only magnifies antidemocratic trends that underlie the pretense of options. Ben Bagdikian has provided eloquent evidence of this in the realm of media ventures. In "Lords of the Global Village," he chronicles the rise of transnational information giants which, today, dominate much of what people see, read, and hear on television, in film, in newspapers and magazines, in recorded music. Behind the apparent kaleidoscope of choice, stand the boardroom decisions of a smaller and smaller number of colossal corporations. Leading the list are five powerful media oligopolies: Time Warner, Inc.; Bertelsmann AG; Rupert Murdoch's News Corporation, Ltd.; Hachette S.A.; and Capitol Cities/ABC, Inc. The next level of the pyramid is controlled by what Bagdikian terms "midsize" giants, U.S.-based media companies like Gannett, Ted Turner's Broadcasting System, General Electric. "To the eye of the consumer," Bagdikian adds,

> the global media oligopoly is not visible. . . . Newsstands still display rows of newspapers and magazines, in a dazzling array of colors and subjects. . . . Throughout the world, broadcast and cable channels continue to multiply, as do video cassettes and music recordings. But . . . if this bright kaleidoscope suddenly disappeared and was replaced by the

corporate colophons of those who own this output, the collage would go gray with the names of the few multinationals that now command the field.[6]

The charade of choice is but a mask behind which fewer and fewer people and institutions are, in fact, making the choices that count. The inner truth of this development is ironically captured on an advertising T-shirt produced for the music publishing giant, ASCAP. It reads, simply, "There are many alternatives, but only one choice."

Beyond the contours of the market, in the confines of daily life, the proliferation of consumer "preference" coincides with a widespread breakdown of social interdependency. As marketing appeals to individual choice, the rhythms of life become increasingly fragmentary. Television watching—once termed a "family" activity—is today becoming more and more solitary. Televisions, situated throughout the household, provide electric companionship for separate individuals. When families do convene—for dinner—table discussion has given way to television spectatorship.

Not only has TV viewing become more insular, but the act of watching itself has evolved into an assembly of fragments. Increasingly, people tend to juggle several shows at once. As maestros of the remote transport themselves across the dial—from *choice* to *choice*—instantaneously, a cacophony of images becomes the norm. The environs of daily life mimic the patter of the spectacle. The sound (and visual) bite becomes not only the preferred medium of television news directors, it becomes a vernacular aesthetic. On the creative side, this montage of fragments has inspired rap music sampling. On the side of social pathology, it reinforces a culture with, as Josh Meyerowitz has described it, "no sense of place."

Amid the clatter of images, the cant of *choice*, the religion of the *new*, lies a general atmosphere of bewilderment, a sense of numbness. It is experienced on the level of inner life, expressed in the syndromes of estrangement and free-floating anxiety that mark the psychology of our time. "These days," notes social psychologist Robert Cialdini, "there are so many choices; so many options; so much information, so much stimulation that we must deal with activity in a less fully considered way."[7] Closeted within all the choice is a gnawing sense of powerlessness. To a large extent, this condition is wedded to the often-trivial nature of the choices available, and to the absence of more consequential options. While we are continually bombarded by incantations to change the things we can (hair color, style of dress, the car we drive), the notion of improving the realm of social possibility has disappeared from view.

Even pressing social issues tend to be seen as a parade of discrete products being sold. In the process they are trivialized. This can be heard in the words of Nadine Threadgill, a Silver Springs receptionist recently interviewed by the *New York Times*:

> I get home, and my mailbox is filled with little envelopes from the cancer fund, the wildlife fund, the alumni fund all asking me for money. There's the homeless problem, the drug problem, the AIDS crisis, the abortion issue. And then someone wants me to get worked up about Eastern Europe.[8]

Overwhelmed by a world depicted as a catalog of products, Ms. Threadgill eloquently demonstrates the way in which that world loses coherence, defies systematic understanding. "Infomercials" emerge as a new vehicle of public address; a sense of the distinction between reality and public relations evaporates. Products, ideas, social problems, politics come at people with the speed of light, collapsing into visual havoc, producing confusion, encouraging people to retreat into a cautious inactivity—a defensive shell of indifference.

Though much of the ennui may result from the customs and mores of contemporary culture, for the pundits of the media industries, the epidemic of disaffection is notable primarily insofar as it leads to people's tuning out of sales pitches. This can be seen in the lament of one market researcher who expressed his concern that "the American public, by nature of the assault they take from commercial ads, have become passive." Elsewhere, in business news sections and trade journals, the passivity is not complete enough; the *zapping* of television commercials assumes the urgency of a major social crisis. Marketing analyst Mona Doyan reports that many in the television audience "simply don't see [television commercials] . . . anymore. They don't have to zap them out by remote. They have tuned out mentally."[9] The *Wall Street Journal* provides a diagnostic term for alienation from endless salesmanship: "*Ad nauseum*," they call it.[10] As democracy is diminished to the language of *consumer choice*, general feelings of disengagement are described as problems of *consumer recalcitrance*.

Within the publicized expansion of choice there resides a potentially toxic narrowing of vision. Nowhere is this contradiction more evident than in the overflowing landfills and garbage dumps that serve as the unseen graveyards of discarded choice. When Simon Patten, one hundred years ago, described the coming of a new standard of living that would be "determined, not so much by what a man has to enjoy, as by the rapidity with which he tires of the pleasure," he may have unwittingly written the eventual epitaph for our *culture of choice*. Trendy, often-transparent hype of "green marketing" notwithstanding, the identity between choice and consumption inevitably harnesses human desire to a machinery of waste. Within each new *choice* being offered is the implicit invitation to dispose of yesterday's *choices*. At the heart of this perpetual cycle is a market economy whose health depends upon the growing infirmity of the planet.

The Culture of Violence

The commercial panorama of choice stands today at the center of the American ideal of the "good life." Defined by its products and advertisements, it has come to symbolize common yearnings for freedom, material security, individual success. In short, the *culture of choice* lays claim to a promised land of abundance and gratification. Yet close beneath the luster—perched in the split subjectives of people caught between longings for satisfaction and the realities of a decaying social world—there exists a condition of disquietude and fear that has come to mark the current American temper.

Within the vast orbit of the mass media—concurrent with the vision of commercial utopia—lies a steady stream of countervailing images that interact with this underlying climate of anxiety. In these images, an audience of consumers receives a picture of everyday life that tacitly reinforces the logic of an escape into the world of goods. If media images of commercial choice provide us with a rendition of the world in which *meaningful* and *rational* individual solutions are readily at hand, the picture of the social world—beyond the radius of these goods—is most often portrayed as spinning out of control.

Journalistic visions of society become increasingly chaotic, disorganized, unstable. Story by story, the disjointed format of "objective" news reporting—whether in the *National Enquirer* or the Network News—incrementally affirms the sense of chaos, posing it as truth. Bits and pieces, fragments composed of sound and sight bites, present a confusing compendium. A broader understanding is continually defied by the standards by which we are informed. If the advertisements, which punctuate the news, offer a readily available catalog of options from which to choose, the jagged presentation of "reality" defies any sense of individual comprehension or response.

On urban newsstands, tabloid journalism contributes eloquently to this splintered perspective. In these newspapers, and on local television news programs, city dwellers receive a portrait of their environment, and their experience, that only intensifies the dread and difficulty of the world in which they live. Whatever their own troubles may be, those living beyond city limits—in suburbia or small-town America—only thank their stars for having escaped the nightmare. With the police blotter serving as the primary source of information for these media, the city is reduced to the lowest common denominator: a den of criminals and monsters. Tabloids and local news programs provide a gory tableau that competes with the most vicious scenes of Hollywood *slice and dice.*

LOVERS SLAIN IN LOVERS' LANE.
WOLF PACKS ROAM SUBWAYS.
CAR TRAPS WOMAN IN HER BED!
HE CUT UP HIS GIRLFRIEND.

Against the endless backdrop of abomination, acts of compassion and community become trivialized under the rubric of "good samaritanism."

Within the city, according to this vision, horror is the norm. Likened to a powerful force of nature, it is uncontrollable and unstoppable. If people like *us*—the media narration goes—live responsibly, according to the dream of choice, those dark inhabitants of the urban nightmare are known, primarily, by their *otherness*. Presented according to well-worn stereotypes of horror-movie demons, this otherness is continuously reinforced. It is always possible to separate *ourselves* from *them* in the great chain of being. To some extent, this image is built on an actual quality of contemporary life. Within a mass society, inhabited by people who are—for the most part—strangers to one another, this sense of disconnectedness is embedded in the terms of everyday life. The British writer Raymond Williams wrote suggestively of this condition:

> The masses are always others, whom we don't know and can't know. Yet now, in our kind of society, we see these others regularly in their myriad variations; stand physically beside them. They are here, and we are here with them. And that we are with them is, of course, the whole point. To other people, we also are masses. Masses are other people. . . . In an urban industrial society there are many opportunities for such ways of seeing.[11]

Here, Williams offers a thoughtful suggestion as to why—in an urban (or suburban, for that matter) industrial society—we are so willing to ascribe *otherness* to people. We do so, he argues, because we understand on a visceral level that we too are *others* in the eyes and minds of those who do not know us, who regard *us* as strangers. This predisposition to ascribe *otherness* to others is, to a large extent, because we have internalized *otherness* as part of the way we see ourselves.

This sense of *otherness*, endemic to media portrayals of the city, provides a picture of a world gone mad, dangerous and predatory. At day's end, a half hour with the *New York Post*, or with the local evening news, makes one feel lucky to have arrived home in one piece. This sense of security is fleeting, however. With the new day will come renewed anxiety. Such a vision is not new. In times past, cities were likewise portrayed as teeming with "dangerous classes." From the mid-nineteenth century on, it was the Irish who fulfilled this propensity to demonize. Early in this century, Italians, Jews, and other "swarthy types" were inserted into the script. Today, this role has been inherited by blacks and Hispanics. In the United States, where people of color comprise an increasing percentage of the population, anxious white alarm, more and more, activates the phantasm of *otherness*. While the majority of crime in America is perpetrated by whites, the media promote the hallucination that crimes of violence are mainly the province of dark-skinned people. Novelist Ishmael Reed characterized this prejudice bitingly when he wrote that the primary "difference between white pathology and black pathology" in America "is that white pathology is underreported."[12]

Violent crime reportage has been a mainstay of popular journalism since the middle of the nineteenth century. Recently, however, this proclivity has been magnified and invigorated by the media of fantasy, particularly film, and television, creating a seamless cultural partnership between realms of fact and fiction. From the gloomy, dystopian, and desolate urban set designs of *Batman*, *Escape from New York*, and *Terminator 2*, to the seedy environs of TV police dramas, the popularly consumed image of the city is inextricably linked to violence and chaos. A subtext running through much of our media drama is one of a world reeling out of control, abandoning civilization and embracing barbarism.

This vision is also seeping into the American heartland. Even the suburbs—once a cliché for peace and safety—have assumed an atmosphere of foreboding hidden close beneath their manicured surfaces. While this theme found early expression in some fifties horror films (*The Incredible Shrinking Man*, *Invasion of the Body Snatchers*), today such visions permeate Hollywood fantasies and their countless sequels (*Poltergeist*, *Halloween*, *Friday the Thirteenth*, and the like). Television and tabloid news stories ape the openings of such tales: "On this quiet and peaceful street . . . "; "In this out-of-the-way residential neighborhood . . . " While violence is essential to the alleged nature of the city, now it has oozed into the bedrock of America. *Something's rotten in the state of Levittown!*

Surely life is filled with contingencies. It is also true that as the social fabric unravels, violence impinges upon daily life. Yet the vision of a world out of control that we see is not merely a picture of things as they are. The *way* that violence is regularly depicted within our society — as a hostile force of nature, or as a problem bred by *others* — tacitly makes an argument for a particular approach to redemption, a particular set of solutions. Within the culture of violence lie not only descriptions of things *as they are*, but prescriptions for things *as they ought to be*. Central to these prescriptions is a justification for righteous and unsparing violence as a solution to America's, and the world's, problems.

To a large degree, the flood of action-adventure films that have become the ascendant genre of Hollywood in recent years, provides a metaphorical environment in which such solutions are aestheticized. Plot, if any, is perfunctory. These movies are built a bedrock of pillage. Behind an implausible facade of righteous motives, body count and pyrotechnics are the driving force of contemporary adventures. In movies like *Terminator*, *Rambo*, *Total Recall*, *Hard to Kill*, *Blood Sport*, and *Die Hard* — all box-office bellwethers — killing for killing's sake has become the new aesthetic. Physical prowess and machismo overwhelm the pretense of a moral code; verbal interaction, or character development, is minimal. In a recent interview, Arnold Schwarzenegger, star of the *Terminator* series, enunciated the link between such fantasy dramas and their real-life application: "Everyone wants to be a terminator for a day; a fierce machine that can destroy anything, settle old scores, and get the job done."[13] If ideas of justice were once predicated on notions of social equality and the common good, today justice has become the purview of technicians of violence, *lethal weapons*. In a society where social Darwinism has once again become the prevailing outlook, survival of the fittest has received a new coat of paint.

The predatory world, which calls for Terminators and Rambos, is but a mirror of the world of "reality" that cynically greets us from journalistic venues. Both, ultimately, provide seductive justifications for authoritarianism and martial law. In an environment seemingly overwhelmed by hostile forces and aliens with "no sense of the value of human life," total war against dangerous *otherness* becomes acceptable.

At a time when the great American middle class is feeling squeezed, there are wells of frustration and resentment that are easily channeled into aggression. It is in this context that racism is, once again, *de rigueur*, sexually coded violence is escalating. If blacks and women, not long ago, provided beacons for America, today they are increasingly the scapegoats of a profoundly fragmented society.

If daily experience and the media panorama interact to underwrite the need for some kind of socal unity, fear and hatred are increasingly fashioning the cement that bonds a new consensus. Control and discipline are viewed as the only answers to the fundamental crisis afflicting streets, schools, and community. Calls for more prisons, more police, more regimentation, the death penalty—at the expense of funds for education, child care, health, and housing—reflect the current primacy of draconian models of justice.

As the public sector is dismantled, wages and benefits decline, and many Americans are instructed to live with diminished expectations of what society might be for them, martial solutions provide the new terms of unification. Nowhere was this disturbing tendency more evident than in the American culture of violence that unfolded around the Persian Gulf War.

The war took place against two historical backdrops. The immediate backdrop was a period in which major debates were beginning to open up over social priorities in the United States. Following ten years of Reaganism, and a widening of the chasm dividing rich and poor, there were rumblings over government boondoggles that favored business and military interests at the expense of the "average taxpayer." One of the most egregious areas of favoritism was military expenditure, which—despite the Reagan/Bush rhetoric about slashing government spending—was spiraling out of control. Calls for military cutbacks and an end to the "Star Wars" program were starting to enter public discourse.

A longer-range backdrop was the specter of the Vietnam War, a televised spectacle of defeat for global American power. In large measure, Vietnam threw into question assumptions that had guided foreign and domestic policy since the Spanish-American War. As the historical writings of William Appleman Williams have shown, the link between overseas expansion and domestic prosperity has been the bedrock of the "American Way of Life." With defeat in Vietnam, and the simultaneous emergence of Germany and Japan as formidable rivals to the United

States for global economic dominance, the cocky assurance of world power that had been a venerable American conceit began to deteriorate.

With the rise of Reagan, an agenda was set to reinvigorate the United States as a military power, for the purposes of transcending the "Vietnam Syndrome."[14] The growth of an antiwar movement during the Vietnam War was defined as a sign of a society that had lost its direction and its will. It had spread, like a cancer, throughout the body politic, and needed to be excised. The mass media, according to this logic, were a prime contributor to the problem, presenting cruel pictures of war that shed doubt on the Southeast Asian adventure.

From the mideighties onward, a number of public military spectacles were staged to regain public approval for military solutions. In Grenada, in Libya, and then in Panama, small-scale predictable-outcome military strikes tested the waters for public support, while providing a testing ground for a rigidly enforced system of military censorship over the media. In each case, images of demonic *others* melded with images of righteous violence to provide a filmic mise-en-scène.

Unlike Vietnam, where journalists had relative freedom of movement throughout the war zone, for the Persian Gulf War the media would be reined in, keeping American eyes in uniform.[15] The war was orchestrated from the beginning, a powerful symphony for the culture of violence. The mass mobilization for the Gulf War rested, almost totally, on governmental control and packaging of information. This approach followed guidelines set during the First World War, when the Committee on Public Information (under the directorship of George Creel) seized control of nearly every arena of information and entertainment to promote a moral economy of war. As in the case of World War I, the media, almost without exception, accepted the propagandistic agenda.

Heroic videographic logos and musical themes introduced the new coverage. Joining news teams across the television dial, retired generals provided play-by-play commentary. Pictures of Baghdad evoked strains of "bombs bursting in air." Nintendo-esque graphics of high-tech weaponry coded the ethos of a totally efficient machinery of combat.

As a war for oil, and to protect the interests of potentates, there was little about the war that could fit the mold of a war "to make the world safe for democracy." While questions were raised by a peace movement that stirred some at the grass roots, the image of virtuous indignation was in full regalia. It was Our Way of Life against The Heathen. It was Democracy and decency against the congenital corruption of the Arab horde. This was a battle between good and evil, and when George Bush (white hat) gave "Saaddim" (black hat) twenty-four hours to get out of town, the genre and the script (*High Noon*) became all the more familiar. It was, to quote Gil Scott Heron, *"nothing but a movie."*

Opinion polls proclaimed an 85–90 percent approval rating on the part of Americans, furnishing a statistical applause track for the entire show. They also reinforced dominant social psychologies of unity and isolation. If one agreed with the military expedition, one found fellowship and authorization for bloodlust in the polls. If one had questions, one was visited by a hollow sense of isolation, of being under siege by the "people's will."

In times of war, it is customary that soldiers carry pictures of women to the battlefield. Some pictures are of particular "loved ones" back home. Others are of "pinups," idealized female embodiments of *what we are fighting for*. According to tradition, these pinups depicted voluptuous femininity, a comely conception of womanhood, one evoking feelings of sentiment, pleasure, and warmth. The most popular pinup for Desert Storm, however, was a woman who had left such traditions behind.[16] Her name was Jacqueline Guilbord. Her picture originally appeared in a magazine ad for Wrangler jeans; soon it was pasted all over the war zone. She stood, slim and lanky, attired in weathered denim, leaning against a police car; hanging easily from her hand, a carbine. Today's pinup was tough, fit, cool, and lethal. Soldiers wrote to her, proclaiming that "your picture is a constant reminder of why we are here." In a photograph, fierceness and desire, a unity forged by the culture of violence, had become the stuff that dreams are made of.

In the 1930s, appraising the rise of fascism in Germany, Walter Benjamin argued that it was war that could most effectively mobilize national fervor while leaving entrenched social and economic inequities intact.[17] The Persian Gulf War, and its marshaling of national zeal, follows the core of Benjamin's insight to a "T."

The drums of war began to sound their captivating tocsin. The ugly head of the demonic *other* was raised, for all to see, as a target for common loathing. A right-wing administration, whose social policies recall those of the robber barons, had taken America to war. A regime that had risen to power on a slogan of "No more government spending!" shelled out a billion dollars a day on a ghastly consumption and human waste. A population lined up behind the pictures. Rule by the iron hand was validated. Amid the florid culture of violence, America's gardens remain untended.

The Culture of Ignorance

On a hot summer day, two men convene at a newsstand and discuss the front page of the *New York Post*.

Looming above a photograph of Donald and Ivana Trump, turned away from each other, is a banner headline: "IVANA AND DONALD UNTIE THE KNOT." The announcement, with its extreme sense of moment, overwhelms the page. At the bottom of the page, a small headline reports: "Nelson Mandela is Free."

One man shrugs his shoulders and remarks to the other, "Freedom doesn't seem very important these days." "Yeah," notes the other with irony, "today we're only interested in the freedom of the rich and famous."

This is a quintessential encounter of our time. It is often said that we are living in the middle of an "information age." The media are everywhere. Computer technology permeates more and more of the fibers of life. More and more industries are involved in the traffic of information: collecting, processing, and disseminating data. Yet while pundits and futurists celebrate the information age, much of the information that circulates throughout society leaves people profoundly ignorant of their world.

To a large extent, this unawareness is a by-product of media driven by market considerations. In a world where attracting ever-larger audiences is the key to survival, the media tend to package "truth" in such a way that will sell. The "age of information" is, for most of us, an age of sensationalism. It plays on emotions, placing feeling above intellect, and elicits visceral responses above rational considerations. Alongside the spectacles of choice, and of violence, the popular media present a picture of what is important by fixating on the phenomenon of celebrity. Celebrity faces dot the media landscape. Intimate details of their lives — love affairs, income figures, cosmetic surgery — enter into the gossip networks of everyday life. *Will "The Donald" marry Marla? Did Frank and Nancy get it on while Ron was taking a nap? Is Roger Clemens worth $2,000 a pitch?* Such questions light up the screen, and often receive more coverage than events affecting the lives of millions. Fatuous soap operas of private life provide more gripping drama than the complexity of consequential public issues. Amid the rhetoric of "information," the ability to think is overcome by waves of trivia and superficiality.

Nowhere is this cultural trend more disturbing than in the ways it compromises the arena of politics, the possibilities of democratic life. In his first inaugural address, delivered in 1801, Thomas Jefferson spoke of democracy as a system that depends upon an informed and intelligent citizenry, capable of evaluating and acting upon the issues before them. "The diffusion of information and the arraignment of all abuses at the bar of public reason," he intoned, "should be the creed of our political faith — the text of civil instruction."[18] In our era, the *text of civil instruction* is the sound bite. The *bar of public reason* is the photo opportunity.

At the center of this development lies the evolution of the mass media as the prime apparatus of public address. Building on developments that unfolded from the mid-nineteenth century onward, a reciprocal relationship between politics and the mass media has marked the dynamics of power in twentieth-century American life. From the time he was Police Commissioner in New York City, Theodore Roosevelt curried an unprecedented familiarity between himself and newspaper reporters, assuring constant and favorable coverage of his activities. His distant cousin Franklin D. Roosevelt continued to cultivate the press corps, ingeniously using radio and other media to promote New Deal policies. It is part of the folklore of modern politics that without television John F. Kennedy would never have been elected president.

The 1980s, however, witnessed a sea change in the relationship between media and politics. Advertising and public relations experts, pollsters and spin doctors, political consultants and cosmeticians were now beginning to script the political process itself. With the decline of ward heelers and old-style party machines, the mass media, with television as the prime venue, were emerging as the environment in which all public politics were taking place. As the late Lee Atwater, a point man in the Reagan offense, noted, television "drives the system now."[19] If in the era of FDR, or even of Kennedy, economists, intellectuals, and engineers constituted the requisite "brain trust," today's inner circle is made up of pollsters and image consultants.

With such advisers, political wisdom is increasingly infused with a Nielsen ratings mentality. This environment accomplishes the idea that an image *that will sell* overrides considerations of fundamental issues or long-term social objectives. Representative David Obey, Democrat from Wisconsin, describes the way in which media considerations not only affect, but shape and ultimately debilitate the political process:

> When the main question in a member's mind every time he votes is, "What kind of a thirty-second spot are they going to make out of this vote?," then truly the ability of the political system to make tough decisions in the long-range interest of the United States is atomized.[20]

At a time when a wide range of social issues demands serious deliberation and action, the context for substantive political discussion has given way to an image-laden ratings war. This development, however, is not merely the intrinsic outcome of the media themselves. It is intimately connected to the increasing use of the media as a weapon of political power.

The rise of comprehensive strategies of image management coincided with the reemergence of the political right wing in the period following the Watergate debacle. In a society permeated by doubts regarding its political ethics, the right wing rose to power following a blueprint for the reconstruction of public imagination. Building on people's frustrations and mistrust, and drawing upon a panoply of maudlin symbols — most of which had been market-tested by Hollywood and the *Saturday Evening Post* for decades — an iconography aimed at *gut feeling* began to assemble a new political constituency. While commentators initially made light of this politics of image, and the intelligentsia decried crass appeals to sentiment, the landslide election of Ronald Reagan demonstrated the effectiveness of this game plan. Watergate might well have led to the destruction of the Republican party. Instead, the very disaffection and cynicism that Watergate helped to engender became capital out of which a Republican revival was manufactured.

Reagan didn't just use *image*, he was *image*. A likable, not particularly bright, sometimes bumbling man, he was like somebody's uncle. He had a lot of weird ideas, but he was familiar, comforting to many. His lapses and his confusions could always be excused. When members of the public objected to his policies, it was a problem of "perception," he had merely been misunderstood. The tilt of his head and his way of speaking as if he were always about to spin a yarn ("Well . . . ") provided a tolerable facade for social policies that, meanwhile, were destroying the nation. Fortunes were built on pyramids of thin air, while many Americans lost their livelihoods and their homes.

Reaganism set a dangerous tone in the United States. It established the legitimacy of pure, disembodied symbolism as the prime political instrument. Democracy was no longer a process, it was but one in a grab bag of catch words. Conviction was no longer something that resulted from thought and contemplation, it was a feeling that welled up in the eyes and left a pleasant ache in the pit of the stomach. As this became the triumphant norm, political consultants became ever more avid students of trigger-point rhetoric and telegenic images. Writing in the *New York Times* in 1990, Robin Toner corroborated the trend, reporting that "political strategists are on an increasing quest for the image, the code, the word, the value, the picture that moves voters."[21] The semiotics of influence were emerging as the prime political exercise.

As the essence of political wisdom is reduced to the manufacturing of catch phrases and carefully staged visual representa-

tions, language is eviscerated of all meaning. The connection between actuality and description is severed. Powerful examples of
this can be culled from any day's newspaper.

When, for example, the United States contemplated a resump-
tion of the bombing of Iraq in July 1991, government doctors of
euphemism searched for the right phrase to name the planned assault. Initially, drawing upon the rhetoric of righteous violence,
they came up with "Poised Hammer." After further thought, it
was decided that this name "sounded too bellicose." In an attempt to provide the proposed bombing with a "kinder, gentler
name," the pillage would be dubbed "Provide Comfort II."[22] For
the sake of projecting an aura of peace upon military schemes,
the dictates of the *culture of ignorance* outweighed those of the *culture of violence*.

At the hub of such enterprises lies the incessant employment
of stereotypes as tools for building political consensus. Within
American mass culture—particularly with the evolution of
Hollywood movie-making techniques—the stereotype has been
a primary device by which tales are told. In a coded image, a
whole set of feelings and loyalties is evoked. The "man in the
white hat," or "the man in the black hat," for example, allows an
audience to identify immediately elements of good and evil
within the drama. Racial stereotypes—the black pimp, the
greedy Jew, the Italian gangster—provide pregnant visions of
villainy, while at the same time reaffirming the idea that character and ethnicity are inescapably intertwined. Simplistic designations of self and other, good and bad, patriotic and un-American
are easily communicated to an audience, engendering instant
feelings of affection or repulsion. Stereotypes rest on no middle
ground, they are the currency that impressions are made of. A
way of seeing the world is fixed wordlessly within them, while
other ways of seeing or understanding are silently eclipsed. Already by 1992—writing about the ways that political and
spiritual leaders build their followings—Walter Lippmann observed the ways that the use of stereotypes communicates the
semblance of a coherent perspective, simultaneously shutting
out those outlooks that might throw that perspective into
question.

When a system of stereotypes is well fixed, our attention is called to those facts which support it, and diverted from those which contradict it. . . . What is alien will be rejected, what is different will fall upon unseeing eyes. We do not see what our eyes are not accustomed to take into account. Sometimes consciously, more often without knowing it, we are impressed by those facts which fit our philosophy. . . . This philosophy is more or less organized series of images for describing the unseen world. But not only for describing it. For judging it as well. And, therefore, the stereotypes are loaded with preference, suffused with affection or dislike, attached to fears, lusts, strong wishes, pride, hope. Whatever invokes the stereotype is judged with the appropriate sentiment.[23]

Since Lippmann's day, this reflexive approach to communicating ideas — using symbols that suggest implicit ideas and feelings — has now become a studied political science.

In large measure, the choice of which symbols to use is the outcome of "focus groups," opinion polls, and other social instruments for measuring and fine-tuning the crowd appeal of politicians and political policies. Such techniques are rooted in developments that were initiated seventy years ago in the field of product merchandising. Beginning in the twenties, advertising, marketing, and public relations experts began to construct a utilitarian taxonomy of human response. Over the past twenty-five years, these methods have been avidly adapted to the political realm.

Today, more than anything else, politics is the work of what Robert Cialdini has called "compliance professionals." They search for triggers of "automaticity,"[24] stereotypes that will evoke an impulsive response from an audience or an electorate. Their tools — opinion polls, focus groups, and so on — are not designed to discern or encourage patterns of logical thinking, but are intended to elicit quick emotional replies. Thought is too unpredictable, dangerously empowering. Instinct is will-less. The consequence of this political trajectory is that the public begins to consume an image of itself as the abstract embodiment of visceral attitudes, authenticated and confirmed by the announced results of opinion polls. As Harry Boyte, Senior Fellow of the Hubert H. Humphrey Institute at the University of Minnesota, has observed, "We have public opinion now, which is people's private reflexes. But we don't have public judgment. So everything is broken down into market segments. You have no political process."[25] As prime-time political promotionalism takes over, the disconnection between the public and politicians becomes acute; for many, passive disengagement sets in. For others, democracy is reduced to cynical spectatorship.

Within this alienated political context, "compliance professionals" attempt to grab hold of the viewer/voter, who is increasingly disdainful about politics and likely to zap the commercial. By appealing to emotions, gossip, and stereotypical response, consultants hope to connect to an audience in much the same way that action movies and celebrity close-ups commandeer viewers' attentions.

Within campaign advertising, the recourse to stereotypes is conspicuous. Campaign ads for Ronald Reagan, for example, were assemblages of familiar, sentimental visual clichés, evoking easy-to-read, if corny, caricatures of heartland America. *A New Beginning*, Reagan's half-million-dollar 1984 campaign film, was a visual *piñata* of packaged goose bumps. As Joanne Morreale has desribed it in her detailed study of the film:

> It begins in darkness; the first image is light, as the brilliant sun blazes in the sky. Throughout, the images in the film are bathed in the sun's rays. Reagan's America is bright and sunny, that is, good, happy, healthy, optimistic. For the most part, the film is packed with familiar, positive clichés: babies, smiling children, flowers, a wedding, people hugging, touching, smiling, looking up, gesturing up, building, working. All of these images have appeared time and again on greeting cards, on television, in movies. They invoke knee-jerk associations with the way people "remember" it to be, or, more likely, with the way that they would like it to have been.[26]

Part of the power of such emotive reveries is that they are continually posed against clichéd stereotypes of *otherness*. Familiar and reassuring American platitudes were set against the backdrop of a society in trouble, racked by doubt and the search for meaning. Against images of self-satisfied government bureaucrats doling out the public trust to lazy, unworthy recipients, *A New Beginning* offered a sense of rejuvenated purpose. Against images of moral corruption and a loss of faith, we were presented with a return to the moral radiance of white picket fences. To cure a mood of shrinking economic possibility, we saw pictures of happy families moving into new homes, in soft-focused communities where father still knew best. Against the Evil Empires of the heathen, good Christian, picnic-going folk represented a conspicuous ray of hope.

By the 1988 presidential election, that feeling of orchestrated warmth gave way to the use of colder and starker images. If Reagan's campaign had plucked Americans' heartstrings, George Bush's played to their fears. Built around negative images, this campaign mined mean-spirited anxieties that lurk in the heart of America. Bush's opponent, Michael Dukakis, was continually associated with alarming images of *the other*. The most notorious example of this technique was the Bush campaign's evoking of Willie Horton as the fiend who stalked ominously within the Dukakis camp. Horton, a convict in Massachusetts who committed a violent crime while on a state-sanctioned weekend furlough program, became a symbol of the marauding black criminals who would be roaming the streets, entering your homes, should Dukakis be elected. Playing on deep-seated racist feelings, a Bush campaign ad showed a column of hulking black men passing through a revolving prison turnstile into the streets. Another ad, which appeared in Illinois, superimposed a cutout of Dukakis's face over a picture of a Massachusetts prison. The text read: "All the Murderers and Rapists and Drug Pushers and Child Molesters in Massachusetts Vote for Michael Dukakis. We in Illinois Can Vote Against Him."[27]

These ads, and others like them, were like political hand grenades, making it appear that Dukakis was not merely "soft" on crime, but he was, moreover, *one of them*, not *one of us*. This use of stereotypes follows Lippmann's description to the letter. They were "loaded with preference, suffused with affection or dislike, attached to fears." Placed on the defensive, Dukakis spent much of the campaign trying to demonstrate—through his own employment of visual clichés—that he was just as *American*, just as intolerant of alien forces, as Bush. Dukakis was forced to bear the historic burden of the immigrant, hoping against hope to gain acceptance.

Drawing heavily on stereotypes intrinsic to the culture of violence, George Bush as president has continued to place a priority on visceral response over thought. In the Persian Gulf War, he was the purposeful western hero, facing down the bad guy with an unswerving sense of righteousness. In his day-to-day life, this instinctive quality is embodied by Bush, the breathless athlete. Bypassing all opportunities to present himself as a man of thought, Bush's photo opportunities regularly depict him as "the frantic sportsman—golf, tennis, horseshoes, boating, fishing. The pace is so frenetic, so dizzying, he seems to be running from something." Embedded within such an identity is a vision of leadership that is primarily physical. Columnist Richard Cohen reached the heart of the matter when he described Bush as a man who "appears to leave little time for reflection, for mulling, for wondering." He elaborates:

> He is a man of action, running incessantly—but to where? The very terms "vision" or "goals" seem to spook him. Hurry, it's time for horse-shoes. . . . [We] get no hint that any intellectual activity is balancing the physical activity. Indeed, there seems no balance at all.[28]

This essentially physical ideal—one that today permeates American society in its obsession with fitness—is, in many ways, a stereotype that speaks volumes about contemporary culture. Insofar as it places the body principle above that of the mind, it is a telling metaphor for a political culture in which *gut response* is the quintessential building block of political power. Elevating mindless activity to a godhead status, ours is a political culture increasingly impatient with thought. The *text of civil instruction* makes war on *public reason*. Amid it all, a culture of ignorance, one that assembles emotions at the expense of deliberation, becomes the norm.

This is not necessarily what ordinary people want, though they are often held to blame. It is commonplace for pundits to argue that the magnification of feeling over thought is the price that is paid for living in a mass democratic culture, one that tries to include—and please—everyone. Despite this incantation, it is not the population at large that determines the prevailing universe of discourse. It is, for the most part, established by the agenda of entrenched social and economic elites, seeking to package their particular interests as the general will. Whether selling soap to consumers, politicians to the electorate, or warplanes to the Pentagon, this means packaging motives in a way that will trigger popular desires, generate suitable public reactions.

Ultimately this represents the implicit triumph of Pavlovian psychology as the ruling principle of current-day political science. In this sense, politics and commerce live by an identical faith. As the ringing of bells spontaneously set off the digestive juices of Pavlov's dogs, contemporary forms of communication are often designed to elicit similarly conditioned responses. Invariably this requires the suppression of thought.

For the most part, the suppression of thought is an implicit dimension of cultural life. When countervailing ideas begin to percolate within the general population, however, the implicit becomes explicit. When Reaganite flag-waving becomes the subject matter of critical artists, who examine the flag as an instrument of social regimentation, censorship of the arts becomes public policy. When the supremacy of Anglo-American cultural ideals is questioned by those who seek to understand and explore the varieties of human experience, these questioners are characterized as intolerant storm troopers for "political correctness," as PC "thought police." Amid a storm of obfuscation and incongruous rhetoric, the "universe of discourse" becomes more and more "closed."

Such an overt move to suppress critical—or *irregular*—thoughts raises the culture of ignorance to a rallying cry, one that seriously endangers America's future. "Used as an epithet," Joel Connarroe (president of the Guggenheim Foundation) has warned, "the phrase 'politically correct' has become a lethal weapon for silencing anyone whose ideas you don't like. To end an argument before it has begun, one need only cry PC."[29]

At a time when many Americans are nervous about whether American preeminence will persevere into the next millennium, the culture of ignorance promotes and ignites xenophobia—fear of *otherness*—and the restoration of jingoistic *know-nothingism*. It can be heard in the ways that protests against the growing use of racial and sexual epithets (*nigger, faggot*, and so on) are characterized as assaults on "free speech," while declarations on behalf of the homeless, disenfranchised minorities, pregnant teenagers contemplating abortion, people with AIDS, or countless casualties of U.S. carpet bombing in Iraq, are abruptly characterized as being driven by moral degeneracy, indolence, or un-Americanism.

Joel Connarroe perceptively diagnoses this dialectic as capping a grave reversal in the social climate of America, one that threatens to undermine the practice of democracy and return us to a time when *everybody knew their place.*

> People used to feel a bit uneasy about racist, sexist and homophobic remarks, but now such comments are apparently beyond reproach and are even tolerated, the anthropologist Richard Perry suggests, as a matter of high principle: civil liberties for the politically dominant.[30]

In 1964, a now woefully neglected philosopher, Herbert Marcuse, wrote trenchantly of the ways that mesmerizing shadows of freedom may ultimately serve as an underpinning for estrangement. "Under the rule of a repressive whole," he observed, "liberty can be made into a powerful instrument of domination." He continued:

> The range of choice open to the individual is not the decisive factor in determining the degree of human freedom, but *what* can be chosen and what *is* chosen by the individual. . . . Free election of masters does not abolish the masters or the slaves. Free choice among a wide variety of goods and services does not signify freedom if these goods and services sustain social controls over a life of toil and fear—that is, if they sustain alienation.[31]

Insofar as the *culture of choice*, the *culture of violence*, and the *culture of ignorance* have become broadly promoted expressions of American freedom, they provide a powerful laboratory in which Marcuse's hypothesis can be tested. To do so, we must reject the *culture of ignorance* and embrace the emancipating powers of critical thought and meaningful action.

Notes

Prologue

1. This newspaper article was brought to our attention by journalist Les Payne, speaking at the American Writers Congress, New York City, October 10, 1981.

1. The Bribe of Frankenstein

1. Mary Wollstonecraft Shelley, *Frankenstein, or The Modern Prometheus* (1831 ed.; New York, 1961), p. 41.

2. Ibid., pp. 142–43.

3. See Langdon Winner, *Autonomous Technology: Technics-out-of-Control as a Theme in Political Thought* (Cambridge, 1977), for a review of literature on technology superseding human power.

4. Carlo Cipolla, *Clocks and Culture, 1300–1700* (New York, 1967), p. 34.

5. Raymond Williams, *Keywords: A Vocabulary of Culture and Society* (New York, 1976), p. 167.

6. John F. Kasson, *Civilizing the Machine: Technology and Republican Values in America, 1776–1900* (New York, 1976), pp. 161–65.

7. Elizabeth Eisenstein, "Some Conjectures about the Impact of Printing on Western Society and Thought: A Preliminary Report," *Journal of Modern History* 40 (March 1968), pp. 1–56. Further study along these lines has led to the recent appearance of a major, two-volume study by the same author; see Elizabeth Eisenstein, *The Printing Press as an Agent of Change: Communications and Cultural Transformation in Early-Modern Europe* (Cambridge, England, 1979). See also Lucien Febvre, *The Coming of the Book* (London, 1977); Frederick Hamilton, *A Brief History of Printing in England* (Chicago, 1918); Agnes Allen, *The Story of the Book* (New York, 1967); Marshall McLuhan, *The Gutenberg Galaxy* (New York, 1962); S. H. Steinberg, *Five Hundred Years of Printing* (Harmondsworth, England, 1955). For some provocative thoughts on printing, set within the framework of a more general, contemporary essay, see George Gerbner, "Television: The New State Religion?" *Etc.*, (June 1977), pp. 145–50.

8. See Dan Schiller, *Objectivity and the News: The Public and the Rise of Commercial Journalism* (Philadelphia, 1981), for a valuable contribution shedding light on nineteenth-century American developments.

9. Herbert I. Schiller, *Mass Communications and American Empire* (New York, 1969). Also by this author, *The Mind Managers* (Boston, 1973); and *Communication and Cultural Domination* (White Plains, New York, 1976). Schiller's work, widely read internationally, provides the best rundown currently available on the U.S. information structure.

10. See Immanuel Wallerstein, *The Modern World System* (I), (New York, 1975).

11. Frederick Douglass, *My Bondage and My Freedom* (New York, 1969), pp. 145–46.

12. See Christopher Hill, *The World Turned Upside Down* (New York, 1972), pp. 106–7.

13. Thomas Paine, *Common Sense* (Harmondsworth, England, 1976), p. 100.

14. Erik Barnouw, *A Tower in Babel: A History of Broadcasting in the United States* (New York, 1966).

15. Karl Marx, *Capital* (I) (New York, 1906), pp. 805, 834.

16. *Survey* magazine, May 3, 1913.

17. Founding *Manifesto* of the IWW, January 1905. In Joyce Kornbluh, ed., *Rebel Voices: An IWW Anthology* (Ann Arbor, 1964), p. 7.

18. D. Schiller, *Objectivity and the News.*

19. It is worthy of mention that from its inception in the 1840s, *Scientific American* had been one of the most prominent voices of free enterprise. Rarely, throughout the nineteenth century, had it veered from its enthusiastic commitment to the mechanical worldview. Amid the rise of factory capitalism, its lack of social concern was conspicuous. See James Shenton, ed., *Free Enterprise Forever! Scientific American in the 19th Century* (New York, 1977).

20. Albert A. Hopkins, ed., *The Book of Progress* (I) (New York, 1915).

21. See Stuart Ewen, *Captains of Consciousness: Advertising and the Social Roots of the Consumer Culture* (New York, 1976), pp. 77–80.

22. Erik Barnouw, *The Magician and the Cinema* (New York, 1981).

23. Hopkins, *Book of Progress.*

24. If *Scientific American* envisioned the transcendent capacity of cinema images as consistent with maintaining industrial discipline, it should be mentioned that others did not. For some, in those early years of the movies, the ability of screen imagery to battle the constraints of daily ritual pointed toward its potential as a revolutionary tool. For Dziga Vertov, the revolutionary Soviet film director whose brother performed his labors in Hollywood, the movie camera provided a device by which the chains of oppression could be broken; dominant modes of perception, transcended. Here, in an essay of 1923 [taken from John Berger, *Ways of Seeing* (London, 1972), p. 17], Vertov assumes the voice of the camera:

> I am an eye. A mechanical eye. I, the machine, show you a world the way only I can see it. I free myself for today and forever from human immobility. I'm in constant movement. I approach and pull away from objects. I creep under them. I move alongside a running horse's mouth. I fall and rise with the falling and rising bodies. This is I, the machine, maneuvering in the chaotic movements, recording one movement after another in the most complex combinations. . . . Freed from the boundaries of time and space, I co-ordinate any and all points of the universe, wherever I want them to be. *My way leads towards the creation of a fresh perception of the world.* Thus I explain a new way the world unknown to you (Emphasis added.)

There is a discomforting similarity between Vertov's description of the camera as a machine in the service of social revolt, and *The Book of Progress*'s interpretation of the camera as a mechanism of illusion and control. For one, the ability to rearrange reality suggests that same ability to its audience. For the other, the ability to rearrange reality placates and structures its audience. While there is a wide range of powerful and compelling cinema, providing new and expansive ways of seeing, Vertov's revolutionary hopes are, as of yet, largely unmet.

2. Consumption as a Way of Life

1. Interview with Anna Kuthan done by Karen Kearns, on file with the Oral History Project, CUNY, New York City.

2. Elizabeth Gurley Flynn, *The Rebel Girl* (New York, 1955), p. 134. See also Grazia Dore, "Some Social and Historical Aspects of Italian Emigration to America," originally in *Journal of Social History* (Winter 1968); as reprinted in Francesco Cordasco and Eugene Bucchioni, *The Italians: Social Backgrounds of an American Group* (Clifton, New Jersey, 1974), p. 20.

3. Herbert Gutman, *Work, Culture and Society in Industrializing America* (New York, 1977), pp. 174–75.

4. Though the United States had (and still has) an agricultural working class, it was (is) a class that was largely assembled as integral to a cash-crop economy. From its beginnings, America had built much of its economic vitality on the foundation of a capitalist agriculture. Slavery in the Americas, standing at the heart of the development of a capitalist world market, while obviously not wage labor, was a decidedly capitalist labor system. It is no irony that the New York Stock Exchange stands today at a site originally haunted by slave traders and their pirate cohorts. [For the site of the New York Stock Exchange, see Matthew Josephson, *The Robber Barons* (New York, 1956), p. 16.] Designed for the forced production of a cash crop, the slave labor system was one that bound people to owners, not to land. In many ways more akin to a factory work force than a peasantry, slaves embodied transportable and exchangeable labor; they had in fact been transported to the production site, the plantation. There people were mobilized by systems of discipline and observation that are more familiar in the industrial factory than to those that prevailed on the feudal lands of Europe. [For the role of slavery in the development of capitalism, see Eric Williams, *Capitalism and Slavery* (New York, 1966), and Immanuel Wallerstein, *The Modern World System.* Slavery as a capitalist labor system is a theme developed by George Rawick in *From Sundown to Sunup* (Westport, 1972). This is one of the few books on the subject of slavery to address this issue frontally. Also, William Eric Perkins, in discussion, helped to shed light on this subject.]

Similarly, the rise of great portions of the United States as a grain belt, a "breadbasket" for the world, by the end of the nineteenth century, was not the result of an initiative by small, independent, "Yankee" farmers, as is the myth. Rather it was the result of a governmentally enforced integration of large-scale capitalist agriculture with highly industrialized networks of transportation (railroads, which were granted vast farmlands on both sides of the tracks) and communications (telegraphy). The American environment to which many Europeans came in the years at the turn of the twentieth century, even in its agriculture, was at sharp variance from their own historical experience, and from the social forms that had shaped that experience. [Regarding the question of the capitalist roots of American agriculture, William Appleman Williams has most clearly perceived and addressed the connection. His *Roots of the Modern American Empire: A Study of the Growth and Shaping of Social Consciousness in a Marketplace Society* (New York, 1974) is an important contribution. Lawrence Goodwyn's *Democratic Promise: The Populist Movement in America* (New York, 1976) also provides important insights into the rise of American capitalist agriculture and the radical response. See also Sigfried Giedion, *Mechanization Takes Command*, Part 4 (New York, 1948), for an analysis of the importance and almost vanguard role of the American mechanization of agriculture. For contrast, see William I. Thomas and Florian Znaieki, *The Polish Peasant in Europe and America*, Vol. 1 (Boston, 1919), or Leonard Covello, *The Social Background of the Italo-American Child* (Totowa, N.J., 1972).]

5. The obvious significant exceptions to this general pattern were Eastern European Jews whose migration to the United States was permanent.

6. See John Berger and Jean Mohr, *A Seventh Man: Migrant Workers in Europe* (New York, 1975), for a vivid portrayal of current conditions among Europe's migratory workers.

7. Mike Gold, *Jews without Money* (New York, 1930), p. 151. See also Antonio Mangano, *Sons of Italy* (New York, 1917), p. 23; Antonio Stella, "Tuberculosis and the Italians in the United States," *Charities and the Commons* 12 (1904), pp. 486–89; and Isaac Hourwich, *Immigration and Labor* (New York, 1912), p. 272, for discussions of the social contradictions of being simultaneously engaged in the Old and the New worlds.

8. R. Williams, *Keywords*, pp. 68–70.

9. In the past twenty years the words "consumer" and "consumerism" have taken on a new meaning connoting the advocacy of consumer rights. In popular terminology and in the mass media, being a "consumer" now refers to people or organizations seeking legal and social protection from the more overt abuses of the marketplace. Here, however, we mean a historically defined social relationship in which people's needs are increasingly encompassed by the mass production and distribution of goods and services.

10. Raymond Williams, "Problems of Materialism." *New Left Review*, 109 (May-June 1978), p. 8.

11. Edgar D. Furniss, *Labor Problems* (Boston, 1925), p. 176.

12. Simon Lubin and Christina Krysto, "Cracks in the Melting Pot," *Survey*, 43 (1923), p. 258.

13. Robert E. Park, "The City: Suggestions for the Investigation of Human Behavior in the Urban Environment." In Robert Park, Ernest Burgess, and Roderick McKenzie, *The City* (Chicago, 1925), pp. 16–17.

14. *New York Times*, November 10, 1979.

15. *New York Times*, January 22, 1980.

16. By *customary*, we mean the varied and intricate patterns of life and survival that predominated among people in preconsumerist societies. These patterns varied, but often combined small-scale agriculture and goods production; the production of vital necessities in the home; and word-of-mouth networks of information through which skills, techniques, and knowledge of survival were exchanged and passed on as a regular part of the culture of daily life.

17. Edward Devine, *Charities and the Commons*, 17 (1907), p. 502.

18. See J. R. Dolan, *The Yankee Peddlers of Early America* (New York, 1964), for a discussion on the many-faceted activities of peddlers.

19. See Robert Hendrickson, Chapter 1, *The Grand Emporiums* (New York, 1979). For a firsthand account of the general store, see P. T. Barnum, *Barnum's Own Story* (New York, 1961), pp. 12–27.

20. Dolan, pp. 254–55.

21. Ibid., pp. 245–47.

22. Barnum, p. 26; Hendrickson, pp. 206–7.

23. In 1946, the Grolier Club Book Society selected the Ward's Catalog as one of the hundred most influential books on American life—a catechism of "the standard of American middle-class living," an apostle of "creature comforts." See Hendrickson, p. 223. For a history of Montgomery Ward, see Hendrickson, pp. 205–33.

24. Gordeon L. Weil, *Sears Roebuck, U.S.A.* (New York, 1977), pp. 5, 25–27. This book offers an informative account of the Sears, Roebuck company. See also Norman Cohn, *The Good Old Days* (New York, 1940), and Hendrickson, pp. 236–53.

25. Weil, pp. 62–64; Hendrickson, pp. 212–17.

26. For a description of Wanamaker's, see Hendrickson, pp. 75–81. See also the excellent article by Susan Porter Benson detailing the development of American department stores, "Palaces of Consumption and Machine for Selling: The American Department Store, 1880–1940," *Radical History Review* (Fall 1979), pp. 199–221. For Macy's ad as well as another description, see Sheila Rothman, *Woman's Proper Place* (New York, 1978), pp. 18–22.

27. Simon Patten, *The Consumption of Wealth* (New York, 1892), p. 51.

28. Ibid., p. 34.

29. Ibid., p. 51.

30. J. Strummer and M. Jones, "Lost in the Supermarket." Recorded by The Clash, *London Calling*, New York, CBS Epic Records, 1979. Copyright 1979 Nineden Ltd/Virgin Music Publishers Ltd. Lyrics reproduced by kind permission of the publishers.

31. Quoted in *The New Yorker*, May 18, 1981, p. 35.

3. City Lights

1. Some of the material used in this essay comes from Elizabeth Ewen, "Immigrant Women in the Land of Dollars, 1890–1930" (Ph.D. dissertation, State University of New York at Stony Brook, 1979). The references are primarily to the experiences of Italian and Jewish women migrating to New York City during this period. In order to highlight the mother-daughter relationship, the role of fathers in family life has been deemphasized. For an exploration of this theme, see Alice Kessler-Harris's introduction to Anzia Yezierska's *Breadgivers* (New York: Doubleday & Co., 1925; reprint ed., New York: George Braziller, 1975), as well as the novel itself. The source material documenting the lives of immigrant women comes mainly from three sources; contemporary novels and autobiography, social work material, and oral history. Extensive use was made of the archives of the Oral History Project 1890–1930, City University of New York, New York City, directed by Herbert Gutman and Virginia Yans-McLaughlin from 1974 to 1976. For secondary materials, see Virginia Yans-McLaughlin, *Family and Community: Italian Immigrants in Buffalo, 1890–1930* (Ithaca, New York, 1977); Charlotte Baum, Paula Hyman, and Sonya Michel, *The Jewish Woman in America* (New York, 1976); and Judith Smith, "Our Own Kind: Family and Community Networks in Providence," *Radical History Review* 17 (April 1977), 99–120.

2. Viola Paradise, "The Jewish Girl in Chicago." *Survey* 30 (1913), 700–703; see especially p. 701.

3. Malcolm Wiley and Stuart Rice, "The Agencies of Communication." In *Recent Social Trends in the United States: Report of the President's Research Committee on Social Trends* (New York, 1933), p. 209.

4. For Italian women, see Phyllis Williams, *South Italian Folkways in Europe and America* (New Haven, 1938), pp. 19–24; Leonard Covello, *The Social Background of the Italo-American School Child*, pp. 210–20; Yans-McLaughlin, *Family and Community*, pp. 25–35. For Jewish women, see Baum et al., pp. 66–74; Mark Zborowski and Elizabeth Herzog, *Life Is with People* (New York, 1952; reprint ed., New York, 1972), pp. 131–35.

5. Louise More, *Wage Earners' Budgets: A Study of Standards and Cost of Living* (New York, 1907; reprint ed., New York, 1971), p. 28.

6. Mary Simkhovitch, *The City Workers' World* (New York, 1917), pp. 79–80.

7. Robert Chapin, *The Standard of Living among Workingman's Families in New York City* (New York, 1909; reprint ed., New York, 1971), pp. 249–50.

8. Flynn, p. 133.

9. Elsie Clew Parsons, "The Division of Labor in the Tenements," *Charities and the Commons* 15 (1905), 443.

10. Since men were more irregular in turning over their wages in full, the mother-daughter bond was vital to the economic viability of family life [see E. Ewen, pp. 123–31; and Louise Odencrantz, *Italian Women in Industry* (New York, 1919), pp. 175–77). For cultural conflicts see E. Ewen, pp. 276–323; Marie Concistre, "A Study of a Decade in the Life and Education of the Adult Immigrant Community in East Harlem," Ph.D. dissertation, New York University, 1943, reprinted in part in Cordasco and Bucchioni, *The Italians*; Belle Israels, "The Way of the Girl," *Survey* 22 (1909), 494–97; Baum et al., pp. 115–17.

11. Lewis Palmer, "The World in Motion," *Survey* 22 (1909), 357.

12. Lewis Jacobs, *The Rise of American Film* (New York, 1939; reprint ed., New York, 1969), p. 12.

13. Mangano, pp. 6–7.

14. Cited in Russell Nye, *The Unembarrassed Muse* (New York, 1970), p. 365.

15. Palmer, p. 355.

16. Cited in Irving Howe, *World of Our Fathers* (New York, 1976), p. 213; see also Odencrantz, p. 235; and P. Williams, pp. 117–18.

17. Jacobs, p. 17; see also Robert Sklar, *Movie Made America* (New York, 1975), pp. 18–30.

18. Jacobs, pp. 69–71. Robert Bremer, *From the Depths: The Discovery of Poverty in the United States* (New York, 1956) argues that the early movies made a real contribution to the social understanding of poverty as environmental (see pp. 110–12).

19. For another account, see Jacobs, pp. 47–48.

20. Ibid., pp. 70–71.

21. John Spargo, "Common Sense of the Milk Question," *Charities and the Commons* 20 (1908), 544–96; see especially p. 595. For another account of this powerful movie, see Vachel Lindsay, *The Art of the Motion Picture* (New York, 1922), pp. 70–71.

22. See Jacobs, pp. 71–72.

23. Maria Ganz with Nat Ferber, *Rebels: Into Anarchy and Out Again* (New York, 1919), pp. 77–78.

24. Gold, *Jews without Money*, p. 94.

25. Cited in Edward Wagenknecht, *The Movies in the Age of Innocence* (Norman, Oklahoma, 1962), p. 41. See also Sklar's discussion of the relationship between comedy and audience, pp. 104–21. For a feminist counterpoint, see Molly Haskell, *From Reverence to Rape* (Middlesex, England, 1973), pp. 61–74.

26. See Alice Kessler-Harris, "Organizing the Unorganizable: Three Jewish Women and Their Union," *Labor History* 17 (Winter 1976), 5–23.

27. Ruth S. True, "The Neglected Girl." In Pauline Goldmark, ed., *West Side Studies* (New York, 1914), p. 116.

28. Jerry Mangione, *Mount Allegro* (Boston, 1943), p. 228.

29. Sophonisba Breckinridge, *New Homes for Old* (New York, 1921), p. 175.

30. True, p. 112. See also Breckinridge, p. 170; and P. Williams, p. 36.

31. Oral interview with Agnes Mazza, CUNY Oral History Project, May 1975. See Yezierska, pp. 35–36, for a fictional rendition of this theme.

32. See Robert Park and Herbert Miller, *Old World Traits Transplanted* (New York, 1919; reprint ed., New York, 1971), pp. 79–80; Baum et al., pp. 116–17.

33. Sklar, pp. 88–91.

34. True, pp. 58–59.

35. Ibid., p. 67.

36. Interview with Filomena Ognibene, March 1975.

37. Interview with Grace Gello, April 1975.

38. For a particularly useful analysis, see Sumiko Higashi, *Virgins, Vamps and Flappers* (Montreal, 1978). See also Haskell, pp. 42–89.

39. Wagenknecht, p. 181.

40. Cited in Higashi, p. 61.

41. For accounts of Theda Bara, see Wagenknecht, pp. 179–81; Higashi, pp. 55–62; and Jacobs, pp. 266–67.

42. Mary Pickford, *Sunshine and Shadow* (New York, 1955), p. 31.

43. Higashi, p. 43.

44. James Card, "The Films of Mary Pickford." In Marshall Deutelbaum, ed., *"Image" on the Art and Evolution of the Film* (New York, 1979). For accounts of Mary Pickford that stress this theme, see also Higashi, pp. 41–52; Haskell, pp. 58–61; Wagenknecht, pp. 159–63; and Jacobs, pp. 264–66. Card, Higashi, and Jacobs all stress Pickford's popularity with working-class audiences.

45. Pickford, pp. 350–51.

46. Higashi, pp. 1–15; Hasket, pp. 49–57. For a discussion of the ambiguities of the virgin theme, see Russell Merritt, "Mr. Griffith, *The Painted Lady* and the Distractive Frame," in Deutelbaum, pp. 147–51. In *The Painted Lady*, Blanche Sweet, as the good girl, is driven mad by sexual contradictions, caught as she is between a repressive father, an unscrupulous lover, and the new sexual world represented by makeup and clothing. For analysis of the good–bad girl, see Martha Wolfenstein and Nathan Leitesm, *Movies* (New York, 1950), pp. 25–46.

47. See Stuart Ewen, *Captains of Consciousness*, and Helen Lynd and Robert Lynd, *Middletown* (New York, 1929).

48. Benjamin Hampton, *History of the American Film Industry* (Covici, New York, 1931; reprint ed., New York, 1970), p. 221. For an analysis of this change, see Hampton, pp. 197–215; Sklar, pp. 88–92, 122–34; Jacobs, pp. 287–301; and David Robinson, *Hollywood in the Twenties* (New York, 1968), pp. 26–41.

49. Hampton, p. 222.

50. Higashi, pp. 136–42; Hampton, pp. 220–26; Sklar, pp. 91–96; Haskell, pp. 76–77; Jacobs, pp. 335–41, 401–3.

51. Wagenknecht, p. 207.

52. Hampton, p. 224.

53. Cited in Jacobs, p. 401. The sexual relationships depicted in these films bear a striking resemblance to the critique of male-female relationships developed by Charlotte Perkins Gilman in *Woman and Economics* (Boston, 1898). Gilman argues that male capitalist greed and gain in the market and female "sex attraction" in the home constitute the grid of dependency relationships in modern society and create a market for "sensuous decoration and personal ornament" (p. 120). See pp. 110–20.

54. See also Michelle Mattelart, "Notes on 'Modernity': A Way of Reading Women's Magazines," in Armand Mattelart and Seth Siegelaub, eds., *Communications and Class Struggle*, (Paris, 1979), 1:158–70. She argues that "change, in as much as it affects women, becomes synonymous with integration into the 'modern.' And it is the image of the happy woman, the woman dazzled by the desires and possibilities of consumption, and progress . . . which is the best publicity for modernity" (p. 160). See also Higashi, p. 142.

55. Hampton, p. 225; Higashi, pp. 102–4.

56. Interview with Maria Zambiello, January 1976.

57. Interview with Maria Frazaetti, March 1976.

58. Interview with Filomena Ognibene, March 1975.

59. Sklar, pp. 44–45. See also Nye, *The Unembarrassed Muse*, pp. 377–79; and Hampton, p. 172.

60. Cited in Nye, p. 378.

61. Lloyd Lewis, "The Deluxe Picture Palace," *New Republic* (March 1929), pp. 174–76; reprinted in George Mowry, *The Twenties* (New Jersey, 1963), p. 59.

62. Ibid., p. 58.

63. Walter Benjamin, "The Work of Art in the Age of Mechanical Reproduction." In Hannah Arendt, ed., *Illuminations* (New York, 1968), p. 223.

4. Fashion and Democracy

1. A fairly detailed description of the rise of the blue jean may be found in Ed Cray, *LEVI's* (Boston, 1978).

2. Paul H. Nystrom, *Economics of Fashion* (New York, 1928), p. 278.

3. Estelle Ansley Worrell, *American Costume: 1840–1920* Harrisburg, Pennsylvania, 1979), p. 38.

4. Ibid., pp. 28–29.

5. The term "dungaree," although it sounds as though it may derive from a close proximity to dung, is instead of Hindi origin: a reference to a rough cotton fabric imported from India, commonly worn by sailors.

6. Horatio Alger,Jr., *Ragged Dick and Mark, The Match Boy* (reprinted New York, 1962), p. 58.

7. Amy Pagnozzi, "Jeans: No Stone Unturned in Fight to Cover the Rear," *New York Post*, July 15, 1980.

8. William Thomas, "The Jeans of Summer," *Back Stage*, July 18, 1980, p. 1.

9. Ibid.

10. Craig Whitney, "Moscow Bracing for Big Influx of Western Influences," *New York Times*, July 3, 1980.

11. Paul H. Nystrom, *Fashion Merchandising* (New York, 1932), p. 31.

12. Ingrid Brenninkmeyer, *The Sociology of Fashion.* Ph.D. dissertation, Fribourg, 1962, p. 115.

13. Ibid.

14. Quentin Bell, *On Human Finery* (New York, 1976), p. 141.

15. Thorstein Veblen, *The Theory of the Leisure Class* (New York, 1899).

16. Brenninkmeyer, p. 115. Bernard Rudofsky, in *The Unfashionable Human Body* (Garden City, New York, 1974), relates that, according to medieval Christian doctrine, sexual distinctions between Adam and Eve were minimal before the fall from Paradise. Illustrating his contention with a fourteenth-century woodcut, we see Adam and Eve as a "sexless couple," devoid of any clear sexual definition. In another illustration, a thirteenth-century miniature, we see an Adam and Eve both painted with hermaphroditic sexual organs (combination penis and vagina) (pp. 16–17). According to such scriptural interpretations, physiological sexual distinctions were, themselves, largely a result of the fall from grace.

17. Anne Hollander, *Seeing through Clothes* (New York, 1978), pp. 23, 36.

18. Frances Elizabeth Baldwin, "Sumptuary Legislation and Personal Regulation in England," *Johns Hopkins University Studies in History and Political Science*, Series XLIV, No. 1 (Baltimore, 1926), p.10.

19. Pearl Binder, *Muffs and Morals* (New York/London, 1953), p. 157.

20. Kent Roberts Greenfield, "Sumptuary Law in Nürnberg: A Study in Paternal Government," *Johns Hopkins University Studies in History and Political Science*, Series XXXVI, No. 2 (Baltimore, 1918), p. 7.

21. Baldwin, p. 23.

22. Ibid., pp. 231–32.

23. Ibid., pp. 228–29.

24. Ibid., pp. 228.

25. Brenninkmeyer, p. 132. The word "damast" probably refers to "damask," a silk imported from Damascus, woven with patterns. The appearance of this and other luxury items is an indication of mercantile trade, and gives some inkling as to the heightened status and power of an emergent bourgeoisie.

26. Baldwin, pp. 248–49. Under a law, "1 James I, c25," it is stated that "all acts heretofore made concerning apparel . . . shall . . . henceforth be repealed and void."

27. Bell, p. 115.

28. See Werner Sombart, *Luxury and Capitalism* (Ann Arbor, 1967; 1913).

29. Brenninkmeyer, pp. 58–59.

30. Ibid.

31. Larzer Ziff, *Puritanism in America: New Culture in a New World* (New York, 1973), p. 19.

32. James J. Flink, *America Adopts the Automobile* (Cambridge, Mass., 1970), p. 65.

33. Rudofsky, 159–60; Brenninkmeyer, 137–38. See also Albert Soboul, *The Parisian Sans-culottes and the French Revolution* (Westport, Connecticut, 1979).

34. See Max Weber, *The Protestant Ethic and the Spirit of Capitalism* (New York, 1958). See also R. H. Tawney, *Religion and the Rise of Capitalism* (New York, 1926).

35. Benjamin Franklin, *Autobiography* (reprinted in New York, 1962), p. 69.

36. Frederick B. Tolles, *Meeting House and Counting House* (New York, 1948, reprinted New York, 1962), p. 123.

37. Bell, pp. 119, 124–25, 148.

38. Hollander, p. 75.

39. Brenninkmeyer, p. 140.

40. Bell, p. 141.

41. Nystrom, *Economics of Fashion*, p. 316.

42. Stuart Chase, *Prosperity: Fact or Myth* (New York, 1929), p. 64. See also Eugene Genovese, *The Political Economy of Slavery* (New York, 1965).

43. Jane Addams, *Twenty Years at Hull House* (New York, 1910), pp. 6–7, 13–14.

44. Allen F. Davis, *American Heroine: The Life and Legend of Jane Addams* (New York, 1973), p. 20.

45. Theodore Zeldin, *France 1848–1945: Ambition and Love* (Oxford, 1979).

46. Charlotte Perkins Gilman, *Women and Economics.*

47. See Rudofsky. See also William A. Rossi, *The Sex Life of the Foot and Shoe* (New York, 1976).

48. Rudofsky, pp. 100–111. See also Binder, p. 123.

.49. Havelock Ellis, *Studies in the Psychology of Sex*, vol. II, part I (New York, 1942), p. 172. See also Binder, p. 114.

50. Nystrom, *Economics of Fashion*, p. 264.

51. Binder, p. 123.

52. Ibid., p. 125.

53. David L. Cohn, *The Good Old Days: A History of American Morals and Manners as Seen through the Sears, Roebuck Catalogs* (New York, 1940), p. 376.

54. Bell, p. 141.

55. Elizabeth B. Hurlock, *The Psychology of Dress: An Analysis of Fashion and Its Motive* (New York, 1929), p. 198.

56. Rudofsky, p. 46.

57. Karlyne Anspach, *The Way of Fashion* (Ames, Iowa, 1967), p. 69.

58. Burton Y. Pines, "Reagan's Money Machine," *Time*, July 7, 1980. The article reports that while Nancy Reagan enjoys her husband's affluence in her five-thousand-dollar dresses, Ronald Reagan "has to be prodded into buying a new suit."

59. "The Very Thing That Makes You Rich," written by S. Bailey, Screen Gems-EMI Music Inc.-BMI. Recorded by Ry Cooder on *Bop Till You Drop*, 1979, Warner Brothers Records, Inc.

60. Cohn, p. 309.

61. Hurlock, pp. 130ff.

62. Hollander, pp. 133–34.

63. See Paul Poiret, *King of Fashion: The Autobiography of Paul Poiret* (Philadelphia, 1931).

64. Louis Levine, *The Woman's Garment Workers: A History of the International Ladies' Garment Workers' Union* (New York, 1924), pp. 1–2.

65. Egal Feldman, *Fit for Men: A Study of New York's Clothing Trade* (Washington, D.C., 1960), p. 1.

66. Bertha June Richardson, *The Woman Who Spends: A Study of Her Economic Function* (Boston, 1913), pp. 77–78.

67. R. S. and H. M. Lynd, *Middletown*, p. 162.

68. Harry A. Cobrin, *The Men's Clothing Industry: From Colonial through Modern Times* (New York, 1970), p. 19.

69. Pauline Arnold and Percival White, *Clothes and Cloth: America's Apparel Business* (New York, 1961), p. 84. See also Nystrom, *Economics of Fashion*, pp. 411ff. There is some dispute as to when slop shops made their first appearance in the United States. While most sources indicate a beginning date of about 1800, one writer places the first slop shop in New Bedford, Massachusetts, in 1822. See Hurlock, p. 88.

70. Brenninkmeyer, p. 147.

71. Feldman, pp. 59–68. See also Brenninkmeyer, p. 147.

72. Nystrom, *Economics of Fashion*, p. 408.

73. Feldman, p. 49.

74. Ibid., p. 48.

75. Ibid.

76. Ibid., pp. 47–48.

77. Nystrom, *Economics of Fashion*, p. 410.

78. Ibid., p. 452.

79. See Hill, *The World Turned Upside Down*.

80. See John Berger, *Ways of Seeing*. The entire book makes valuable reading for any student of images; see particularly pp. 88, 109–10.

81. Ibid., p. 106.

82. Peter C. Marzio, *Chromolithography 1840–1900: The Democratic Art* (Boston, 1979), p. xi.

83. Ibid., p. 5.

84. Ibid., p. 104.

85. Elsa G. Herzfeld, *Family Monographs* (New York, 1905), pp. 14–15.

86. Marzio, p. 2.

87. Ibid., pp. 125–26.

88. Brenninkmeyer, pp. 145–46.

89. Chase, *Prosperity*, p. 65.

90. Bell, p. 31.

91. Nystrom, *Economics of Fashion*, p. 26.

92. Cohn, p. 461. See also Weil, *Sears, Roebuck, U.S.A.*, p. 43.

93. Cohn, p. 387.

94. Ibid.

95. Allen Devere, "Personal Decoration," vol. 8, *The World Tomorrow* (New York, 1925), p. 77. Cited by Cohn, p. 309.

96. Weil, p. 42; Cobrin, p. 49.

97. Weil, p. 43.

98. Cohn, pp. 290–91.

99. Levine, pp. 12–17.

100. Ibid., pp. 15–16.

101. Ibid., p. 398.

102. Ibid., p. 405.

103. Jacob Riis, *How the Other Half Lives* (New York, 1890), p. 108.

104. New York Bureau of Labor Statistics Report, 1885. Cited by Levine, pp. 18–23.

105. Levine, pp. 171–72.

106. Ibid., p. 37.

107. Ibid., pp. 108–9.

108. Ibid., pp. 30–31.

109. Ibid., pp. 122–23.

110. Arnold and White, pp. 104–5.

111. Cobrin, p. 105.

112. Hurlock, pp. 26–28.

113. Hollander, p. 391.

114. John William Ferry, *A History of the Department Store* (New York, 1960), p. vi.

115. See Ferry, entire; Anspach, p. 172.

116. Ferry, p. 23.

117. Nystrom, *Economics of Fashion*, p. 409.

118. Ferry, p. 42.

119. Ibid., p. 47.

120. John B. Swinney, *Merchandising of Fashions* (New York, 1942), p. 6. See also Ferry, p. 40.

121. Weil, Chapter 3.

122. Ferry, p. 16.

123. Hurlock, pp. 130ff.

124. John F. Kasson, *Amusing the Million* (New York, 1978), pp. 17–18.

125. Nystrom, *Economics of Fashion*, pp. 88–92.

126. Robert S. and Helen Merrell Lynd, *Middletown in Transition: A Study in Cultural Conflict* (New York, 1937), p. 175.

127. Hollander, p. 154.

128. Hurlock, pp. 115–16.

129. Hollander, pp. 34–35.

130. Arnold and White, p. 91.

131. Nystrom, *Economics of Fashion*, p. 434.

132. Brenninkmeyer, p. 163.

133. Nystrom, *Economics of Fashion*, p. 212.

134. Cecil Beaton, *The Glass of Fashion* (Garden City, 1954), p. 116.

135. Nystrom, *Economics of Fashion*, p. 339.

136. Gold, *Jews without Money*, pp. 60–61.

137. Richard Gambino, *Blood of My Blood* (New York, 1974), p. 175.

138. Park and Miller, *Old World Traits Transplanted*, p. 147.

139. Caroline Ware, *Early New England Cotton Manufacture: A Study in Industrial Beginnings* (New York, 1931; reprinted 1966), p. 215.

140. "The Pretender," by Jackson Browne. Swallow Turn Music/WB Music. ASCAP.

141. Jervis Anderson, "That Was New York: Harlem," Part I, "The Journey Uptown." *New Yorker*, June 29, 1981, pp. 43–44.

142. Ruth S. True, "The Neglected Girl," p. 60.

143. Ibid., pp. 66–67.

144. Richardson, pp. 77–78.

145. Jane Addams, *Democracy and Social Ethics* (Cambridge, Mass., 1902; reprinted 1964), pp. 34–35.

146. Chase, p. 80.

147. Hurlock, p. 3.

148. Leonard Covello, *The Teacher in the Urban Community* (New York, 1958), p. 22.

149. Richardson, pp. 75–77.

150. Beaton, p. 26.

151. Anspach, p. 34.

152. Poiret, pp. 265–66.

153. Ibid., p. 275.

154. Christian Dior, *Christian Dior and I* (New York, 1957), pp. 42, 48.

155. Nystrom, *Fashion Merchandising*, p. 31.

156. Hurlock, pp. v–vi.

157. Louise Odencrantz, *Italian Women in Industry*, p. 229.

158. Anspach, p. 40.

159. Nystrom, *Fashion Merchandising*, pp. 218–19.

160. Brenninkmeyer, pp. 65–67.

161. Hurlock, p. 175.

162. Ibid., pp. 176–77.

163. Mangano, *Sons of Italy*, p. 21.

164. Hurlock, p. 183.

165. R. S. and H. M. Lynd, *Middletown in Transition*, pp. 171, 200.

166. Nystrom, *Economics of Fashion*, p. 73.

167. Poiret, p. 271.

168. Cohn, p. 285.

169. Nystrom, *Fashion Merchandising*, pp. 43, 47.

170. Ibid., pp. 70–81, 127–53.

171. Hurlock, p. 143.

172. Nystrom, *Fashion Merchandising*, p. 189.

173. Nystrom, *Economics of Fashion*, pp. 479–80.

174. Stuart Ewen, *Captains of Consciousness*. See pp. 31–39, "Mobilizing the Instincts."

175. Nystrom, *Economics of Fashion*, pp. 55ff, 67ff.

176. Ibid., p. 69.

177. Vance Packard, *The Hidden Persuaders* (New York, 1957), pp. 144–48.

178. "The Lush New Suburban Market," *Fortune*, November 1953, p. 128.

179. Allen Ginsberg, "America." In *Howl and Other Poems* (San Francisco, 1956).

180. Michael McClure, "Nights in North Beach." In Lynda Rosen Obst, ed., *The Sixties: The Decade Remembered Now, By the People Who Lived It Then* (New York, 1977), p. 28.

181. Diana Vreeland, "Chatting About Style." In Obst, p. 146.

182. Carrie Donovan, "The Way to Dress Today," *New York Times Magazine* (Fashion Supplement), August 24, 1980, p. 137.

183. Enid Nemy, "Looking Like Somebody," *New York Times Magazine* (Fashion Supplement), August 24, 1980, pp. 186–87.

184. Donovan, p. 137.

5. Shadows on the Wall

1. O'Brien, pp. 43–53.

2. Walter Lippmann, Chapter 1, *Public Opinion* (New York, 1922).

3. Ibid., pp. 91–92.

4. David Goslin, "Decision Making and the Social Fabric," *Society*, 2 (2) (New Brunswick, 1985), p. 9.

5. The major book in the field of "life-style" market segmentation is Arnold Mitchell, *The Nine American Lifestyles* (New York, 1983). In this work he divides the population into nine American life-styles which he calls VALS (values and life-style): *Survivor, Sustainer, Belonger, Emulator, Achiever, I-Am-Me, Experiential, Societally Conscious*, and *Integrated*. Since the book's publication, there has been a reconfiguration of the system, VALS 2, which attempts to refine a more specific relationship between attitude and purchase behavior. The refined VALS 2 system segments the population into eight consumer categories: *Actualizers, Strugglers, Fulfilleds, Believers, Achievers, Strivers, Experiencers*, and *Makers*. For a description of VALS 2, see Rebecca Piirto, "VALS: The Second Time," *American Demographics*, July 1991. For a more detailed description of the development of market segmentation, see William Meyers, *The Image Makers: Power and Persuasion on Madison Avenue* (New York, 1984).

6. Ben H. Bagdikian, "The Lords of the Global Village," *The Nation*, June 12, 1989, p. 819.

7. Robert Cialdini, quoted in the *New York Times*, December 6, 1989, p. C16.

8. Lena Williams, "Free Choice: When Too Much Is Too Much," *New York Times*, February 14, 1990, p. C10.

9. Ibid.

10. Quoted by Deborah Baldwin, "The New Marketplace," *Common Cause Magazine*, May/June 1991, p. 16. This article is an excellent survey of these new marketing trends and their effects.

11. R. Williams, *Culture and Society*, pp. 299–300.

12. Ishmael Reed, "The Black Pathology Biz," *The Nation*, November 20, 1989, pp. 597–598.

13. Arnold Schwarzenegger interview, "Late Night with David Letterman," July 2, 1991.

14. Noam Chomsky in *Media Control: The Spectacular Achievements of Propaganda*, Open *Magazine* pamphlet series, California, 1991, pp. 9–10, quotes Reaganite intellectual Norman Podhoretz's definition of the Vietnam Syndrome as "the sickly inhibitions against the use of military force." Chomsky comments, "There were these sickly inhibitions against violence on the part of a large part of the public. People just didn't understand why we should go around torturing people and killing people and carpet bombing them. It's very dangerous for a population to be overcome by these sickly inhibitions, as Goebbels understood, because then there's a limit on foreign adventures. It's necessary, as the *Washington Post* put it the other day, rather proudly, to 'instill in people respect for the martial virtues.' If you want to have a violent society that uses force around the world to achieve the ends of its own domestic elite, it's necessary to have a proper appreciation of the martial virtues and none of these sickly inhibitions about using violence." A T-shirt

commonly seen on the street in 1991 provides ample evidence for Chomsky's argument. It portrays a red, white, and blue American flag with an eagle bursting out its middle. Underneath the image, the text reads, "These Colors Don't Run."

15. See, for example, Jason De Parle, "Long Series of Military Decisions Led to Gulf War News Censorship," *New York Times*, May 5, 1991, pp. A1 and A20. While administration officials called this policy a triumph, a "model for the future," and the majority who work in the media stepped into line, a few journalists dissented. "I'm not sure the public's interest is served by seeing what seems to have been such a painless war, when 50,000 to 100,000 may have died on the other side," said Ted Koppel, host of the ABC news program *Nightline*. "Obviously this was done so they could maintain the closest possible control over public opinion, to increase support for the war."

16. *New York Times*, February 15, 1991, p. A16. The shift toward women as embodiments of the culture of violence represents an interesting change in the traditions of body image. Historically, within patriarchal cultures, male body ideals have served as common expressions of ideas about power. Female ideals within patriarchal body politics have served as sites for ideas of value: aesthetic, moral, and economic. This association between female body ideals and systems of value is probably rooted in the history of women as objects of sexuo-economic exchange. As a sense of patriarchal values has unraveled, and as issues of power have become increasingly prominent within American culture, female body ideals have come, more and more, to mimic a conventionally male aesthetic of power. Beyond Jacqueline Guilbord, women are increasingly depicted according to the ideal of extreme muscle definition and express a bodily rhetoric of power, intrinsic to the culture of violence. This tendency can be seen in films like *La Femme Nikita*, *Thelma and Louise*, and *Terminator 2*. For a description of these new images see Julie Baumgold, "Killer Women: Here Come the Hardbodies," *New York* magazine, July 29, 1991, pp. 24–29.

17. Walter Benjamin, pp. 243–44.

18. Thomas Jefferson, "Inaugural Address," March 4, 1801, reprinted in Adrienne Koch and William Peden, eds., *The Life and Selected Writings of Thomas Jefferson* (New York, 1944), p. 324. For a historical analysis of the shift in public discourse from the language of reason to the language of emotion see Kenneth Cmiel, *Democratic Eloquence* (New York, 1990).

19. Lee Atwater, quoted in Michael Oreskes, "America's Politics Loses Way As Its Vision Changes World," *New York Times*, March 18, 1990, p. 22.

20. Ibid.

21. Robin Toner, "Wars Wound Candidates and the Process," *New York Times*, March 19, 1990, p. B6.

22. *New York Times*, July 25, 1991, p. A3.

23. Lippmann, p. 119.

24. These terms come from Robert Cialdini, *Influence: The New Psychology of Modern Persuasion* (New York, reprint ed., 1990).

25. Oreskes, p. 22.

26. Joanne Morreale, *A New Beginning: A Textual Frame Analysis of the Political Campaign Film* (New York, 1990), p. 76.

27. *Newsweek*, September 26, 1988, p. 25. See Toner for more description of "negative campaign" commercials.

28. Richard Cohen, "It's Time for Horseshoes," *Westsider*, July 25–31, 1991, p. 7.

29. Joel Connarroe, "How I'm PC," *New York Times*, July 12, 1991, p. A29. For more on this controversy see the report of President Bush's speech warning the public of the "abuse" of free speech, *New York Times*, May 5, 1991, p. A1. Also see Michael Berube,

"Public Image Limited: Political Correctness and the Media's Big Lie," *Village Voice*, June 18, 1991, pp. 31–37; Richard Goldstein, "The Politics of Political Correctness," *Village Voice*, June 18, 1991, pp. 39–41. For an explanation of how this issue was used by the right wing see the *Boston Globe*, July 8, 1991, pp. 1 and 7. For the reshaping of American culture into a common culture based on inclusion and tolerance, see Henry Louis Gates, Jr., "Whose Culture Is It, Anyway: It's Not Just Anglo-Saxon," *New York Times*, May 4, 1991, p. 23.

30. Connarroe, Ibid.

31. Herbert Marcuse, *One-Dimensional Man* (Boston, 1964), pp. 7–8.

Index

Compiled by Eileen Quam and Theresa Wolner

Act I dresses: ad for, 102–5, *104*
Addams, Jane: on clothing, 75, 95–96, 114, 157–58, 176
Advertising: and capitalism, 20; and consumption, 29, 44, 47; for dresses, 102–5, *104*; for films, 58; industry, 20; for jeans, 75–76, 79; for lingerie, 102, *103*, 111; in magazines, 199; magnetism of, 47; and modernity, 28, 44; opportunities for, 195–96; and passivity, 201; by peddlers, 37, 38; for ready-made clothing, 145; vs. traditional culture, 70. *See also* Commerical imagery; Marketing; Merchandising
Agassi, Andre: in commercial, 194
Agriculture: and capitalism, 29, 223n; mechanization of, 223n
Alger, Horatio, 77
Amagoalik, John: on cultural disruption, 35
Amateur Wife, The (film), 70
"America" (Ginsberg), 180
American Revolution: vernacular literature and, 10
American Telephone and Telegraph. *See* AT&T
Americanization: in film, 68, 70; of immigrants, 32–35, 42, 68, 70; in suburbs, 178
Anarchism: and labor, 138–39
Anspach, Karlyne: on fashion imagery, 160
Appearance: and rise of fashion, 140–42
Art. *See* Visual art
ASCAP, 200

AT&T, 23, 24, 29
Atomic bomb: and consumerism, 173
Atwater, Lee: on television, 212
Autobiography (Franklin), 92

B. Altman (department store), 142
Babbitt, Benjamin: marketing techniques of, 38, 39
Babblers. *See* Lollards
Bagdikian, Ben: on mass media, 199
Baldwin, Frances Elizabeth: on sumptuary law, 85–86
Bara, Theda, 66–67
Barnum, P. T.: and advertising, 39
Barter, 37
Batman (film), 205
Beat culture, 180–81
Beaton, Cecil: on fashion imagery, 160; on Irene Castle's appearance, 151
Behold My Wife (film), 70
Bell, Quentin: on conspicuous consumption, 106; on military attire, 93; on nobility and labor, 84
Benjamin, Walter: on distraction, 196; on mechanical reproduction of images, 47, 168; on war, 209
Benson, Susan Porter: on department stores, 225n
Bergdorf Goodman (department store): and fashion imagery, 160
Berger, John, 222n; on oil painting, 125
Bertelsmann AG, 199
Bertha, the Sewing Girl (film), 59
Bible: on clothing, 81–82, 85; interpretation and power of church, 5; vernacular translations of, 6

Bicycle: and women's clothing, 113
Binder, Pearl: on sumptuary law, 86; on
    women's appetites, 101
Birth of a Nation (Griffith), 66
Blood Sport (film), 206
Bloomer, Amelia: on clothing, 112
Bohemianism. *See* Beat culture
Bok, Edward: on women's fashion,
    108–9
Bon Jour jeans, 76, 79
Book of Progress, The, 18–19, 222n
Boussac, Marcel: and mass-produced
    clothing, 163
Boyte, Harry: on public opinion,
    215–16
Brand names, 27, 28, 40. *See also*
    Trademarks
Brando, Marlon, 78
Brooks Brothers, 119
Browning, John H.: overalls by, 76, 120
Brummell, Beau, 93
Bullock's (department store): on cus-
    tomer types, 170–71
Bush, George: media use by, 217–18,
    234n; and military power, 207, 209
Business suit: prototype for, 77
Bustles, 75, 99, 106, 131
Butterick's: clothing patterns of, 149

Calvin Klein jeans, 75–76, 163
Camera: as machine of social revolt,
    222n; as mechanism of control and
    order, 17–19; perception of, 222n.
    See also Film; Photography
Canadian Northwest Territories: cultural
    transformation in, 34
Capitalism: and agriculture, 223n; and
    choice, 197; and consumerism, 68;
    and fabric, 91; factory, 2–3; and
    fashion, 80; and images, 127; indus-
    trial, 3, 48; and labor, 138; and mass
    communication, 3–4, 12–13, 16, 18,
    21; and mechanical control, 20;
    popular perceptions of, 15, 16;
    reference-idea of, 13, 20; and slavery,
    223n; social-democratic, 20. *See also*
    Democracy
Capitalism and Slavery (Williams), 223n
Capitol Cities/ABC, Inc., 199
Carroll, Dan: on jeans advertising, 79

Castle, Irene: style of, 151
Catalogs. *See* Mail-order merchandising;
    Montgomery Ward's (department
    store/catalog); Sears, Roebuck &
    Company
Caxton, William, 4
Celebrity: in news, 210, 211
Centennial Exposition. *See* Philadelphia
    Centennial Exposition
Chapin, Robert: on working class, 55
Chase, Stuart: on clothing of poor, 158;
    on function of clothing, 130
Childbearing: and women's sexuality,
    97–98
Children: and clothing, 177
Choice: culture of, 194–202, 220
Chomsky, Noam: on propaganda,
    233–34n
Chromolithography, 125–30, 146
Church: attack on, 6. *See also* Clergy
Cialdini, Robert: on choice, 200; on pol-
    itics, 215
Cinema. *See* Film
Cipolla, Carlo: on mechanization, 2
Civil War: and garment industry,
    122–23, 129, 149
Clash, The, 50
Clergy: clothing of, 84–85; and literacy,
    8; and monopoly over word, 5;
    power of, 5, 8
Cloth: abundance of in clothing, 76, 85,
    97; and capitalism, 91; decreasing
    amounts in clothing, 150; develop-
    ment of synthetics, 163; and sumptu-
    ary law, 88
Clothing: ceremonial, 93; for children,
    177; in Communist countries, 80,
    164; consciousness, 172–87; and con-
    spicuous consumption, 84, 105–6,
    107, 180–81; development of size
    standards, 122–23; and dress reform,
    111–14; emergence of in Bible,
    81–82, 85; function of, 130; home-
    made, 92, 116, 123; of immigrant
    daughters, 64–65, 70; importance of,
    xix; Ivy League, 186; man-style for
    women, 111–14; men's, 92–95, 152,
    176–77; military, 93; and morality,
    91–95, 97, 176; patterns for, 123,
    149–53; peasant, 83–84; plain style,

90, 92–93, 96, 105, 111, 114; preppie, 186; ready-made, 92, 115,
116–23, 129–36, 143–46, 154–56;
and revolt, 183–84, 185–86; and sin,
82, 85, 97, 102–5, 106–7; and socio-
logical standing, 75–81, 84–85, 155;
tailor-made, 115, 116–23; and taste,
169; weight of, 106; women's,
75–115 passim, 131–32, 151–52,
175; of youth, 164–65, 182. *See also*
Fashion; Garment industry; Textile
industry
Cohen, Richard: on Bush, 218
Cohn, David: on use of rouge, 132
Colbert, Jean-Baptiste: and fashion, 89
Columbian Exposition, 146–47
Commercial imagery: and choice,
194–202; and consumption, 24. *See
also* Advertising
Commercialization: by peddlers, 38
Common Sense (Paine), 9
Communication technology: and capitalism, 3–4, 12–13, 16, 18, 21; and
commerce, 11–13; and mass culture,
20. *See also* Mass communication
Conformity: and fashion, 80, 173, 178;
in suburbs, 173, 178, 179
Connarroe, Joel: on "politically correct,"
219, 220
Consumer: choice, 199, 200, 202;
defined, 31, 224n; life-styles, 198–99,
233n. *See also* VALS
Consumerism: x, xxii, 23–51; antisocial
and destructive premises of, 48; and
atomic bomb, 173; and choice, 197,
200, 202; and citizenship, 30; and
class, 82, 85; and clothing, 84,
105–6, 107, 115, 158, 182; and commercial imagery, 24; "consume"
defined, 31; definition of, 224n; and
fashion, 81, 84; history of, xxii; and
industrialism, xxii, 29, 47–51; life-
styles, 198–99; magnetism of, 35;
and modernity, 44; vs. nature, 29,
31, 36; in New World, 30; politics
of, 51; portrayed in film, 70; and
production, 36; social process of, 46;
in suburbs, 178–80; and survival, 30,
32, 197; transcending, 51
Corliss Engine, 3

Corsets, 75, 99, 100, 101, 114, 131
Cosmetics, 132, 175
Cotton industry, 91, 121
Covello, Leonard: on immigrants and
clothing, 159
Creel, George, 208
Critical thought: importance of, 220
Critique of Pure Reason (Kant), 189
Cultural transformation, 30, 34–35, 62
Customary: defined, 224n

Darwinism, 206
De Mille, Cecil B.: films of, 68–70
Dean, James, 78
Democracy: and choice, 202; and fash-
ion, 75–187 passim; images of,
123–34; industrial, 15; and politics,
210–20; war for, 209
Democratic Promise (Goodwyn), 223n
Demon Seed (film), 2
Denims. *See* Jeans
Department stores, 44–47, 225n; clien-
tele of, 44; and fashion, 142–44; and
mass marketing, 46, 47
Desert Storm. *See* Persian Gulf War
Devere, Allen: on fashion and democra-
cy, 133
Devine, Edward: on consumption, 36
Die Hard (film), 206
Diggers, 8
Dior, Christian: on American fashion,
161; and mass-produced clothing,
163
Domination: male over female, 82
Douglass, Frederick: on chromolithogra-
phy, 127–28; on literacy and free-
dom, 7–8
Doyan, Mona: on television commer-
cials, 201
Dress reform, 111–14
Dresses: ad for, 102–5, *104*
Du Bois, W. E. B.: on migrants from
South, 156
Dukakis, Michael: use of media by, 217
Dungarees. *See* Jeans

Eleventh Hour (film), 60
English Channel: telegraph cables across,
12

Enlightenment: and universe mastered by laws, 1

Entrepreneurs: and mass media, 10–11; mechanical worldview of, 11

Escape from New York (film), 205

Ethnicity: and clothing, 183

Eugénie, Empress: yardage of dresses for, 76

Eviction, The (film), 59, 61

Exports: to European society, 27

Expositions, 146–47

Fabric. *See* Cloth

Fact: reproduced image as, 191, 192

Factory: capitalism, 2–3; vs. home, 36; industrialism, 4; printshop as, 4

Family Monographs (Herzfeld), 128

Fantasy: as truth, 192

Fashion: antifashion, 181, 182; and appearance, 140–42; commerce of, 167–72; and democracy, 75–187; as escape, 155, 171–72; exploitation in, 134–42; jobbers, 135–36; imitation of, 161–63; and industrialism, 149–53, 173, 184; mass, 130–31, 142–49, 177, 184, 187; and mass media, 20; meaning of, 80–81; merchandising, 135–36, 185; miniatures, 146; and personality types, 169–72; and poverty, 130; tyranny of, 158–59; and women's health, 100–1; and youth, 164–66. *See also* Clothing; Garment industry

Fawcett, Brian: on American culture, xi, 189

Feminism: and clothing, 79, 108, 111–14

Femme Nikita, La (film), 234n

Feudalism: and literacy, 5–6, 8; and printing, 5

Field, Marshall, 45

Filene, William, 142

Film: advertisements for, 58; audience, 54, 62, 66, 72; authority of, 192; as community, 59; consumption portrayed in, 70; vs. family authority, 65; and fashion, 148–49; feminine archetypes in, 66–68; formula for, 68; and immigrant experience, x, 53–73; and mass culture, 72–73; as mechanism of order and control, 17–19, 20; product placement in, 195; sexuality in, 66–72, 227n; and social understanding of poverty, 59–61, 226n; stereotypes in, 214; tenements portrayed in, 59–61; and utopian possibility, 18–19; violence in, 205, 206; women portrayed in, 66–72, 234n. *See also* Camera

Fisk, Jim: marketing techniques of, 39

Flapper style, 152

Fool There Was, A (film), 67

Foot-binding, 75, 98–99

Forbidden Fruit (film), 68, 69, 70

Ford, Henry: and assembly-line development, 42

Fortune (magazine): on suburbia, 178

Fox Studios, 66

France: *haute couture* in, 80, 89; revolution and clothing, 90–91

Frankenstein (Shelley): on creation, 1, 13; social relations expressed by this legend, 2; on technology out of control, 1, 20; on utopian potential, 1

Franklin, Benjamin: on appearance, 92, 95

Frazaetti, Maria, 71

French Revolution: and clothing, 90–91

Freud, Sigmund: on gratification, 49

Friday the Thirteenth (film), 205

Frobisher Bay, Canada: cultural transformation in, 34

From Sundown to Sunup (Rawick), 223n

Furniss, Edgar: on Americanization, 32

Gannett Company, Inc., 199

Ganz, Maria: on tenement life, 61

Garment industry: changes in, 131, 134–42; during Civil War, 122–23; growth of, 136; labor in, 136–40; strikes in, 139; and slavery, 120–22; sweatshops of, 14, 131, 137, 140. *See also* Clothing; Fashion; Textile industry

Gello, Grace, 66

Gender: and clothing, 82, 85, 89, 96, 112–14, 173

General Electric, 199

General store: as early marketplace, 38; vs. national marketplace, 43–44

Gerard, Frantz: on corsets, 101
Germany: and economic dominance, 207–8; fascism in, 209
Giedion, Sigfried: on mechanization of agriculture, 223n
Gilbreth, Frank, 19
Gilbreth Chronometer, 19–20
Gilman, Charlotte Perkins: on dependency relationships, 227n; on women, 98
Ginsberg, Allen: on America, 180
Gish, Lillian, 67
Gloria Vanderbilt jeans: ads for, 75
Godkin, Edwin: on chromolithography, 128
Gold, Mike: on community support, 62; on cultural disruption, 30; on immigrants and fashion, 153–54
Goodman, Theodosia. *See* Bara, Theda
Goodwyn, Lawrence: on capitalist agriculture, 223n
Goslin, David: on choice, 196, 197
Grecian bend, 75, 76, 78, 99
Grenada: media coverage of, 208
Griffith, D. W., 66
Grolier Club Book Society: on Ward's Catalog, 224n
Guggenheim Foundation, 219
Guilbord, Jacqueline, 209, 234n
Gulf War. *See* Persian Gulf War
Gutenberg, Johann, 4, 6
Gutman, Herbert: on ads of utopian promise, 28; on immigrants, 225n

Hachette S.A., 199
Halloween (film), 205
Hamilton, Alexander: on homemade clothing, 116
Hard to Kill (film), 206
Haute couture, 80, 89, 163
Health: and women's clothing, 100–1
Hearst, William Randolph: yellow journalism of, 16–17
Hegel, G. W. F.: on concept and reality, 189
Heron, Gil Scott, 209
Herschel, John: telescopic explorations of, 190–91
Herzfeld, Elsa: on chromolithography, 128

High heels, 75, 175
High Noon (film), 209
History: fact as, 192
Hobble skirts, 75, 114
Hollander, Anne: on clothing and status, 85; on film and fashion, 148; on French cancan, 110
Hollywood, 66, 213. *See also* Film
Home buying parties, 186
Horton, Willie, 217
House of Worth, 101
Hurlock, Elizabeth: on clothing and appearance, 140–41; on fashion as liberation, 161–62; on film and fashion, 148; on power of fashion, 158

Ignorance: culture of, 210–20
Immigrant Protective League, 54
Immigrant, The (film), 60
Immigrant women, x, 53–73, 225–27n; and film, x, 53–73; purchases by, 44; and sexual revolution, 54
Immigrants, x, 17; Americanization of, 32–35, 42; and consumer society, 30, 31, 33, 44; and fashion availability, 154–57, 159, 162, 165; in garment industry, 134–36; integration of, 33; as subject in film, 59–61
Ince, Thomas, 60
Incredible Shrinking Man, The (film), 205
Individualism: in suburbia, 174, 178
Industrial Workers of the World (IWW): on machine, 15
Industrial working class: and capitalism, 13; and marketplace, 36; social crisis of, 13–14; and technology, 2, 13–14
Industrialization: and communication technologies, 12–13; and consumption, xxii, 29, 31, 47–51; and fashion, 149–53, 173, 184; and image production, 123, 127; machine and, 3–4; and progress, 29; social experience of, 13, 47, 123
Infomercials, 195, 201
Information age, 210
International Ladies' Garment Workers' Union, 137
Inuit: and cultural transformation, 34
Invasion of the Body Snatchers (film), 205
Iowa: Sears merchandising in, 42–43

Iran-Contra scandal, 195–96
Italian, The (film): working class portrayed in, 60, 61, 69
IWW. *See* Industrial Workers of the World

Jacobs, Lewis: on poverty and struggle as dramatic themes, 59
Japan: and economic dominance, 207–8
Jeans: designer, 75–76, 79, 160; as egalitarian, 185; history of, 75–81
Jefferson, Thomas: on democracy, 211
Jews: and rise of fashion goods, 135–36
Jews without Money (Gold), 30, 62, 153–54
Josephson, Matthew: on New York Stock Exchange, 223n
Journal of Science (Edinburgh), 191
Journalism: and reporting of violence, 203, 205. *See also* Newspapers; Yellow journalism
Junk mail, 195

Kant, Immanuel: on representation, 189
Kasson, John: on Columbian Exposition, 147
Kenealy, Arabella: on corsets, 101
Kennedy, John F.: use of media by, 212
Klausner, Samuel Z.: on cultural disruption, 35
Klein, Calvin. *See* Calvin Klein jeans
Kleptomaniac, The (film), 59, 60
Knights of Labor, 139
Koberger Press (Nuremberg), 4
Koppel, Ted: on media coverage of Persian Gulf War, 234n
Krysto, Christina: on Americanization, 32
Kuthan, Anna, xiii, 24–28, 46

Labor: in garment industry, 136–40
Ladies' Home Journal: and fashion, 145
Land. *See* Real estate
Lawrence, Mass.: woolen mills in, 28
Leisure: and clothing, 84, 106, 175, 177–78; of nobility, 84
Levi Strauss: overalls by, 76, 120
Levine, Louis: on labor in garment industry, 137
Libya: media coverage of, 208

Lily of France: ad for, 102, *103*, 111
Lingerie: ad for, 102, *103*, 111; fabric of, 132; women's use of, 99–100, 108, 110
Lippmann, Walter, 195; on public opinion, 192, 193; on stereotypes, 214–15, 217
Literacy: and feudalism, 5–6, 8; and freedom, 7–8; history of, ix; and knowledge, 5, 6; and printing, 5, 7, 124
Lithographer's Journal: on chromolithography, 128
Little Annie Rooney (film), 67
Locke, John, 191
Locke, Richard Adams: on Herschel, 191, 192
Lollards: and social revolt, 6
Lord and Taylor (department store), 143–44
Louis XIV: and luxuries, 89
Lubin, Simon: on Americanization, 32
Lynd, Robert and Helen, 117, 166

McCarthyism, 178
McClure, Michael: on suburbia, 180–81
Machine, 1–4; and bourgeoisie, 2–3, 13–14; control by, 3; as domination, 2; as reference-idea, 2, 3, 13; as social instrument, 3; vs. working class, 2–3, 13–14. *See also* Technology; World-machine
Macy, R. H., 142; and advertising, 145; and retailing techniques, 45–46, 194
Mail-order merchandising, 40–44; catalogs, 41, 47, 144–45; and mass marketing, 46
Makeup. *See* Cosmetics
Male and Female (film), 68, 69
Malls, shopping: and imagery of commerce, 48
Manchester, England: working class in, 3
Mangano, Antonio: on motion pictures, 58
Manifesto (IWW), 15
Marconi, Guglielmo, 12
Marcuse, Herbert: on freedom, 220
Marketing: by peddlers, 38–39; principles of, 39; segmentation, 198–99,

233n; for suburbs, 178. *See also* Merchandising; Retailing
Marketplace, 35–46; evolution of, 46; national, 43, 46, 48; propaganda of, 197; and utopia, 49; world, 3, 10
Marshall Field (department store), 142
Martineau, Pierre: on dressing men, 177
Marx, Karl, xiii; on capitalism, 13; on concept and reality, 189
Masculine ideal, 176
Mass communication: and capitalism, 3–4, 12–13, 16, 18, 21; and social reform, 16. *See also* Communication technology
Mass culture: and communication technology, 20; and consumption, 35–36, 198; and disconnectedness, 204; film and, 72–73; and industrialism, 35–36; and media, x, xi, 65, 195; power of, 65; reshaping of, 235n; and suburbia, 178, 183; value of, x
Mass distribution, 40, 48–49, 224n
Mass fashion. *See under* Fashion
Mass media, 10–12, 20, 190–93; and commercial choice, 195, 197, 199, 202; control by, 233n; and market considerations, 211; and mass culture, x, xi, 65, 195; money as, xi, 33; as politics, 211–19; power of, ix
Mass production, 25, 34, 40, 44, 45, 47, 48–49, 224n
Mattelart, Michelle: on modernity, 227n
Mazza, Agnes, 64, 226n
Mechanical worldview, 11, 13–14. *See also* World-machine
Mechanization Takes Command (Giedion), 223n
Media. *See* Mass media
Media Control (Chomsky), 233n
Melting pot: promise of, 33
Merchandising: and choice, 194; fashion, 135–36, 185. *See also* Marketing; Retailing
Merchants. *See* General store; Peddlers
Meyerowitz, Josh: on culture, 200
Middletown (Lynd and Lynd), 117, 166
Migrants. *See* Immigrants
Miser's Hoard, The (film), 59
Misfit Wife, The (film), 70

Modern World System, The (Wallerstein), 223n
Modernity: advertising and, 28, 44; and consumption, 44; vs. traditional culture, xxii, 72; women and, 70, 227n
Money: and consumption, 29–30, 33; as mass medium, xi, 33; transformative powers of, 33–34. *See also* Wages
Montgomery Ward's (department store/catalog): and commercial power, 44; and immigrant market, 42; as influential on American life, 224n; and mail-order merchandising, 41–42, 44; as reference on material culture, 41
Morality: and clothing, 91–95, 97, 176
Moresco, Filomena, 63
Morreale, Joanne: on Reagan's campaign ad, 216
Mother-daughter relationship: of immigrant women, x, 53, 56–57, 62–65, 68, 70, 72, 225n, 225–26n
Motion pictures. *See* Film
Movies. *See* Film
MTV, 195
Murdoch, Rupert, 199
My Bondage and My Freedom (Douglass), 7–8

Nash, Beau, 93
National Enquirer, 203
National Lithographers' Association: on chromolithography, 126–27
Nationalism, 32
Need for Gold, The (film), 59
Neighbors Who Borrow (film), 59
Nemy, Enid: on fashion, 187
New Deal: promotion of, 212
New World: consumption in, 30; vs. Old World, 54
New York Post, 204, 210
New York Stock Exchange: site of, 223n
New York Sun, 190–91
New York Times, 34–35, 201, 213
News reporting. *See* Journalism
Newspaper: and commerce, 10–11, 13, 44; and truth, 192; and worldview, 11. *See also* Journalism; Penny press
Nielsen ratings, 212

900 telephone numbers, 195
Nobility: clothing of, 84–85, 90; leisure of, 84; vs. peasants, 5
North, Oliver, 196
Nystrom, Paul: on fashion, 80, 100, 130, 152, 162, 166, 170, 171

Obey, David: on media and politics, 212
Ognibene, Filomena, 65, 71
Old Wives for New (film), 68–69
Old World: vs. New World, 54
On Human Finery (Bell), 84
Original sin: and clothing, 82, 85, 97, 102–5, 106–7, 111
Otherness, 204–5, 206, 208, 216, 219

Pacifism: and clothing, 183
Packaging: allure of, 27, 38–39; by media, 218–19; by peddlers, 38–39
Paine, Thomas: on democracy, 192; on tyranny, 9–10; on vernacular literature, 9
Painted Lady, The: virgin theme in, 227n
Pamphlets: and social revolt, 8–9
Panama: media coverage of, 208
Paper dolls: and spread of fashion, 146
Paradise, Viola: on immigrants, 54
Park, Robert: on Americanization, 33, 34
Parsons, Elsie Clew: on tenement families, 56
Patten, Simon: on industrial consumerism, 47, 48, 50, 202
Pavlov, Ivan Petrovich, 219
Peasants: clothing of, 83–84; and consumer society, 29; vs. nobility, 5
Peddlers: as forerunners to marketplace, 37–40; and chromolithography, 128
Penny press: and commerce, 11, 16
Perception, xxii; vs. reality, 189
Perry, Richard: on civil liberties, 220
Persian Gulf War: media coverage of, 196, 207, 208, 209, 214, 217, 234n
Philadelphia Centennial Exposition (1876), 3, 147
Photography: as authority, 192; in journalism, 17. *See also* Camera
Photoplay magazine: on clothing of youth, 164
Pickford, Mary, 67

Plain style clothing, 90, 92–93, 96, 105, 111, 114
Plato, 189
Poiret, Paul: on designer labels, 160; fashion design of, 114, 150, 167–69; on fashion imitation, 160–61, 172
Politics: and democracy, 210–20; and media, 211–19
Poltergeist (film), 205
Poor Men's Wives (film), 70
Pope Gregory XI: and condemnation of Wycliffe, 6
Porter, Edwin S.: on justice in class-defined society, 60
Presses. *See* Penny press; Printing; Printshops
Printing: as authority, 192; and commerce, 4, 10; and democracy, 6, 7; and emancipation, 7; history of, ix, 4; and imagery, 124; and literacy, 5, 7, 124; and mass communication, 192; and mercantilism, 7; and popular discourse, 5; printing press and power, 8, 124; and revolution, 4, 5
Printshops: as factories, 4
Products: as magical, 26
Proletarianization, 14
Propaganda: of marketplace, 197; by media, 233n; of yellow journalism, 17; of war, 17, 208
Prosperity. *See* Wealth
Prostitutes: clothing of, 100, 108–9
Protestant Reformation: on sumptuousness, 92
Public opinion, 192, 215, 234n
Public relations: by peddlers, 37, 39
Pulitzer, Joseph: yellow journalism of, 16–17
Puritans: clothing of, 90; revolution, 9

Racism, 204–5, 206, 214, 217, 219
Radio: and commerce, 11, 12
Ragged Dick (Alger), 77
Rags (film), 67
Railroads: and mass distribution of goods, 40; and telegraph, 11, 12
Rambo (film), 206
Rap music, 200
Rawick, George: on slavery and capitalism, 223n

Ready-to-wear. *See under* Clothing
Reagan, Nancy, 211; clothing of, 107
Reagan, Ronald: capitalist ethics of, 107; and military power, 207, 208; use of media by, 211, 213, 216, 217, 219
Real estate: value of, 29–30, 31
Reality: vs. imagery, 25
Reason: and creation, 9; vs. emotion, 234n; vs. tyranny, 9
Rebel without a Cause (film), 78
Reed, Ishmael: on prejudice, 205
Religion: and clothing, 82–83; and social hierarchy, 83
Representation, 189, 190, 193
Republic, The (Plato), 189
Retailing: innovations in, 40, 45. *See also* Department stores; Marketing; Merchandising
RFD. *See* Rural free delivery
Richardson, Bertha June: on clothing of poor, 116–17, 157; on tyranny of fashion, 159
Robber Barons, The (Josephson), 223n
Roosevelt, Franklin D.: use of media by, 211–12
Roosevelt, Theodore: use of media by, 211
Roots of the Modern American Empire (Williams), 223n
Rosenfeld, Morris: on machine, 14, 19; on sweatshops, 14
Rosenwald family: and garment industry, 134–35
Rudofsky, Bernard: on monobosom, 106
Rural America: mass images in, 28
Rural free delivery (RFD): and mail-order merchandising, 43
Ruskin, John: on clothing, 93

Salesmanship: techniques, 36; visual, 195. *See also* Merchandising; Retailing
Saloons, 58
Saturday Evening Post, 213
Schiller, Herbert I.: on capitalism and world information order, 4, 221n
Schwarzenegger, Arnold, 206
Schwarzkopf, Norman, 196
Scientific American: on cinema images, 18,

222n; on free enterprise, 222n; on industrial culture, 20
Sears, Roebuck & Company, 41–44, 132; catalogs, 42–44, 144; Iowaization scheme, 42–43
Sensationalism: of information age, 211
Sexuality: and childbearing, 97; and clothing, 97–115, 173; of women, 97–98, 109–11
She Won't Pay Her Rent (film), 59
Shelley, Mary Wollstonecraft, 1
Shopping centers: and imagery of commerce, 48
Silent films, 54, 58, 62; and sexual issues, 66
Skirts: hobble, 75, 114; flounced, 76–77, 131
Slavery: as capitalist labor system, 223n; and chromolithography, 127–28; and cotton industry, 91, 121–22; and literacy, 8; philosophy of, 7–8
Slop shops, 119, 129
Smith, Gladys. *See* Pickford, Mary
Social reform: and industrial democracy, 15; and mass communication, 16
Social revolt, 6, 8–9
Socialism: and labor, 138–39
Society magazine, 196
Sons of Italy (Mangano), 58
South: migrants from, 156–57
Soviet Union: clothing in, 80
Spanish-American War, 207; journalism and, 17
Spargo, John: on immigrants, 60–61
Sports: and women's clothing, 113
Stanton, Elizabeth Cady: on clothing, 112
Statue of Liberty, 17
Stereotypes: in media, 214, 217
Stewart's (department store), 142, 143
Strand Theatre (New York), 71
Strikes: in garment industry, 139
Suburbia: and clothing, 175, 180–81, 183; life-style of, 174–81; rise of, 174–75; violence in, 205
Sullivan, Gardner, 60
Sumptuary law, 85–88, 155
Survey magazine: on consumption, 36; on motion pictures in tenement districts, 57–58

Swanson, Gloria, 69
Sweatshops. *See* Garment industry

Technology: control by, 1–2, 3; and
    progress, 1, 11. *See also* Machine;
    World-machine
Telegraph: and commerce, 11–12
Television: and choice, 200; and politics,
    212; power of, 193; violence on, 205
Tenements: family life in, 56, 60; in
    films, 59–61. *See also* Immigrants
Terminator/Terminator 2 (film), 205, 234n
Textile industry, 91–92, 112–13, 116–23
Thelma and Louise (film), 234n
Threadgill, Nadine, 201
Time Warner, Inc., 199
Toner, Robin: on political strategy, 213
Total Recall (film), 206
Trademarks, 28, 40. *See also* Brand
    names
Transatlantic cable, 12
Traveling salesmen. *See* Peddlers
True, Ruth: on working class, 63, 65,
    157
True Levellers, 8
Truth: fantasy as, 192
Turner, Ted, 199

Underground literature, 10
Underpants. *See* Lingerie
United Fruit Company, 12
United Parcel Service: founding of, 144

VALS (values and life-style)/VALS 2,
    233n
Vanderbilt, Gloria. *See* Gloria Vanderbilt
    jeans
Veblen, Thorstein: on conspicuous con-
    sumption, 84; on emulation and fash-
    ion, 157
Vernacular literature: commercial ap-
    propriation of, 15; and literacy, 5,
    6–10; radical, 6–7, 14
Vertov, Dziga: on camera, 222n
Vietnam War, 207, 208, 233n; media
    coverage of, 208
Violence: culture of, 202–10, 220,
    233–34n
Virgin theme: ambiguities of, 227n

Visual art: availability of, 124–30; pos-
    session of, 124–25

Wages: and consumer society, 30, 36; of
    immigrant daughters, 63–64; of im-
    migrant families, 54–55; as utopian
    promise, 28–29. *See also* Money
Wall Street Journal, 202
Wallerstein, Immanuel: on modern
    world system, 5; on slavery and
    capitalism, 223n
Wanamaker, John: and retailing, 45; and
    rural free mail delivery, 43
Wanamaker's (department store), 45,
    142, 225n
War: media coverage of, 17, 207–10,
    234n
War Industries Board: on clothing, 153
Ward, Montgomery. *See* Montgomery
    Ward's (department store/catalog)
Watergate: media coverage of, 212–13
Watt, James: on consumerism, 50–51
Wealth: art as, 124–25; and clothing,
    76–77, 84–85, 88–89, 106
Weber, Max: on Ben Franklin, 92
Western Union: as first industrial mo-
    nopoly, 12
Wheeler, Elmer, 39
White terror: machine as, 13
Whittle Communications, 195
Why Change Your Wife? (film), 68, 69, 70
Wigs: of nobility, 90
Wild One (film), 78
Williams, Eric: on capitalism and slav-
    ery, 223n
Williams, Raymond: on consumer
    (word), 31, 48; on mass society, 204
Williams, William Appleman: on capital-
    ism and agriculture, 223n; on over-
    seas expansion, 207
Winstanley, Gerard: and social revolt,
    8–9; worldview of, 8–9
Wireless. *See* Radio
Woman and Economics (Gilman), 227n
Women: body ideals and values, 234n;
    and clothing, 96–115, 175–76; and
    consumerism, 37–38, 45, 70; in film,
    66–72; in garment industry, 138; and
    home production, 37; models of
    liberated, 100; and modernity, 70,

227n; as objects of sexuo-economic exchange, 234n; and patriarchy, 34, 234n; as possession, 97; retailing techniques for, 45; sexuality of, 97–98, 109–11; suburban, 176; and violent culture, 234n; in work force, 112–13. *See also* Immigrant women; Mother-daughter relationship

Working class, 55, 63, 65; agricultural, 223n; and capitalism, 13–14, 15; and fashion, 91–92, 115–23, 172–73; in film, 60, 61, 69; industrial, 2–3, 13–14, 36; literate, 10; vs. machine, 2–3, 13–14; urban, 16

World-machine: challenge to, 14–15; communication technology and, 20–21; management of, 13, 16; and power, 8; rationalism of, 19. *See also* Machine; Mechanical worldview; Technology

World War I: promotion of, 208

Wycliffe, John: and social revolt, 6

Yellow journalism, 16–17; as propaganda, 17

Zambiello, Maria, 70–71

Zeldin, Theodore: on bourgeois men/women, 97

Stuart Ewen is professor of media studies at Hunter College, and professor in the Ph.D. program in sociology at the City University of New York Graduate Center. For nearly twenty years he has been one of the leading historians and critics of American consumer society, and an important innovator in the fields of media and cultural studies. He is the author of *All Consuming Images: The Politics of Style in Contemporary Culture*; this book provided a foundation for Bill Moyers's four-part PBS series, "The Public Mind," which won Peabody, Emmy, and National Education Association awards and in which Ewen appeared. Stuart Ewen's other books include *Captains of Consciousness: Advertising and the Social Roots of the Consumer Culture*. He writes a regular column — "The Public Eye" — for *ARTFORUM* magazine, in which he examines issues and enigmas in the mass media and contemporary consumer culture. His writings appear in French, Italian, Spanish, Finnish, German, Norwegian, and Japanese translation. He is currently writing a social history of public relations, to be entitled *Controlling Chaos*.

Elizabeth Ewen is a professor in the American studies program at SUNY/Old Westbury. She teaches American history and cultural studies. She is also director of Old Westbury's General Education Program. Her other books include *Immigrant Women in the Land of Dollars: Life and Culture on the Lower East Side, 1890–1925*. In addition she has written extensively on the social history of the mass media, on women's studies, and on film. Currently she is working on a book entitled *The Rise and Fall of the Suburban Dream, 1945 to the Present*.